P9-DTL-564

After Kilvert

After Kilvert

A. L. Le Quesne

READERS UNION
Group of Book Clubs
Newton Abbot 1979

First published by Oxford University Press

This edition was produced in 1979 for sale to its members
only by the proprietors, Readers Union Limited,
PO Box 6, Newton Abbot, Devon, TQ12 2DW.
Full details of membership will gladly be sent on request

Reproduced and printed in Great Britain
by A. Wheaton & Co Ltd Exeter
for Readers Union

For Mary
who encouraged me to do it
and to the memory of
R. F. K.
with gratitude, affection
and respect

Preface

I owe a large debt of gratitude to a great many people for their help in enabling me to write this book. It seems appropriate to start with the Kilvert Society, to whom my obligations are manifold: for one thing, they have supplied the originals for several of the illustrations, but apart from that I cannot begin to list all those of the Society's members who have helped me on with interest, encouragement, or information. I hope they will take pleasure in recognizing my debt to them in some of the pages that follow; and I think well enough of them to believe that they will have no objection to joining me occasionally in that very Kilvert-like activity of raising an eyebrow of mildly ironic humour at some of our own Society activities. I am bound to mention two names in particular: Charles Prosser, for more than twenty years the indefatigable Secretary of the Society and legendary source of Kilvert lore, to whom I am as indebted as every other Kilvert inquirer has been for his unfailing readiness to put his stores at our disposal, but who has unhappily not lived to see this book's publication; and Frederick Grice, the Deputy President of the Society, to which he has devoted so much energy and enthusiasm in recent years, to whom I personally am indebted for the stimulus of both his conversation and his own researches on Kilvert.

I am grateful to all the present-day (or at least recent!) inhabitants of Clyro who made our all-too-short residence there the happy memory that it is; many of them, wittingly or unwittingly, have walking-on parts in this book, and I hope I have given none of them cause to hold it against me. Here again, once I start naming names there will be no end to it; but I must particularly thank Joan Harris of Crossway for her enthusiastic typing of the manuscript, and both her and her husband Trevor for allowing me to reproduce the illustrations of Clyro Court and the village blacksmith from postcards in their possession. In this connection, I should also like to thank David Harling for his readiness at short notice to come to the help of a perfect stranger too incompetent to supply his own illustrations.

It was an old friend and colleague, Stacy Colman, who originally suggested that I should submit *After Kilvert* to the Oxford University Press, and without him it is unlikely that I would have had the temerity to do so. As it is, I owe him my gratitude not only for the book's appearance in print, but also for a new friendship with its editor, Richard Brain. I am more grateful than I can say to him, to Susan le Roux, to Judith Chamberlain, and to all those of their colleagues in the O.U.P. with whom I have had any dealings for the energy, charm, and tact with which they have pursued the interests and soothed the tender sensibilities of a middle-aged new author.

Like all good prefaces, this one comes finally to my family – to M, C, and E, who flit erratically and uncomplainingly through its pages, and latterly to J, who arrived too late to have that uncertain pleasure, but in time to share with the rest of them the unpredictable temper and irregular attentions of a father with his mind on other things and a universe of family discourse heavily haunted by the figure of Kilvert. Thanks to them all for putting up with it, and even being interested; but especially to M, for accepting with enthusiasm a life shaped round her husband's desire to write a book, and one that was often more fun for him than for her.

A. L. Le Quesne

Shrewsbury
20 November 1977

Illustrations

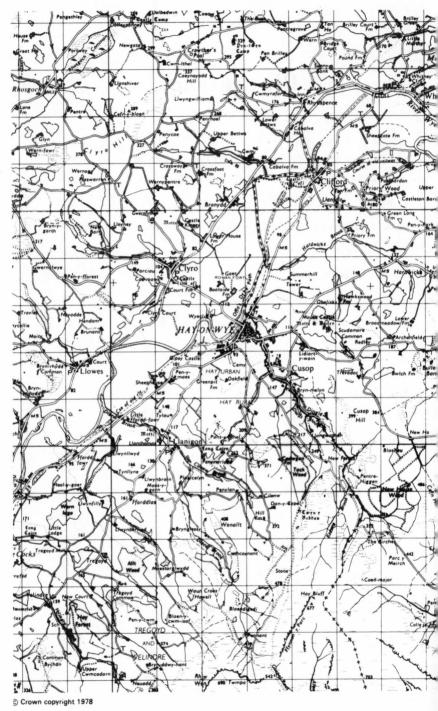

© Crown copyright 1978

The area round Clyro as it is today: taken from the current edition of the 1:50,000 O.S. map (reduced).

1970 *1 January.* On New Year's Day of 1970, I was at home with my family in Jersey, about to move to Clyro to live in the house where the Revd. Francis Kilvert had been living a hundred years before – the consummation of a long period when his life and mine, though a century apart, had been moving steadily closer together. I suppose there are some likenesses between us. We were both born of the professional upper middle classes; both clerks in the ancient sense, though not in my case in holy orders; both read history at Oxford; both had long bachelorhoods before marriage in our later 30s (though I was 41 in 1970, to his 29 in 1870). But it was not these trivial likenesses that drew me to him and to his Clyro, but the no doubt casual enough decision that he made at the start of 1870 to try keeping a diary. I have been a diary-keeper myself since my youth but this too might have been no more than a casual coincidence if I had not by 1970 already been conscious of the growing pull of Kilvert upon me for nearly twelve years – a pull whose origin I can date precisely to 30 August 1958.

1958 *30 August.* A bit warmer, and fewer showers. Spent the morning in a Melbourne bookshop; had thought of taking a trip to Geelong, but a headache for the second day in succession and the resultant inertia dissuaded me. In the afternoon, bussed out to see the local rugger semi-final at Orrong Park beyond Prahran, and that was a good idea. A fine English-autumn-like afternoon, warm and golden and grey clouds. But I'm not making much use of this Melbourne weekend; a coach tour from Adelaide might have been wiser. Reading *Kilvert's Diary*, which I bought in Adelaide, with extreme pleasure. His love of landscape is very close to mine, and simple though it is, his descriptive style seems to me beautifully effective. He describes what he sees, not the effect it produces on him – the mistake I often make. But what a superb date for seeing England, and what an Arcadia it sounds!

In August of 1958, I was homesick in Australia. I had left England a year previously to take up a job in Hobart, having never been out of Europe before, and I was miserable; home and

1

friends were ten thousand miles away and felt like it, and the Australian landscape, even in its tenderer Tasmanian version which I later came to love, appalled me. It was the eighteenth-century reaction to wilderness, the fear of chaos; the massive hills shaggy with natural forest terrified me, the featureless tawny grassland dotted with the skeletons of ring-barked gums dismayed me by its dryness, its untidiness, its lack of definition. Even where the landscape had a man-made veneer, it was thin to transparency, rocks and tree-stumps cropping up everywhere. I was accustomed to English landscapes which are soft to the touch, fertilized and ploughed deep by a hundred generations of men, and in the face of the harshness and hardness of a frontier landscape I was lost, without bearings, lonely and homesick. In August 1958, I went to a conference in Adelaide, dropped into a second-hand bookshop, and picked up the one-volume World Book Club selection from *Kilvert's Diary*. Next weekend, in Melbourne on the way back to Hobart, I was already far enough into it for it to leave its first mark on my own diary, and to know that I had met one of my masters.

At that time and place – when a tombstone with an English place-name on it could move me to tears – the Diary caught me at my most vulnerable; but I do not think that it would ever have been very different. It was one of the books – we all have a few – which I was born to live with; one of the shaping encounters which makes you what you are.

1870 *1 January*. On that New Year's Day Francis Kilvert started keeping a diary. I think (though I cannot be sure) that on that day he was at home with his parents in the vicarage of Langley Burrell in Wiltshire. Langley Burrell is just outside Chippenham; the young man's father, Robert Kilvert, was its vicar, and Francis Kilvert was himself curate of Clyro, a village in the upper Wye valley on the Welsh border, just in Radnorshire but within a mile of the point where Herefordshire, Breconshire, and Radnorshire met. Now, as was usual at that time of year, he was at home on holiday, in a place which had been familiar to him all his life; for at Langley Burrell he was little more than a mile from his birthplace at Hardenhuish Vicarage, that being the parish his father held at the time of his birth, on 3 December 1840. Robert Kilvert had been born in 1804, but Francis was only his second child; solidly entrenched though they were in the English middle classes, there was little money in this branch of the Kilverts. Marriage was hardly thinkable without a parish, as the vicar's son was to find in his turn; and even when the parish came, Robert Kilvert still found it necessary to run a small private school for a few pupils who boarded in the vicarage, a common enough arrangement in those days. By then he had taken a wife too, Thermuthis Coleman, a daughter of the country gentry around Chippenham, and in a few years he moved to the Coleman family living of Langley Burrell. It was there that his son Francis was twice to assist him as his curate, and was staying in 1870 for his usual New Year's holiday from Clyro.

Francis's childhood had been spent at Hardenhuish Vicarage, but we know nothing of it directly except that in later years his memories of it were happy ones. He was one of a typical large Victorian vicarage family before long, four girls and two boys – all of whom perhaps, the boys almost certainly, had their early education from their father, together with the rest of his pupils, for money was still not plentiful in the household and the economy on school fees must have been useful. Later he attended the school kept by an uncle and namesake at Claverton Lodge near Bath – it was still a generation before a public-school education would be taken for granted for sons of the vicarage. Knowing what we do of the adult Kilvert, we can be fairly sure he was a gentle, friendly, tractable child. The Kilverts were a closely knit family, and remained so all their lives, and it is not hard to imagine that cheerful, profoundly ordered existence of a Victorian country vicarage, hardly touched by the last faintest ripples of the storms of the outside world. It seems likely that the order was firm, for there are indications that Robert Kilvert ruled his family with a Victorian authority which his elder son never outgrew, though in later life he sometimes escaped it. It may have been from his relationship with his father that he first learned the rules of docile submission to recognized authority, of parents, of religious belief, of social order and convention, that characterized his whole life. We do not commonly look for happiness in submission to established authority nowadays, and it may take an effort to realize that it can be found there as authentically as in other places, and that it was there that Kilvert and many of his contemporaries did find it.

1840 was – in one sense – a good time to be born in England. Between 1815 and 1848, the threat and the fear of revolution were real things in the minds of Englishmen: a long-established social and economic order was breaking up, and what new order would emerge from it, it was still impossible to tell. To the classes who had ruled England till now, the future was black and alarming: chaos and apocalypse at hand. To bold and adventurous men it could be an exciting time, frightening but free, when it was possible to hope for anything, as well as to fear for everything. But the earth trembled beneath the country houses and the vicarages, and there was worried talk over the dinner-tables, of the Reform Bill, the disestablishment of the Church, the repeal of the Corn Laws, Chartists, rick-burnings. A political oligarchy that had ruled England for a century and a half was being challenged by new men and new interests; deeper down and more ominous, the forces of the new industrialism were threatening to blow the existing society apart like steam pressure mounting in a sealed boiler; and everybody remembered what had happened in France fifty years ago. It was a time of fear for the possessors and suffering for the destitute, and a child old enough to be aware of it would always have known what insecurity was.

But Kilvert was not old enough to be aware of it, and he grew up in a tranquil world; there is nothing in his Diary to suggest that he ever saw or guessed at the temperatures and pressures that lay beneath – it is that very unawareness that gives the Diary half its attraction for this more turbulent age. As the young Francis grew to full awareness of the world about him, so that world was settling into its mid-Victorian calm (which perhaps can also be described as the mid-Victorian anticlimax). Everything was getting bigger and better-lit and faster and cheaper and more comfortable, and for the moment it seemed that this had no reverse side, that beauty, liberty, peace, and virtue were fellow-travellers on the train. In 1851, when the boy was 11, the Great Exhibition was held, that gigantic festival of relief and confidence. It would not be surprising if the Kilverts, like so many other families that year, went up to London to see it – we know that Francis saw the Exhibition building itself, the Crystal Palace, re-erected on its new permanent site at Sydenham, in 1854 or 1855.

The benefit of such an upbringing was assurance, its penalty shallowness. Everything we know of Francis Kilvert proclaims a rooted innocent confidence in the structure of his society and the destiny of his nation. He never knew what it was to fear the result of a general election or the headlines of a newspaper. His means were modest, but no threat to them was conceivable; and in all his lifetime, no nation in the world was ever in a position to threaten seriously the borders of his country or the means of its livelihood. The trade winds blew favourably for his class and his nation. Even the technical progress of these years was assured rather than exhilarating. The most dramatic demonstration of violent change, the railway, grew up with him; he must have travelled on stage-coaches in his youth, but the railway was always natural to him – he never saw it naked and new. His world was becoming continually wealthier, its products more varied, but none of them were such as to alter the central routines of his life.

So also with the intellectual world. There were turbulent ideas stirring in the England of the 1840s and 1850s, but the eddies, though violent, were local. Here also it was easy for the moderately intelligent to find themselves being borne along on a broad calm stream of accepted notions. Kilvert's father was a respectable scholar and a schoolmaster, and in this general sense Kilvert's background was that of the academic intelligentsia; but there is no sign that the ideas he had inherited and grown up with were ever severely shaken or even challenged in his mind, still less that he ever did much thinking for himself. The great challenges to the mid-Victorian religious, political, social, economic platitudes did not reach Kilvert's level in his own lifetime. Schooling at the hands of his father and his uncle was not likely to shake many inherited ideas – and Kilvert was a docile inheritor. Following in his father's path, he duly went up to Oxford in 1858, as a commoner of Wadham. But there is no sign that Kilvert's years at Oxford posed any vital challenge to the ideas in which he had grown up or that he ever felt the necessity to fight for them. He studied the recently founded course in History and Jurisprudence, rather than the traditional Classics, but there is nothing in his later career to suggest that either of these disciplines made any lasting impression on his mind. It is fair to note that he had the intellectual ambition to sit for honours, in an age when most undergraduates were still content with a pass course; but he only got a fourth.

In this atmosphere of accustomed things being done in accustomed ways, it was very natural for a docile son to follow his father into the Church; and this Francis Kilvert duly did. We can be reasonably certain that this decision did not spring from any keen and sudden awareness of vocation, from any Evangelical sense of sin and acceptance; all that we know of his attitude to his creed and his calling in later years tells against this. The truths of Christianity and his own dedication to the ministry seem simply to be assumptions that he never questioned or examined, constituents of the air he breathed in the vicarages at Hardenhuish and the neighbouring Langley Burrell, to which his family moved in the 1850s. So a smooth and easy path had brought him to his undistinguished degree in 1862, to ordination as deacon in 1863 and priest in 1864, to a natural two years as his father's curate at Langley Burrell. Then, in the spring of 1865, he took another curacy at Clyro in remote rural Radnorshire. There is no indication that the Kilverts had any previous connection with the area, or any links of blood or friendship with any of its gentry, or with the Vicar of Clyro, the Revd. Richard Lister Venables. One can speculate, but not usefully. All we *know* is that this extremely placid, pleasant, unremarkable young man took up his curacy in the spring of 1865. He was 24; he was living free, away from the sheltering, stifling wing of the family, able to find out who he was and to be himself for the first time in his life. He came, in the spring, to a countryside of romantic beauty, which in 1865 must have been close to the peak of its perfection. It was a new life, and it was to have unexpected consequences.

The years at Clyro soon settled into a routine: his lodgings in the village, the round of services and pastoral visiting, holidays at home or with friends in midwinter and in the summer; once, in the summer of 1869, a trip to Switzerland – apart from one later visit to Paris, so far as we know the only time Kilvert ever went abroad. But as time went by, something apparently began to stir beneath the conventionalities that were all this young Victorian curate had yet to show to the world: something untamed, something real, something strong; an acute, sometimes painful sensibility to the beauties of the natural world, and the idiosyncrasies of the human one, that he had not learned at the vicarage. It was a sensibility descended from Wordsworth, but authentically Kilvert's own; and, in a life crimped by the conventions of what a

AFTER KILVERT

Victorian curate might and might not do, it would one day demand expression. Something socially acceptable, something tolerable to the morality sternly bred into him – for if birth was now demanding its liberty, breeding still kept the upper hand, as it did all his life – something private. On that New Year's Day of 1870, he was about to discover it.

In 1938, Mr. William Plomer of the publishing firm of Jonathan Cape in London received the manuscript of a Victorian diary, submitted to him by the diarist's nephew, Mr. T. Perceval Smith, with a view to publication. At that time, Mr. Plomer has recorded, the Diary consisted of 22 notebooks, containing (apparently) a daily record of the life of a Victorian country parson, the Revd. Francis Kilvert, from 1 January 1870 until March 1879. Although daily, the record was not continuous: there were gaps between September 1875 and March 1876, and between June 1876 and December 1877, and in addition the diary stopped abruptly and without explanation in March 1879. The obvious implication is that some volumes were missing, and there are grounds to suspect very strongly that they were removed, and probably destroyed, by Kilvert's widow before she allowed the Diary to pass into the hands of other members of the family, because she thought their contents too personal to be revealed to anyone but herself.

She put her judgement against our curiosity, as she had a right to do, and she was not the last of those into whose hands the Diary passed to do so. After the death of Mr. Perceval Smith, the Diary came into the possession of his sister, Mrs. Essex Hope, who reputedly had qualms of family conscience about the publication of extracts from it, seeing it as a breach of confidence with the dead; and in 1958 she destroyed all but three of the remaining volumes. The loss cannot be repaired. The original typescript copy of the whole 22 volumes which Mr. Plomer had made in 1938 was accidentally destroyed and no other copy, so far as one knows, was ever made. With the exception, therefore, of three volumes, the manuscript of the Diary is lost, and we shall never have more than the extracts (about one-third of the whole, he estimated) that Mr. Plomer selected for publication in 1939. So we have ten years of a small man's life a hundred years ago snatched back out of the dark into the day, with the sunlight still bright and the dew still fresh on it. But it is glimpses only, and because Mrs. Kilvert and Mrs. Hope acted as they did, the rest even of that ten years is blackness complete and for ever.

Of the first thirty years of Kilvert's life we have nothing but a few grey facts. It is natural to ask whether a man who appears so born a diarist did not discover his gift before the age of thirty; but there is no answer. If he did, no trace of it survives. It is remarkable, too, that an inexperienced diarist should master the form with such ease from the start. Mr. Plomer recalled nothing in the lost first entries to show whether this was the continuation of a long-standing diary, or the beginning of a new one; nor, if it was the latter, as to the motives that prompted Kilvert to start it.

All the same, all the evidence seems to suggest that in January 1870 the Diary was a new enterprise for Kilvert. The fact that it begins on 1 January is significant, for the notebooks do not normally begin or end on any particular date; obviously Kilvert went on to a new one as soon as he had finished the last. It looks, therefore, very much as if he set out from scratch with the New Year. It is noticeable, too, that he nowhere implies that the Diary existed before 1870, and that all his references to events before then are vague as to date – he mentions at most the month, as one does when speaking from memory. Finally, it is also noticeable that the earliest entries are very much the fullest. The three volumes in which Mr. Plomer's edition was finally published represent respectively 8, 8, and 6 of the original notebooks – nearly a third each – yet the first volume covers 20 months, the second 33, and the third, allowing for the gaps, almost four years. It looks very much as if the early notebooks represent the bursting-out of a pent-up volume of impressions that are beginning to run thin as the later notebooks are reached. Nor is it only a matter of volume. There is a magic, a degree of vividness, about the first year that is never wholly recaptured; no later spring is ever quite as green as the spring of 1870.

So it looks as though the curate of Clyro *did* sit down to keep a diary for the first time in the New Year of 1870. Inevitably, one asks why? It was late for the diary-keeping impulse to emerge;

Opposite: Not quite the only known photograph, but the only known portrait, of Kilvert. It must date from the period of the Diary, for Kilvert here can hardly be less than thirty.

and it is worth realizing that it must have meant a sizeable re-ordering of his time. These early entries run to something like 1,500 words a day, and though the writing is unselfconscious, it is not unconsidered; they can scarcely represent less than two hours work. And it is not as though Kilvert had just arrived at Clyro and had not yet established a settled routine for his days. He had already been there over four and a half years; how had his time been spent previously, if he could now – apparently effortlessly – find two hours daily to invest in a diary?

We don't know. One obvious explanation would be that the evenings spent writing in the lamplight (or was it candlelight?) were replacements for some other evening activity that had recently failed him; but what that might be is not easy to say. On the whole, the easiest explanation is probably the prickings of an acute sensual awareness for which the ordinary round of his life provided no sufficient outlet. It is not difficult to imagine its urgings growing more insistent over the years. The conventional vehicle for expressing them would be verse, and we know that Kilvert was trying his hand at that before 1870. But verse, though Kilvert never stopped versifying, was not a weapon that ever fitted snugly to the particular form of his sensibilities, and perhaps it was a realization of this that led him to try another form, and to find that this time he had chosen right. On New Year's Day, 1870, he put pen to paper and began.

The chances of things are so strange. The son of a Wiltshire parson, of a family with a long Shropshire ancestry, lives an obscure life in the nineteenth century as a curate and vicar in villages on the Welsh border, and dies, still young, and is to all practical intents forgotten. And the world goes on and changes, and eighty years later a history teacher, much of Kilvert's own age, descendant of a family which until the last two generations never strayed outside Jersey, finds himself in Adelaide and picks up an old book, and suddenly those two lives apparently so unapproachably remote are crossed and knotted, and the way Kilvert spent his casual summer afternoons a century ago is of interest to me and is echoed in my brain now.

It was more than anything else the power of Kilvert's Diary to bring a lost landscape to life in its full range of evocations and associations that gave it its enchantment for me, when I lit on it in that far and alien country. He fed my nostalgia. None of the other great diaries does this to such an extent, and it is Kilvert's ability to do it, I believe, that accounts for most of his hold over so many people. And that ability in turn lies in his powers of vision and description; though there is more to it than this: the rousing of nostalgia requires a state of mind in the reader as well as a quality in the writer. I read his Diary, and I loved it, and in due course I came home.

In 1962, I was back from Australia in England and found myself teaching at Shrewsbury. Kilvert's two countries – for he had two, Radnorshire and Wiltshire – still dwelt with me, not much less powerfully for my return, and both were still strictly faerylands, places of the imagination only, known to me from the Diary alone. The chance of my travels had never taken me to either, although Radnorshire, at least, was close to Shrewsbury; close, and yet tantalizingly far enough to be beyond the range of casual outings. But I never had any doubt that, when the day came, I must go and see for myself.

1962 *4 July*. Henley whole holiday; an unsettled day, dark clouds and showers, but also some brilliant weather. Set off to visit Kilvert's country and do some branch line travelling that will soon be impossible at the same time. Caught the 8.45 to Newport, changing at Hereford. At Newport caught the 11.15 to Brecon. A tremendously long heavy climb, up through green agricultural land to a country of deep valleys and great frowning flanks of hills, thickly sown with collieries and colliery towns, lines, half of them abandoned and rusting, branching in every direction; up to emerge on bare open featureless grass uplands, where the collieries and their villages squat, but have no real hold on the landscape, over Dowlais Top to the more striking country of the Brecon Beacons, nobly sculpted on the grand scale, round a big reservoir, and up at last to the summit at Torpantau Tunnel. Emerged to a wonderful view down the valley toward Talybont and the Usk. Changed at Talyllyn to a Builth train, and so through rich farming country dense with trees and foliage, the cuttings purple with foxglove and campions and white with big daisies, to Three Cocks Junction, a delightful station in the middle of nowhere, a meeting-point of three routes all equally unimportant. There caught a Hereford train to Hay, into the Kilvert country at last – followed it with fascination from the map in the Diary. I've never clearly visualized it, and hadn't imagined it as it is – the wide valley of the gravelly Wye flowing between ranges of hills rising to a considerable height, to the south-east to great bare summits – I hadn't thought of *that* as upland. Very remote unspoilt country; most of the views from this line Kilvert must have known so well can hardly have changed. Reached Hay at 2.30, a silvery-grey, very quiet old little town on the banks of a Wye here shallow and very wide. Got a snack in a café, found the castle at the summit of the town where Kilvert's friends the Bevans lived, and had a look at the odd and hideous imitation Norman church. Then set out to walk to Clyro. I've never done a pilgrimage like this before, visiting a place known well to me through the writings of another man. Strange how much Kilvert attracts me. And all the perplexities of time, of going where he went, of passing the gate of Wye Cliff which he mentioned so often, where he called ninety-two years ago to the day – was it a day like this, and what has changed? Now he is only a ghost: he only exists as a reason for my making this walk; and may I sometime be a similar ghost, existing only as a reason for somebody else's walk? A dizzy thought. Clyro itself a remarkably plain little village, with a main road carving through it. Saw what I took to be Clyro Court, Caemawr, and the vicarage where the Venables lived. The church was being decorated, swarming with people carrying things and smelling of distemper – a plain, restored, uninteresting little building. But as I walked back to Hay, it was a superb afternoon, that Kilvert would describe so much better than I. The sun was out and very hot, bright on the Castle and the town across the river (Kilvert's bridge has been replaced), while great blocks of cloud shadow trailed over the high dark hills behind it. The road rises and dips delightfully, and the wide gentle valley is immensely peaceful and fertile. Caught the 5.02 to Hereford and as far as Whitney this was all country intensely familiar to Kilvert; the Wye flashing brilliant silver beside the train, and the houses, Rhydspence and Cabalva, by the road at the foot of the hills on the far bank, along which he used to walk home from Whitney Rectory, which I think I recognized. Abandoned branch lines go off north and south into the hills. Caught the 6.20 home from Hereford.

So the threads of Kilvert's life and mine drew a little closer: ninety-seven years after he first saw Clyro, I followed him. I came by train, as he always did, but at the time of his coming to Clyro the railway from Hereford was brand new, opened only the year before his arrival, whereas when I came it was within two years of its closure, and I was never to travel by it again; at my next visit, the lines were already lifted, grass growing along its former track under Hay bridge. I am glad that I came that way once, for these things make a difference. The route by which you habitually approach a place, the colour a house is painted, the note of the church clock striking, these things, and a million others like them, all minute to insignificance in themselves, nevertheless contribute something to the impression a place leaves on the palm of your mind.

It was summer when I first saw the place and it struck its first bold outlines on my mind. You never outlive these first impressions – different enough, in many particulars, from the picture my imagination had drawn. I had known nothing before of the immense brooding presence of the Black Mountain that glowers over the valley from the south. I had never seen the Wye, and the breadth and the richness of the valley, the scale of the river flashing and sparkling over its shallows, were surprises to me, something I had not learned from the Diary. How did it look to Kilvert, I wonder, that day in the early spring of 1865 when he came here for the first time? Stranger and more exciting than to me, I think, for Kilvert was a young man coming to his first job away from home, and in 1865 England was a wider and less tame country than it is today, distances longer, dialects stronger, regional identities more pronounced; and Kilvert did not know it already through the eyes of another as I did, although he knew and loved his Wordsworth, who himself knew and loved the Wye, and the Wye must still have ranked high among the best-known and most publicized beauties of England in the 1860s.

The buildings of Hay sat a little lower then, I think – the Crown Hotel had not yet gone up in Broad Street to dwarf everything else with its scale and its ugliness. The town must have felt more secret than now, with a more intense private life, and less open to the world; and he crossed a different bridge, though on the same site as today's. But as far as sheer appearances go, I think that what I saw as I walked out to Clyro that first day, a long switchback mile from Hay, is very much what he saw – until I came to the village.

For Clyro itself is a disappointment, when after a long acquaintance with it in the Diary you first see it as it now is. The Clyro of the Diary is a village in Arcadia. The Clyro of today is what I called it when I first saw it, a plain little village, a crook-legged street which has lost all the coherence and most of the character it must have possessed in Kilvert's time, a succession of strangely unrelated buildings in incompatible styles, non-styles, and building materials. Kilvert's Clyro must at least have had in common the shaly grey sandstone of the neighbourhood, the invariable building material for everything from a pigsty to a church until a hundred years ago – until the railway, in fact; and I suspect that its buildings were spaced out with some degree of companionship, of instinctive relationship. Today it is a ragged street of odds and ends: some houses advance threateningly to the very edge of a mean little pavement, others lie back behind their gardens, the village hall stands aloofly up a bank, the desolate gloom of its design and its dull red brick weighing heavily on the street and the spirit, and the new vicarage turns its back resolutely on the village like the prim little middle-class villa it is; a dusty bow window is veiled in plastic, the brisk and awful post-war police house is painted in blue and pink and yellow. Nothing relates; the buildings ignore each other; the street is a heap of fragments. Only a group of cottages up the Painscastle road, beyond the churchyard, retain a natural seemliness; and another group at the far end of the village street too, the hotel, a gaunt stone house opposite, the post office, and a little wayward cluster of cottages,

---

Opposite: Clyro: the view from the centre of the village looking up the Painscastle road, as it was early in the century and as it is today. Apart from the felling of the trees, there has been little change here. The building on the left is the old smithy; the picture of the village smith (p. 176) was taken immediately in front of it.

are likewise still on speaking terms and keep the coherence of the old order – though chaos threatens here too, in the spreading asphalt of the hotel car-park and the bright trim little modern bungalow beyond it.

An order has dissolved here; and the disintegration must have started just after Kilvert's time. Indeed, with a sure eye he recognized the start of it when one day in August 1878 he came over to visit Clyro from Bredwardine ten miles down the valley, where he was then the vicar.

1878 *28 August*. The Anthonys live now in the hideous huge staring new cottages which dwarf and spoil the village. [The Anthonys still live there.] They ought to have been built further back from the road with some pretty little flower gardens before the doors. Old Hannah Whitney's cottage, at the door of which she used to sit knitting so cheerfully in mob cap, crossover shawl and spectacles, is alas pulled down.

His judgement did not fail him. The new houses, no doubt, were a row of model estate cottages in the 1870s – they bear the crest of the Baskervilles, the owners of the Clyro Court estate which comprised most of the parish – and their occupants probably thought better of their 'hugeness' than Kilvert did; but they were built with no eye to their effect on the appearance of the village. Though they are still built of local stone, they are probably the last buildings in Clyro that were and already they are disfigured by the use of a dull red brick for the window dressings.

Even the church was disappointing to me that day in July 1962. I had assumed, from one's general notion of Arcadia rather than from any definite passages of the Diary, that it would be old. It stands handsomely enough in the middle of the village, in the midst of the crowded headstones of Kilvert's 'sleeping folk', an avenue of yews leading to it from the lych-gate (though the wych-elms of Kilvert's time are all gone), and it is dignified by a western tower of fine proportions; but, inside and out, it is essentially a nineteenth-century building, architecturally too late for Arcadia. In Kilvert's time it was nearly new. It is, as a matter of fact, a moderately successful piece of Victorian Gothic. well proportioned, light, and well kept, but it is not what your imagination has led you to expect. There are a dozen churches of greater interest within a radius of ten miles, as there are a dozen more picturesque villages.

I do not think it can ever have been an especially beautiful village; rather, Kilvert's Clyro must have been a modest and seemly little place set in a magnificent landscape. But, though the landscape is unchanged, the Clyro we see is not Kilvert's Clyro, and considering how lightly, relatively speaking, the hand of the last hundred years has brushed over Radnorshire and the upper Wye Valley, we may justly feel that it has rested cruelly hard here. Cruellest of all, it has brought the road. What to Kilvert was just the road to Llowes in one direction, the road to Whitney in the other – for if you were going further in either direction, you went by train – is now the A438, Hereford to Brecon, and along it from Willersley westward pours a formidable stream of heavy truck traffic from Leominster and the Midlands to industrial Wales, Llanelly, Neath, and Swansea. The impartial factuality of the invention of the internal combustion engine and the relative economics of rail and road transport have left the railway track at Hay a grass-grown path and come close to devastating Clyro. The mounting weight of traffic pouring down the narrow village street induced the County Council in the 1960s to build a short bypass through the fields on the east of the village, and since then the village street has regained a lot of its old peace, but at the price of a desert of asphalt, where the bypass diverges from the village street, that desolates the approach to the village from Hay; at the price too of being cut off by the broad channel of roaring tarmac from the green fields that lapped up to the houses in Kilvert's day.

But if Clyro was a disappointment that day, the general landscape was not; this is something that a hundred years have hardly touched. The Wye here, a broad, flashing, gravelly river, runs north-east down a wide valley backed by powerful hills. The hills west of the river are the lower, but they still go up to over a thousand feet, and in Kilvert's time the tops were for the most part bare moorland. The slope down to the valley bottom is convex, wrinkled with narrow wooded dingles, and scattered over it are the modest little white and grey hill farms and cottages that Kilvert knew so well. Gwernfythen, Llwyngwilliam, Wernypentre, and so on, most of them approached up narrow high-banked lanes; these are the hillsides that he quartered so densely in his walks as he did the rounds of the parish. The hillside steepens, falls over a brow, and comes down to the valley floor in a rush, and plump at the foot of it sits Clyro, like a village with its back to a wall; from the top of the Bron you could almost pitch a stone down the chimney of the Baskerville Arms. Nearly a mile of valley bottom still separates you from the river; but, while most of the Wye Valley hereabouts is flat meadowland, much subject to flooding, a low bumpy ridge reaches out from Clyro to Hay bridge. The cross-valley road follows it, and has done for a long time. The Romans too crossed the river here – the site of their camp, the Gaer, is in the fields near the road, beside Boatside Farm, where the Hamars lived – and when the Normans built their castle at Hay that too must have been to protect the river-crossing. They built another one at Clyro itself; the motte stands just opposite the group of council houses at the point where the Hay road leaves the village, and a widening of the road has exposed one flank of the mound. It bore fine trees in Kilvert's time, which he saw felled; today it is covered with a jungle of scrubby elder, but it is still the Castle Clump. In winter, when the valley is under snow, it serves as a nursery slope for the village children on their sledges and fertilizer-bags; and did then, I dare say.

Beyond the Clump the cross-valley road dips into the hollow of Peter's Pool, a boggy wooded bottom beside the road, now fast being filled up by a local authority rubbish dump; then rises quite steeply for a quarter of a mile or so. This is the Longlands pitch, where Richard Meredith the land-surveyor once delayed Kilvert with his speculations on whether animalculae had the power of feeling. (Any sudden steep rise in the road is a 'pitch' hereabouts – the sudden rise of the Rhosgoch road, as it slants up the hillside from the north end of the village, is 'Tom the Cutter's Pitch', whoever Tom was.) As you top the rise, away to your right on a clear day you glimpse, far away on the south-western horizon at the head of the valley, the graceful line of the Brecon Beacons, shaped like little waves rippling in from two sides on the central peak of Penyfan, and frozen in the moment before breaking. At your feet the road falls away again equally steeply to the river and Hay bridge; and on the far bank lies Hay, in the noblest setting that a little town could ask for. It is a view that has naturally the quality that the eighteenth-century landscape

designers valued so highly and sought so ingeniously – unexpec-
tedness; however well you know it, there is still surprise and
delight as you top the hill and there it is at your feet. Hay lies on a
steep little boss of ground above the river; its grey stone houses,
their slate roofs catching the light at every angle, huddle up
round the half-ruined castle with its group of stately trees that
crowns the boss – the castle where the Bevans lived. But it is the
backcloth that gives the view its quality.

Beyond the Wye the hills go up again immediately, and
grandly, in two colossal steps. The farmlands slope up steeply to
about a thousand feet, the slopes steepening as you climb, till just
below the crest the fields refuse at it, and the escarpment breaks
out in patches of common, rough wood, and occasional crags of the
living rock, the red marls that compose it. Here and there the
wall is broken by the valleys of fast tumbling streams – Devon
would call them combes, Shropshire batches, but here they are
always dingles – and between them the escarpment thrusts out in
abrupt headlands, wooded on the crest – the Welsh word is 'allt',
and it appears more than once hereabouts. Between these headlands the escarpment is broken by several breaches, and the
broadest of them is Cusop Dingle, behind Hay itself. As you look
down on Hay from the top of the Longlands pitch, it lies gazed
down on by a lordly ring of hills. Cusop Dingle cleaves back deep
to the roots of the escarpment, rising evenly to nick the skyline at
its top; on each side of it the flanking hills fall back, the valley
broadening out as it sinks, and there plumb in the mouth of it on
its hillock, like a diminutive actor on the stage of a Greek theatre,
is little Hay, demure but dignified in this huge presence.

If that was all, this would already be a grand landscape; but it
is not all, though if you are walking out from Hay to Clyro, as I
did that day, you may think it is – until, that is, nearing the top of
the Longlands pitch from the Hay side, you look back over your
shoulder, and find that a more formidable presence yet is upon
you. Above the plateau at the top of the escarpment, the hills go
up again in a second step of another thousand feet of bare
moorland, the Black Mountain. Its forbidding scarp looks north-
westward across the valley and at its northern tip ends in two
final headlands, the immense black bastion of the Tumpa, and,
last of all, the long prow of Hay Bluff, thrust forward to overlook
Hay itself. The mountain closes the Clyro landscape with drama-

tic finality; it also introduces into it a new quality. It is hugely naked, a vast whaleback clothed only in bracken and whortle-berry, treeless, unwalled, uncultivated, untamed; it brings into the landscape something rare in southern Britain, the elemental, the non-human, and it brings it gigantically. As you walk out from Hay along the Clyro road, the lower escarpment almost hides the mountain until, as you climb the hill up from the bridge, abruptly the stark triangular hump of Hay Bluff thrusts up over nearer hills like a giant looking over his garden wall. It is a rare and memorable trick of landscape formation, and it commands awe, the rising of this immense pagan presence, as you realize that the world is a full dimension larger than you thought and contains things stranger and more powerful than you knew. It is the same emotion, undoubtedly, that went to the making of one of the most perfect romantic images in English poetry, the famous passage in *The Prelude* in which Wordsworth describes the night when he took a rowing-boat out into the moonlit Ullswater, until –

> from behind that craggy steep till then
> The horizon's bound, a huge peak, black and huge,
> As if with voluntary power instinct
> Upreared its head. I struck and struck again,
> And growing still in stature the grim shape
> Towered up between me and the stars, and still,
> For so it seemed, with purpose of its own
> And measured motion like a living thing,
> Strode after me.

This was Kilvert's familiar landscape. In its outlines he never describes it, for when he started his Diary, it had already been familiar to him for five years, and a diary's function is to describe the new, not the familiar. But the form of the Clyro landscape lies behind and is taken for granted in every entry of the Diary. It is the things that go unmentioned because they are most familiar

---

Opposite: Clyro, the valley, and the Black Mountain, from the Bron behind the village. Ashbrook is visible in the extreme bottom left-hand corner, and the village school where Kilvert taught is directly above the church tower. Castle Clump is in the middle of the picture; the council housing estate just in front of it has gone up since 1970. The outskirts of Hay can be seen in the middle distance, just above the bend of the river; on the skyline beyond is Hay Bluff.

that are the ones that are always with us and leave the deepest mark on us. But it was to be seven years before I next saw Clyro.

Australia again. Sydney. Spicer Street, Woollahra. Remorseless blue skies and heat. The Eastern Suburbs – Italian greengrocers, Greek milk-bars, the Cypriot hairdresser, the German delicatessen. Going to the laundrette in Paddo. Poor old fly-blown Centennial Park. Charlie Connolly our neighbour hopefully writing songs for Joan Sutherland. Umpiring cricket. The University – lunches with Geoff in the Staff Club. Carlyle, praise be, Acton, Macaulay, Maitland. The psychology department's white rats in cages. Flying paper darts out of the window. Marriage. M. Children, C, E. Not very homesick now; married, you're like a snail and carry your home with you. But still wanting to come home.

1967 *31 December*. The stream of our life in Sydney seems to be running dry: it's time to move. We are on the very brink of a decision to go back to England. I have various things in mind – chiefly the idea of going to live near Clyro for a year or two, and doing a new, retrospective version of Kilvert.

The two lives were drawing a little closer; the lines tightening a little. The instinct, impulse, whatever it was that in January 1870 had led Kilvert to start keeping a diary was now, a hundred years later, having its effect in Sydney; the ripple had taken its time, but it had crossed the world.

To go back and see how things were at Clyro now. *To go back:* the very idea is retrograde, an idea typical of a man, a class, a time, a time above all. My nostalgia at Adelaide was a nostalgia of place, but beneath it there lay a nostalgia of time, and this now was working itself out. For what gives Kilvert's world its magic, as he described it in the Diary, is of course that it is the garden from which we have gone out, and looking back to it we recognize its beauty and our loss. It is the sense of loss that is haunting, the sense that something we once had has slipped from us; and no gain is compensation. Gain or no, that loss should occur is an outrage and a cause for question. The mood itself is a token of the gap between now and then, for it is something that Kilvert very rarely felt, I think – this sense of concern for the Clyro of a century before, this sense that that former Clyro is in some way an indictment that must be answered. The mood of the Diary is

Arcadian, not nostalgic; it is because of that that it can feed nostalgia so powerfully. Not, certainly, that nostalgia was not alive in the England of 1870: witness Tennyson and Matthew Arnold; it had come at the latest with industrialism fifty years before. But Kilvert's background was the country rectories of rural southern England, where the sense of change and loss came late and slowly, and there is little of it in him. He brings a Wordsworthian sensibility to a landscape that itself did nothing to arouse nostalgia; for what evidence was there of recent change, of an older order lost, at Clyro in 1870? The railway had just come to Hay with all the presence and dignity that characterized railways in the nineteenth century, when they monopolized long-distance land transport as nothing ever will again; but the railway's power of infecting a landscape is modest. I have myself seen in India how it can co-exist for decades with a primitive countryside; and here on the Welsh border in the 1870s, in spite of the daily passage of the trains, change crept on in the valley and the village with seemingly geological slowness. Even the eighteenth-century enclosures had not touched this border country. Kilvert found a village in full touch with its past, and not aware of an unbridgeable 'then' and 'now', where only the most sensitive indicators suggested anything different – the miller no longer saw fairies dancing at night at the Rhosgoch; the folk were forgetting their songs. Was it perhaps a premonition of the storm brewing over Christian Malford that enabled Kilvert to see so intensely the May landscape while the hammerheads were building up over the horizon, to see it and to write it and hand it down? But a middle-class middle-aged Englishman in the 1960s looked at Kilvert's Clyro with a sense of conscious loss, and felt the need to know how much had gone.

1969 *24 April*. Set off from Shrewsbury about 11.30, the object being to look for a house near Clyro. The day, though occasionally showery, was superb, bright with windy light: beautiful sun and shadow on the flanks of the Lawley and Caradoc as we went south. Ludlow, where we stopped briefly, was looking splendid, quite unchanged, its hill crowned by the grand serene lines of that wonderfully-riding church. And on south on a road I've never travelled before, over the sad remains of the Wyre Forest branch at

Woofferton and across through magnificent pastoral country whose churches no longer looked Shropshire, past
Weobley, till the Brecon Beacons gathered on the dim
skyline and at Whitney we joined the Kilvert world, where
I came before – by the railway whose bridge over the Wye
is now a gaunt ruin. Past Rhydspence, a fine but tumble-
down black and white inn, and Cabalva, a stone farmhouse, to Clyro – appalled by the mass of heavy truck
traffic the road carries. We were directed up to Cae Mawr,
a beautiful early 19th century house high on the hillside –
the drive climbs between crowds of daffodils under a grand
avenue of beeches and elms and the view over the valley is
immense. A nice woman showed us the old gardener's
cottage, which is for sale – a squalid little place, but with
the accompanying stable block and walled garden and a
beautiful position it has wonderful romantic possibilities if
one had the money. We wandered round it, but it won't do
for us (Kilvert must have known it in its glory).

He did. He saw it – the garden from which we have gone out – in
spring too. Ninety-nine years ago he was here, solicitously
looking round the garden for Cooper, the head gardener, to
enquire whether he had completely shaken off that fine Victorian
complaint, 'stoppage'; it was all in glory and order then, the day
so fine and hot, the fruit-trees in blossom on the rosy brick walls.
Demolished railway bridges, ruined gardens – we live among
ruins, as Kilvert did not. True, Whitehall was a hollow shell and
up on Clyro Hill Maria Lake's cottage was crumbling away, but
these were mere individual losses; he did not have, as we have,
the relics of a whole lost order of things before his eyes. To him,
this order must have looked natural, the tip of the shoot, the
growing-point of a long history; whereas we know and see ours to
be built on ruins. No wonder if we think much of the past, and
almost always of it as something alien and severed from us rather
than as the stock from which we grow.

(*We* – but who are we?)

As it happened, we were treading very closely in Kilvert's
footsteps that day when we went up to Cae Mawr, for it was the
home of the Morrells, who seem to have been the closest of his
many friends at Clyro, and he must have known every step and

turn of that drive up the hill; though the avenue of fine beeches in whose tops the rooks nest and behind which the sun sets in winter can only have been young then. But the Morrells have gone, and in April 1969 the old walled garden that Cooper tended for the Baskervilles of Clyro Court was a wilderness, his cottage squalid in its dereliction. Our hunt that day was to have a different and more surprising conclusion.

> We asked a woman at the house if there was anything else going in the village, and she told us that Kilvert's own house, opposite the pub, is for sale! We can't get the key till tomorrow: it's a big, grim, shabby stone house, too close to the main road, but what a temptation!

Strange that on my first visit to Clyro I had apparently never thought to look for Kilvert's home; yet after all not so very strange. For I had come then to see the Clyro that I had come to know through the medium of the Diary, through Kilvert's eyes in fact, and the house in which he lived was *behind* the eyes; he looked outward from it. It figures very little in the Diary; but it is still there, grey, tall, and gaunt, presenting to traffic coming down the main road from England a broad grim northern wall, relieved only, and most unexpectedly, by a wide-arched Gothic window extending the height of two floors. It is an anomalous, awkward-looking house, its proportions all wrong, its roof-line and the positioning of its windows falling continually into clumsy asymmetries – the work, one would say, of a builder making a blundering attempt to do an architect's job. Socially, too, it is abnormal; it fits into none of the common categories and it seems impossible to say for whom such a house might be intended. It is not a farmhouse, and it had no outbuildings except a ramshackle wooden stable and coach-house at one end in an advanced state of disintegration. It is not a gentleman's country house, placed as it is right on the village street with no grounds and only a small garden. It is not a vicarage – the old vicarage, a much more socially accomplished building, stands a hundred yards up the street. It had, when we first saw it, the desolate air of a house long empty and not in the best repair. But it looked an honest substantial place, built of the local grey stone; the manners, as distinct from the style, of its architecture were decent traditional

early-nineteenth-century manners, and, after all, it was the house Kilvert had lived in, and it was for sale.

1969 *25 April*. . . . over the bridge at Bredwardine (where Kilvert died) and over the very steep Dorstone Hill, with a wonderful view back over the chequered country north of the Wye, down into the Golden Valley, which is smoother and calmer than the Wye valley and along by the old railway, through Westbrook to Hay, where we picked up the key of Kilvert's house, and so on to Clyro. The house is an exciting place. Much of it recently papered, but it very badly needs modernization – a fair bathroom, but plumbing and electricity otherwise fairly primitive, beastly ugly modern fireplaces for heating, a Rayburn in an impossible room in the basement for cooking: patches of damp, some cracks of unknown seriousness etc. But it has considerable charm, and structurally it must be unaltered since Kilvert's time; the floors are good, and the general structural condition seems fair. The garden is a reasonable size; there are some fascinating varieties of level, and a stream running in a channel below the garden level. Some of the rooms are attractive, with decent Victorian panelling. I don't see how we can *not* make an offer.

It was Kilvert's house all right, fallen on sad days, but in all essentials the house he knew so well a century ago. We were to learn a lot more about it in due course (for we made an offer, and it was accepted). It is a house of numerous rooms, all of much the same moderate size and with no perceptible gradations of dignity between them. That is, it is built on the social assumptions of a farmhouse, where all the occupants are taken to be of the same class; there are no segregated quarters for servants. But, as I have said, it is clearly not a farmhouse, and questions

---

Opposite: Ashbrook: the house where Kilvert lived, as far as we know, throughout his years at Clyro, and where we lived after him. Kilvert's sitting-room was the ground-floor room on the left, whose window is obscured by the clematis; his bedroom is immediately above it. By the corner of the house is the door into the room originally designed as the estate office. In the foreground is the parapet of the bridge over the Clyro Brook; in Kilvert's time, the village women used to draw their water from steps beside the bridge.

multiply as one examines it. It presents itself to the world in the dignity of a stone house, yet the roughcast that covers one angle conceals single brick; half the floors are oak and half deal; and here and there, in unexpected nooks and crannies, one comes on bits of handsome, though unsophisticated, oak panelling, mixed in with run-of-the-mill deal boarding. It bears all the marks of divided and uncertain intentions; and the village tells a story about its origins whose truth, so far at least, seems unprovable, but which certainly appears to fit the facts.

The house was built, sometime in the 1850s, by one Peter Chaloner, a man of many functions, joiner, keeper of the village inn across the road whose goings-on Kilvert used to observe from his windows without much enthusiasm, auctioneer, and perhaps also the agent of the Baskervilles – the owners of the big house of the village, Clyro Court, and of a good deal of the land in the parish. So much seems beyond doubt, and there is every sign that it was designed by a local builder following traditional practice and rule of thumb rather than by an architect. The local tradition is that Peter Chaloner built it, with the squire's permission and at his expense, as a house for the bailiff of the Clyro Court estate. Certainly it was part of the estate later on; and, to back up the story, one of the ground-floor rooms, which has a separate outer door approached by a flight of steps, was apparently designed as the estate office, and certainly used as such well within living memory. Peter Chaloner, though, built the house at a time when the squire was not in residence at Clyro Court and seized the opportunity to satisfy what one may imagine to have been long-repressed pretensions to social grandeur. The result was a clumsy rustic imitation of a gentleman's residence – it is easy to see, looking at the house, that Chaloner's, or his builder's, taste and sense of proportion were not quite equal to the strain placed upon them. As luck would have it, the church, also just across the way, was being rebuilt at the same time, and – so the story runs – Peter Chaloner seized the opportunity to appropriate some of the rejected fittings of the old church – the great window that is such a striking feature of the house's northern aspect, a lot of panelling, and the heavy pointed door of the basement kitchen. All this is possible: the church *was* being rebuilt in the 1850s, the fittings in question *do* look as if they might have had such an origin. Unfortunately, in the middle of the works the squire returned.

exploded with wrath at the sight of the grandeur his bailiff had deemed suitable for himself, tore out most of the panelling and sent it up to Clyro Court instead, and had the house finished on the cheap.

The story would explain the numerous oddities of the house; odd it certainly is, and it has always been something of an anomaly in the village. What use Peter Chaloner intended for the numerous rooms it is impossible to say, for he does not seem to have had a large family. In fact, for much of its existence it seems to have been used as a lodging-house, and it still bears numerous signs of this today. Peter Chaloner died in 1860, soon after the house was completed; his widow lived in it for many years, and we know she took in lodgers, for she was Kilvert's landlady. In 1861 she seems to have been living in the house with only a grown-up daughter and a servant for company, so there would certainly have been room to spare; and no more natural place could have been found for a young bachelor curate to take rooms when he came to the village four years later. A hundred and five years after, we followed him.

1970 *7 January*. We made a smart get-away from Hereford, leaving the hotel soon after 8.30 with the beginnings of the light. A beautiful drive up the valley, which was under hard white frost but very little snow, the eastern horizon turning orange behind us as another day of brilliant sun and very sharp cold took shape. Reached Clyro at 9.20, driving straight to the school and dropping C. It has under 50 children and 2½ teachers. Talked a bit with the headmaster, Mr Evans, and liked him. . . .

The school that Kilvert knew and where he taught, the old building still there at the end of the village, where the Hay road joins the main road; even the master's name was still the same.

At Ashbrook [as the house is certainly called now, and may have been in Kilvert's time], half the rooms were piled high with packed furniture and effects, the other half completely bare, and all bitterly cold. But if the house was pretty unwelcoming, the view of the Black Mountain under snow in the south was brilliant, and everyone we met in the village was welcoming and helpful. So we set to work

29

on the immense job of settling in. We're living for the time being in what's to be the kitchen, which is free from furniture and has a decent little open fire – using it squalidly for everything. I set to work unpacking cases, looking for blankets, etc.; then drove into Hay in the afternoon for various essentials. Hay seems more and more enchanting, a tiny maze of doll's-house streets, with the towering castle on top of it all – towering, but still really very modest. . . .

The castle that was almost a second home to Kilvert, when the Bevans lived there – Mr. Bevan, vicar of Hay for years, his wife, and a family of children whose numbers in the Diary seem to stretch to infinity. Young men and women, singing round the organ in the hall.

A very mid-twentieth-century middle-class move. Driving out from Hereford (there is no record that Kilvert ever travelled the length of that road in all his time at Clyro, and it is most unlikely that he did). The do-it-yourself assumption of it all, where a hundred years ago the servants would have been there in advance, unpacking furniture, lighting fires, airing beds. The casual improvisation of driving into Hay to bring home what you wanted in the back of the car, where a hundred years ago a mile's journey was not a negligible matter, and the means of getting your purchases home questionable.

> The house gloomy at present, but not eerie. It was pleasant to see light in the great window as I drove up, after it has been dark for so long. But outside the one or two centres of warmth in the house, it's deadly cold.

When we moved in, in January 1970, Ashbrook had stood empty for nearly two years; it was nobody's house, and beginning to look as if it never would be anybody's again, rain pouring in through the roof, darkness lurking in attics and cellar, paper peeling off the walls. It takes time to make a house your own.

Kilvert was so completely part of it, knew it all so well, the lane beside the house, the Clyro Brook running beneath the garden, the Baskerville Arms opposite (he usually called it by its old name, the Swan), the two rooms in the north-west angle of the house where he lived and slept; and they are all still here, and he is gone as if he had never been. I don't understand this.

1970 *8 January*. I got the Rayburn in the old basement kitchen going in the evening. . . .

Mrs. Chaloner's kitchen, undoubtedly, and probably, like a farmhouse kitchen, her living-room as well; one notes again that, for all its apings of gentility, the house's accent is broadly rustic. Likely enough she had a best parlour on the ground floor as well, which would leave two ground-floor rooms for lodgers' sitting-rooms. In Kilvert's time, the household at Ashbrook consisted of himself, Mrs. Chaloner (a widow in her mid-70s), her invalid daughter Elizabeth, a living-in maid (there seems to have been a rather rapid turnover of these), and usually one more lodger – for part of the time at least, a solicitor's clerk from Hay. The household seems to have been an insular affair. There was no common meeting-place – probably it would have been socially out of the question; meals, one presumes, were taken privately; it is true that the solicitor's clerk once asked Mrs. Chaloner if she thought he might sometimes sit with Kilvert in the evenings but Mrs. Chaloner firmly rejected the proposal, to Kilvert's clear approval, on the grounds of Kilvert's well-known dislike of tobacco smoke. Poor lonely young solicitor's clerk, who perhaps had no taste for reading, and who had *not* got a diary to write in the evenings! No radio, no television, no company of his own sort in the village, the pub perhaps socially impermissible – for him, of an evening, the candles must have burned slowly indeed.

1970 *11 January*. . . . we now have the room inside the front door in full use as a kitchen and dining room . . .

The old Clyro Court estate office, where the tenants came to pay their rents, till the estate was broken up and sold in 1950, and the Baskervilles, after a hundred years, were gone from Clyro.

. . . and the back (dining) room is also largely clear . . .

Kilvert's old sitting-room, where Toby the cat used to come in and purr by the fire, where he wrote the Diary, where he could lean out of the window to chat with passers-by at the gate.

And the house, too, is falling into shape round us. All houses are full of ghosts when you move into them, of old purposes and associations you don't share; but as each room acquires a defined purpose and takes on a new look with your furniture, the place becomes friendly and your own; and already this is happening here.

The house is not haunted. I believe in ghosts on the whole, though I have never seen one; and to go pursuing Kilvert while living in the house where he lived, one would think, might be to do something that would raise an echo. But the house is wholly neutral, empty of its past; it received us passively, as no doubt it has received all its occupiers.

1970 *12 January*. The clop of horses' hoofs in the village street – two girls riding by. A rare, exciting, romantic sound.

– to Kilvert precisely as commonplace as the sound of a passing car today. As commonplace, but not the same: a mind shaped round the sound of horses' hoofs is different from one shaped round the sound of passing cars; it is these minute differences which, in sum, make the experience of every age inaccessible to every other.

Though as a matter of fact the sound of horses' hoofs is still common enough to turn few heads in Clyro. There is a good deal of horse-rearing hereabouts – the professional descendants of Jones the jockey, who lived by the corner of the churchyard wall, still have work to do. Hill ponies graze freely over the Black Mountain; pony-trekking centres proliferate; gymkhanas abound; the local hunts flourish; woodland paths are muddied by hoof-marks; one passes girls riding on the grass verges of the road. But the horses which did the work of society then merely occupy its leisure now; it must be fifteen years or so since the last working horse was seen in Clyro.

1970 *18 January (Sunday)*. I went to matins. The church is clean and well kept, but it's a sad business after Kilvert's time – less than a dozen there, and I the only man apart from the vicar and the organist ...

Except for two or three occasions in the year, church-going is almost over in Clyro: Sunday after Sunday, the numbers vary from a dozen to half a dozen, single figures in separate pews, children, middle-aged, the old. I am a Christian and I am usually among them, but I know that the thing is over and that the folk are not going to come back, that a stream has altered its course and the old bed is drying up. It is not Christianity that is over, but one of its crystallizations is, and that the one that Kilvert knew and probably the only one that he would have recognized.

It is not that the village has formally ceased to be Christian: for christenings, weddings, funerals, it still looks to the Church; the vicar still has a recognized public status and a function in the community; the church itself is still, in some sense hard to define but actual, recognized as a public building in which the community has an interest, as for instance the little Congregational chapel across the brook is not. The church's position, plumb central to the village, is not yet altogether a false claim. Clyro is still a community with a good many common aspirations, beliefs, and emotions, and in so far as they find expression anywhere, it tends still to be through the Church, its rituals and its ministrations. It is this function which, I take it, establishment was meant to symbolize; and in this sense, although the Church here is not the Church of England but the Church in Wales which was disestablished sixty years ago, the Church in Clyro is established yet, for this is not the Wales of the chapels.

But the church-going is something different, and that as I say is over. The vicar's warden, one of a family of ten born in the gardener's cottage up at Cae Mawr in the days when the gardens employed six men, remembers the time when the church was full on Sundays and there was a large and flourishing choir; but the choir's blue cassocks now hang mouldering in the vestry, and the congregation has dwindled to isolated survivors, none of them young – call them a faithful few if you like, but you solve few problems by doing so. Kilvert never gives figures, and he sometimes laments the thinness of congregations and the failure of some of the parishioners to come to church; but the impression one gets is of a church comfortably full on most Sundays, which might, speculatively, mean a congregation of 100 or 150, out of a population of about 650. What brought them? It is hard indeed to say now exactly, when most of them probably could not have told you at the time. A simpler, more concrete religious belief, no doubt; equally certainly, a more coherent, more tradition-bound, more socially disciplined community. By which I don't mean that Squire Baskerville checked up each Sunday to make sure that his tenants were in church (he may have done, but I doubt it), but that Kilvert's Clyro was a community in which prescription still had force and many things were done because they had always been done; in which choices, if not actually made for people, were very forcibly recommended to them by common custom, and most went with the tide. We are very free today.

The building, by its size and its emptiness – it can seat over 300 – retains the memory of the older order of things for which it was designed. Architecturally it is exactly the church that Kilvert knew, a nave and north aisle in plain neo-Gothic. It replaces what was probably a much more modest vernacular building like those that still survive in the hill parishes hereabout – Bryngwyn, Colva, Glascwm. Down in the valley, the parish churches are almost all Victorian rebuildings now. At Clyro, the body of the church was rebuilt in 1853, no doubt mainly at the expense of the Baskervilles; the low western tower, with a saddleback roof, survived until Kilvert's arrival in the parish in 1865, in fact just long enough to be sketched by his sister that spring, but at the end of that same year it was heightened and given a battlemented top, thus completing the church as Kilvert knew it and as we see it today.

> Home through the churchyard in the bright mild morning, down the avenue of yews, past the tombstones of people that Kilvert knew.

1870 *20 January*. Drove to the Academy Rooms, Piccadilly, to see the splendid collection of old masters.

Kilvert was on one of his annual winter visits to London. He seems usually to have had a month's holiday from Clyro in August and another over Christmas and the New Year; in the summer he would stay with friends, in the winter he would spend Christmas at Langley Burrell, where the family hearth still burned brightly – his brother and one or two of his sisters would be there too – and then in January he would come up to town,

---

Opposite: Clyro Church, then and now. The upper picture is from a sketch by Kilvert's sister, Dora, and shows the old tower and one of the avenue of wych-elms which in Kilvert's time led up to the church porch from the churchyard gate. The lower photograph looks up this path, now treeless. The crucifix in front of the tower is the village war memorial. The slope behind the church is the Bron; over the roof of the nave, it is just possible to make out the roof of Penllan, where the Williams sisters lived (see p. 132).

Clyro Church May 25th/68

where he would pay visits, take friends' children to a pantomime (there is no record that he ever went to an adult theatre), attend services at St. Paul's, and, more than anything apparently, visit art exhibitions. He was a devoted picture-viewer – not surprising in a man whose visual sensibility, as the Diary bears witness, was so acute; yet oddly enough, his comments on what he saw are hardly most remarkable for their visual awareness.

> One of the finest pictures and the one which struck me most was a priceless Murillo, 'The Good Shepherd', a child with a crook walking between and guiding two lambs. One of the lambs walks meekly by the child's side. The other looks playfully up into his face. The child's eyes are uplifted and in them and over his whole face there is a marvellous beauty. An indescribable look of heavenly light and purity and an expression in which are blended sweetness and trust, resignation and love. The Good Shepherd whilst guiding his lambs looks upward for guidance himself. . . .

He speaks our language, but the gulf that yawns between that sensibility and ours is appalling. Murillo is not a name of power today. All the art criticism of the past seventy years has taught us to see in a picture a visual object and nothing else, whereas to Kilvert painting is valued for the vividness with which it can evoke a moral or erotic emotion; form is servile to content. It requires an effort of the imagination these days to grasp even that it is a possible function for painting, which it is – to imagine oneself into the interior of a taste so trained is impossible; a whole mode of seeing art has been turned face downward between Kilvert's time and ours.

It is typical of the man that even by the standards of his own time, his tastes were very orthodox. His sensibilities clearly owe nothing to Ruskin: there is no mention of his ever looking at a Pre-Raphaelite picture, still less at a Turner. He held decorous opinions in an ordered age, though it is still fair to add that he looked at his pictures hard and that his excitement at them was a genuine, not a Pontifex, excitement. The passage, too, invites the comment that Kilvert obviously shared the Victorian idealization of infancy (in the days when Freud was undreamed of and there were three nurses at Cae Mawr to keep the middle classes at a comfortable distance from their children) and that, on paper at least, he is liable to gush. Both are true.

He caught a train home to tea with his friends at Mitcham, the Thomases, where he was staying; the wind was bitter from the east, with stray dry flakes of snow.

1970 *22 January*. Set off in the car at 10.15 for Llandrindod: through Glasbury and Boughrood to Llanstephan, where we crossed the Wye by a perilously frail suspension bridge, then up the valley to Builth and over the hills to Llandrindod, 25 miles in all. . . . 2062429

If Kilvert had ever made a similar journey, he would have had to walk a mile to Hay, catch a Hereford, Hay, and Brecon Railway train to Three Cocks Junction, two stations up the line (now closed), thence a Mid-Wales Railway train up the Wye Valley (this line is also closed) to what was then called Llechrhyd but is now Builth Road, and from there finally a London and North Western Railway train to Llandrindod (the line is open but barely, and staggers along from year to year by grace of a large subsidy), and he would have been lucky to do it in two and a half hours.

Cross-country travel for him was generally much slower than for us; it was also much more restricted, since for travel of any distance he was tied to the sparse railways of Radnorshire, where we roam at will over the complex network of roads. Finally, and here the balance of advantage is less obvious, for him travel was public and leisured, whereas for us it is private and demanding. Kilvert's notion of travel involved falling in with friends on the platform at Hay, sharing compartments, and striking up acquaintances with strangers. He bought leisure with his ticket, stretched his long legs, and delighted in the beauties of the Wye fleeting past the window; we shut ourselves up in metal boxes with our wives and our children, devoting our attention to the control of an expensive machine, and travel across country without ever leaving home. A cramped restricted mode of life which yet made for wide human contacts, a broad and free one which yet makes for fragmentation – the contrast may have a more general validity.

Not that Kilvert would have been likely to make a journey to Llandrindod in any case, for in his day it was hardly more than an undistinguished village in central Radnorshire. Llandrindod Wells is a creation of the years at the end of the century, an alien presence in Radnorshire – a late Victorian spa town of three-storied hotels and boarding-houses in staring red brick, later fallen on evil days and thriftily taken over by Radnorshire County Council as the seat of local government for the county. But in 1870 there was no Llandrindod Wells and no County Council; the sheep grazed on the hills, and the county magistrates ruled the land.

1970 *25 January*. After lunch, set out for Bettws chapel up the hill. It turns out to be a very quiet modest little greystone building, restored after Kilvert's time, squatting on its haunches at the edge of a field surrounded by a line of scrubby macrocarpas – the only access is along the margin of the field. Behind, the broken upland country of low hedges and pastures stretches away to the north, and in front the Wye valley lies open at your feet, just emerging from the Welsh hills into the English plain: the river swinging in broad loops between the hills, shining reac. s of it catching the light here and there, one of them spanned by the Whitney toll-bridge. There was heavy cloud over the hills beyond the river, which thrust great dark headlands out to command the valley, but here and there the sun struck through the cloud in rays made visible, touching the landscape with vagrant gleams of light, one falling on Lower Bettws on the shoulder of the hill just below us, another lying all up the length of Cusop Dingle: very lovely. Fallen bracken along the edge of the field, wet and dead, but a magnificent rich dark brown. This Bettws landscape is infinitely less altered than Kilvert's village....

Bettws (the word means 'chapel') is a chapelry of Clyro parish. I do not know its history, but the chapel is old – seventeenth century at the latest, mediaeval very probably – and built, presumably, for the convenience of the scattered homesteads up in this hilly remote corner of the parish, three miles by road from Clyro village. Kilvert and his vicar used to take turns to conduct Sunday afternoon service here, making the long climb on foot in all weathers, including the occasion when it was so cold that Kilvert's beard froze to his mackintosh. Now there is one communion service a month. The chapel was the centre of a vigorous little community then, led by the Walls of the adjacent Chapel Farm and the Dykes (odd coincidence!) of Upper Cabalva, down on the main road at the hill's foot; both prosperous farmers with upwards of 300 acres, who sent their daughters away to boarding-school, and Wall especially one of the pillars of the parish, twenty-five years a churchwarden – the curate was on very friendly terms at Chapel Farm, and would often drop in there after the service. There were the Hodgsons, who were gentry, from Lower Cabalva, and the younger Dykes from Llwyngwilliam, and Wilding, the clerk, from Tybella along the hill, and probably forlorn Emma Griffiths from the Chapel dingle. All gone, of course, long ago; but for the rest, little has changed up here: buildings, landscape, the great view that the chapel over-looks, fall on the eye in the same patterns still as they fell on his then.

1970 *27 January*. Dull and misty when I set off for Shrewsbury at 9.30, but by a happy chance I took the steep lane up from Rhydspence to Cefn, and as I climbed a marvellous view opened behind me. The Wye valley below was almost hidden under a much greater river, of dense white mist which filled it nearly to the brim. Its surface was almost as level as water, only very slightly billowy, and it was flowing downstream very slowly to the point where the valley opens out into the lower country beyond Whitney. At that point it broke up and thinned out and the strong dark headlands of the hills stood firm among the ruins of it. On the other side of the stream of mist, the lower slopes of the ridge that conceals the Golden Valley were milky and dim behind its fringes, but the crest stood out in sharp dark silhouette fringed with trees; and further round to the right the bumpy rugged uplands were wholly above it, stretching away very desolately under a sky of high solid grey.

Here, too, there has been no history for a hundred years: the reigning clock here is the one that shows geological time, and on that dial a century is far too minute for the eye to perceive.

1870 *1 February*. In the evening netting and *Les Misérables*, that extraordinary pathetic [book] with its marvellous touches and descriptions of touching self-denials of the miserable for the miserable.

Kilvert does not seem to have been a great reader. There are a large number of scattered references in the Diary to the books he is reading, but taken as a whole the picture that emerges is not of a man whose first instinct when alone is to reach for a book, and when in a strange town to look for a bookshop. Indeed, if he had been it is unlikely that the Diary would have been so engaging a work, for he would probably not have been prepared to devote so much time to it. Is it surprising that a man with such a natural feeling for the use of words on paper should show comparatively little interest in the books of others? Perhaps not: it is notable that his interest in poetry seems much livelier than his interest in prose literature, and this is a clear indication of the kind of use of language that appealed to him. Otherwise, there seem to have been a good many occupations – his pastoral activities, contacts with other people, writing his own Diary, walking – that for him took precedence over reading. Moreover the impression one gets from the titles that he mentions is that his choice of books was a casual and random business – there are no clearly marked themes to be discerned, and much of what he read was indifferent or ephemeral. Of the approximately forty titles that he mentions, barely half a dozen mean anything to most people today: *Tristram Shandy*; *The Essays of Elia*; Kingsley's *Alton Locke*; Mrs. Gaskell's *Ruth*; Trollope's *Is He Popenjoy?* (but apparently none of Trollope's clerical novels). Even *Les Misérables* was not his own choice: he was still at home at Langley Burrell, and his sister Dora was reading aloud to them in the evening (in translation, incidentally). Nothing theological, political, academic, or polemical; no Dickens; no Thackeray; no George Eliot (of whom he would probably have disapproved); no Jane Austen; no Brontës; no Carlyle; no John Stuart Mill; no Ruskin. As a list of negatives, it is fairly formidable. (It is worth noting, though, that any surprise at the absence of any mention among his reading of the authors who are today most commonly mentioned in the same breath as himself, Dorothy Wordsworth and Parson Woodforde, is misplaced, for neither was published in his lifetime: indeed, it adds to the stature of the Diary to realize how original it was, how the branch of literature it represents scarcely then existed.) He took *The Times*; he was an occasional, but not I think a regular, reader of the *Quarterly* and *Saturday Reviews*; but in the accepted sense of the word, one wouldn't call him a reader.

His admiration for *Les Misérables*, though, is worth noting, as is his reason for it, and both are worth setting beside his similar admiration of Charles Kingsley's 'social novel' *Alton Locke*. One senses here his genuine feeling for the hardships of poverty, and for the readiness of the poor for self-sacrifice to help each other's need, a quality so often remarked on by Victorian social commentators. This was something that Kilvert knew for himself by direct experience, by his tireless visiting round the cottages of Clyro and Langley Burrell; and it's fair to observe that this instinctive sympathy can come close at times to cracking the surface of Kilvert's equally instinctive social conservatism.

1870　*7 February*. A letter from Emmie bringing at last the good news that she, Sam and the children are really coming home next month for two years. Sam is to have half pay £1,000 per year whilst in England. . . .

Emmie was his sister, Sam his brother-in-law, a colonel in the medical service of the Indian Army – the Kilverts thus, like so many English upper-middle-class families of the nineteenth century, had their tie with India, that great mysterious exotic Possession, so much more alarming and so much more deliberately Possessed since the Mutiny a dozen years before. Nevertheless, there is no sign that the idea of it generated in Kilvert any of the emotional excitement that the idea of Empire was to rouse in so many twenty years later; he takes it wholly for granted. From time to time, Sam and Emmie wound their slow way home on leave, by P. & O. and the newly opened Suez Canal, they and their growing family and their native ayah who cut such an exotic figure in the quiet country parsonage at Langley Burrell. Sam had no reason to complain of his half pay, well over £5,000 in the values of a century later (and very little of it liable to be poached by the Inland Revenue); just ten times as much as his brother-in-law's curacy at Clyro was worth.

1870 *12 February*. Met two Miss Llanthomases in the street ...
Heard Mary Bevan's misadventures in going to the
Hereford Hunt Ball ... Dinner at Cae Mawr. Mrs. Ven-
ables there ... The Crichtons there too ...

What Mary Bevan's misadventures were we shall never know:
mild, one suspects. The gentry families towered in unchallenged
splendour over the lowlands of rural society in the 1870s, with
their carriages, their walled gardens, their staffs of ten or a dozen
servants resident in the house; as landlords they owned it, as
J.P.s they governed it, as parsons they ordered its creed. Kilvert,
though a poor relation, was of them by reason of his birth, his
education, and his cloth, and it was among them that he found his
friends. They were an intensely close-knit group, always meeting
each other at the regular round of dinners, balls, and parties that
went on in all these houses, Hay Castle, Llanthomas, Wye Cliff,
Cae Mawr. In this remote Welsh border country their position
was all the more unchallenged, for this was gentry, not aristocratic, country – the truly great, the dukes, the earls, the palace-
dwellers, were to be found nearer London.

On this one day he met almost all the gentry families of the
immediate neighbourhood. The Thomas girls from Llanthomas,
the big house at Llanigon, two miles south-west of Hay, whose
father was vicar of that parish; the Bevans of Hay Castle, another
big clerical family – their father, Archdeacon Bevan, was vicar of
Hay for fifty years, and Kilvert was virtually an honorary
member of the household with its swarm of high-spirited sons and
daughters in their teens and twenties (one of them was later to
become the first bishop of Swansea and Brecon, and lies in Brecon
Cathedral now, mitred, in bronze). Cae Mawr, the handsome
white Regency house surrounded by a wide verandah, up on the
hillside opposite Clyro school, the home of the Morrells, a young
couple of Kilvert's age, offshoots of a landed family from the
Thames valley; the husband, Hopewell Morrell, was perhaps
Kilvert's closest friend in the neighbourhood. They had a large
and constantly expanding family of young children, which gave
employment to a governess and three nursemaids. Mrs. Venables,
the vicar of Clyro's young second wife; her husband was up at
Llysdinam, the Venables' family seat on the Wye above Builth.
The Crichtons, also close friends of Kilvert's and again of about

his age, from Wye Cliff, standing high above the river, set back from the road half-way between Clyro and Hay. Only the Baskervilles were missing, the young squire who lived at Clyro Court with his two unmarried brothers, three unmarried sisters, and an entirely celibate household of eight servants, none of them older than 34. This is not surprising, for the Baskervilles do seem to have held themselves somewhat aloof from the other families of the parish; certainly Kilvert saw little of them. They were the only major landowners among the group, and in those landed days, that probably made the difference.

Of their houses, Llanthomas was destroyed years ago; Hay Castle is now the abode-cum-warehouse of the largest second-hand bookseller in the world; Cae Mawr is intact and privately owned by a naturalized Yugoslav potter of Polish extraction; Mrs. Venables' grandson still lives at Llysdinam; Wye Cliff was burnt down ten years ago; Clyro Court has been a secondary modern school for twenty years. The gentry are here still, but they have left their palaces and they reign no longer.

1870 *14 February.* . . . We propose to spend some of the surplus Communion Alms in bedding for the poor people who want it much this vigorous weather. . . . *19 February.* Next to Mrs. Corfield's, and she was deeply thankful for a blanket and pair of sheets, having only one blanket and a house full of children.

Poverty, that accepted feature of the social landscape then that has become an indecency today. The poor are still with us, but to indicate the fact is to make a universally recognized indictment of society. The agricultural labourers of Clyro in 1870 were not, by the standards of the time, a depressed class: there is no trace of unemployment among them, nor of any protest at their lot. But there was abundant poverty, evidenced by bare feet, leaking roofs, families with one blanket between them – think of that, in bitter February weather! – and Kilvert, a kindly and conscientious man, took it wholly for granted. Not, certainly, in the sense that he made no effort to relieve it, as witness Mrs. Corfield. He recognized the obligation of charity, and carried it out – it is said that when carving a joint at table, he always set aside the first slices to be given away. Yes, but! but! but! – was his dinner much the poorer in consequence, and was the poverty of his parishioners any the less?

It is the twentieth-century comment, and again you have to make your choice between morality and history. Like virtually all his contemporaries, Kilvert did not see poverty as any indictment of the society in which it existed, because every civilized society known to history had always involved poverty and none had ever been wealthy enough for its abolition to be a practical possibility. Industrial England was just reaching the stage when such a thing became thinkable, but it would be hard to blame a country curate of modest intellect for failing to perceive a truth concealed from virtually all his greatest contemporaries. In theological terms, probably, Kilvert would have seen poverty as one of the sad but unalterable consequences of the Fall; in human ones, he would have seen it as balanced by charity. Poverty and charity in a poor society are the equivalents of abundance and equality in a wealthy one, and the differences they make in the human beings who experience them must be considerable. Victorian charity, with its sense of seeking out individuals in need and giving them things, must have been a stern and grinding virtue; if it was only a case of Kilvert giving to Mrs. Corfield a blanket bought out of the Communion Alms, the act of giving and receiving must have made formidable moral demands on both; and no doubt such demands often went miserably unmet. But it is a great deal more facile and less demanding to make your donation to Shelter or Oxfam than to give Mrs. Corfield a blanket, just as it is more facile and less demanding to shoot a man from a distance than to stick a sword into him; and abundance and equality make no demand on direct human relationships at all.

But nobody who has been poor and received charity would prefer that system to an abundance relatively widely shared. The trouble, perhaps, was that it was the Kilverts who did all the giving and the Mrs. Corfields all the receiving; of reciprocity there was none.

1870 *15 February*. Owls hooting in the dusk across the dingles and from the heights of Cefn Cethin. Volunteer band in Hay playing across valley, a review in preparation for a Volunteer Concert tonight.

Sounds of the Victorian night – no traffic on the road.

1870 *17 February*. Market people passing by. . . .

1972 *11 February*. The Prices of Penllan were lamenting the decline of Hay market in recent years, remembering the days when buses used to come in from all the neighbouring villages. . . .

Hay market is still on a Thursday, but year by year it is becoming a smaller thing. The two old market halls are closed, and only a few stalls survive; it is as much habit as anything that still brings a good many farmers and their wives to town that day. Almost everyone has a car, and most prefer to do their shopping in Hereford or to come in on Saturday morning instead.

But a hundred years ago it still performed a vital economic function for the countryside, and its importance seems to have lasted little diminished almost till the Second World War; more than anything, it is the spread of cars that has killed it. People hereabouts can still remember the farmers' wives from miles around pouring into the little town in their bonnets, mounted on ponies or donkeys with their baskets of eggs, butter, and poultry beside them. For them, the market was a vital source of income, for it was an understood thing that household expenses came out of the proceeds of their eggs and poultry, their bilberries and blackberries in season. Many of them probably never shopped anywhere else. And, in Kilvert's time at least, the importance of the market was vastly greater because there were many fewer shops in Hay – especially food shops; perishables had to be bought at the market. There was no refrigeration, and nobody would have thought it worth while importing perishable foodstuffs from a distance into a small country town. Now there are supermarkets and a freezer shop in Hay, and many of the farms are equipped with their own freezers, stocked up for months ahead; and the market languishes.

Bird's Nest ... Cwmbythog ... Kilvert was out that afternoon tramping round the parish visiting his people in a bitter east wind, battling with the pain in his eyes that frequently troubled him – migraine, perhaps? It is possible too to guess at psychological strains in a young man whose instincts were so narrowly penned up by the conventions of his age and calling. But he was a tireless visitor, crossing and criss-crossing his parish by lanes and field paths to call at the remotest cottages up on Clyro Hill or down on the edge of the Rhosgoch bog. It was his job – it looks as though the vicar left almost all the pastoral work of the parish to him and he was lucky enough to love it. He delighted in walking, and the Diary bears abundant testimony to his prowess as a walker: it is easy to believe the old shoemaker of Rhayader who remarked on the number of pairs of boots that his father had soled for 'Mr. Kilbert' when he was vicar of St. Harmon. He had a deep and very sensitive appreciation of the beauty of the countryside over which he walked, indeed a half-mystical adoration of it; and finally, he had become very attached to the farming folk of this border country whom he visited. He loved their quick minds and the beauty of their women and children, contrasting both favourably with the Herefordshire folk over the border; he loved the experience of being welcome everywhere, of being invited in to the farm kitchens while the farmer's wife and her grown daughters went about their work and the farm dogs rubbed his legs.

Was he popular in return? It is frustratingly hard to judge what the parish thought of Kilvert, for we see everything through his eyes, outward; hardly any independent memory of him survives. The village today has its doubts; but the few bits of evidence that survive almost all seem to point one way. Kilvert did the job that the village expected of its clergy with all his heart, and seems to have been respected for it. More than that: I doubt if he spoke from any great depth of religious experience, but he was a man with an unusual gift for affection and he loved and sympathized with his people, and at this simple human level, he received much love back. This was essentially a profane rather than a spiritual quality, and to some extent undoubtedly a sensual one – it was the women and the girls in whose company he most delighted, and who returned his affection most warmly. But he seems also to have had a great gift for friendship with the old; and there is no doubt that, if the zeal, and also one would think the success, of Kilvert's parish-visiting owed much to the instinctive human pleasures for which it gave him the opportunity, there was a strong sense of religious duty in it as well; it was not self-indulgence which took him to visit John Meredith's mad sister, or Edward Evans dying in his stinking hovel.

1870 *21 February*. I joined Mr. Venables at Hay at 1.15 and we
went up to Llysdinam together by that train. . . .

Mr. Venables, Kilvert's vicar, was sixty, by all accounts a
somewhat stern country rector of the old school and clearly a man
of considerable authority in the neighbourhood, a leading magis-
trate on the Radnorshire bench and influential among the gentlemen of the county. He had his own country seat at Llysdinam,
about five miles up the Wye valley above Builth; in the early
1870s the house was being rebuilt and the vicar spent considerable time there, often leaving the parish in Kilvert's hands. He
had married twice; his first wife had been at least half Russian,
and he himself had visited Russia and published a book about his
experiences there; but she had died childless just at the time that
Kilvert came to Clyro, and two years later he had married again,
a woman twenty-five years younger than himself, the 'Mrs.
Venables' of the Diary.

Kilvert was on very good terms with the Venables. Toward Mr.
Venables, a man of much natural authority thirty years older
than himself, his attitude probably had more of respect than of
intimacy in it (in the Diary he is always *Mr*. Venables), and a
good deal of awe as well, but between him and Mrs. Venables the
relationship was equally happy and much more intimate. The
curate and the vicar's young second wife! – a delicious breath of
scandal brushes one's cheek; but not a bit of it. There was nothing
romantic whatever between them (as, for instance, there is
always a hint of romantic might-have-beens in Kilvert's references to another young wife, Mrs. Crichton of Wye Cliff). We hear
nothing of Mrs. Venables' charm or her looks, but much of her
kindness and her sympathy; she was Kilvert's confidante in the
village, whom, when in trouble, he turned to most naturally for
advice and consolation. Essentially, she mothered the somewhat
solitary bachelor curate; she was after all thirty-six and, till the
June of this year, childless. Indeed, in the whole relationship of
the Venables to Kilvert, there is something strongly parental.
The rather remote, awe-inspiring figure of Mr. Venables has very
much the look of that of his own father, might indeed serve as a
paradigm of one common type of Victorian father–son relationship; and it is permissible to think that in Mrs. Venables he found
a second mother in whom, because of her closeness to him in age

and of her very remoteness in blood, it was easier to confide than in his own.

1870 *24 February*. A lovely evening and the Black Mountain lighted up grandly, all the furrows and water courses clear and brilliant. People coming home from market, birds singing, buds bursting, and the spring air full of beauty, life and hope. Farm labourers threshing with the machines at Llowes Court. Ash and beech and elms being felled in Clyro Court lands, and going away in timber carriages. Alders being cut down on the left bank of Wye. A market woman's chestnut horse restive in the road and market folk on foot winding their way home through fields by Wyeside.

One of the joys of the Diary is its acute sensitivity to the seasons: reading it, one has a vivid awareness of the exact stage of the passing year. This derives obviously from the sensitivity of Kilvert's own perceptions – not only perceptions of nature, but also, as here, perceptions of its reflection in human activity, which make one think of a set of mediaeval illustrations of the seasons. Kilvert's excellence as a diarist resides, in a great degree, in his ability to convey a pure vision, to make us see the Clyro of the 1870s through the clear medium of his eyes rather than through the refracting medium of his brain: he is never so good when he starts thinking and the adjectives begin to creep in. The phrases here are pure vignettes, snapshots seized by a very sharply focussed eye and printed in the prose with the vividness of direct experience, as various and as devoid of blurring comment as the seen world itself. The colour and speed of exposure of that market-woman's restless horse could not be bettered. With the coming of the camera and the colour film, this use of language has fallen into neglect, but could even a camera do this more effectively? How much better this sheer observation is than the abstractions and the pathetic fallacy that he wrings out of the spring air! He was too naïve ever to analyse his own writing and see where its strength lay, or we might have had more of his best work; but the naïvety and the strength are so closely related that perhaps, if the one went, the other would vanish too. But it is worth noting that the chief respect in which Dorothy Wordsworth is superior to Kilvert (in others she is often inferior) is that the purity of her observation is *never*, unlike his, overlaid by this heavy Victorian gilding. She had of course the advantage of writing in 1800, not 1870.

I envy that purity of vision; but I am committed to thinking.

Inconspicuous in the middle of Arcadia, here, you notice, the machines are already at work: had been, indeed, for fifty years.

1870 *26 February*. Kilvert walked eight miles over Clyro Hill and Newchurch Hill to the tiny hamlet of Colva, to call at the inn beside the little low whitewashed church.

> Mrs. Phillips, the landlady of the Sun, was much frightened when I asked for her husband, uneasy and nervous lest I should have come to apprehend him for having been in a row or doing something wrong. But when I said I wanted the words of an old song, she was greatly relieved and said at once, 'Oh I know who you are. You are the gentleman from Clyro.' I laughed and she began to smile. Mrs. Phillips took me into the parlour where I sat down, tore a leaf out of my pocket book and wrote with my address a request that Phillips would send me by post 1. the song about our Saviour, 2. the song about Lazarus, 3. the song about King James and the Tinker. . . .

This was a very characteristic excursion for Kilvert, and we note that his reputation had preceded him. He had an indefatigable interest in local folklore and local dialect that crops out again and again in the Diary. In the first place, I suspect, this was because it was so intimate a part of the life of the people that he loved; but he carried it to the point of becoming a serious collector of folklore, and this at a date when very little serious recording of this sort had yet been undertaken and when as an academic subject it did not yet exist. We know that as early as November 1868, he had mentioned to Mr. Venables his notion of writing something about the 'traditions' of the neighbourhood: in 1872 there was some discussion of the possibility of publishing his collection of local folklore in *Archaeologia*, and in 1878 some notes of his on Radnorshire dialect appeared in *Notes and Queries*. It was a collection of a rather indiscriminate, jackdaw-like kind, no doubt; but it seems quite likely that if Kilvert had lived, he might have left behind him a small reputation as a pioneer of folklore research. But it was not to be: the reputation was to be delayed, and of a different kind when it came.

1970 *26 February*. To the Bronith, and took the lane up the hill. The track climbs up the edge of a larch plantation, dips to cross a brook, and comes out in a bare muddy field high on the shoulder of the hill with a fine oak standing alone in the middle of it, and a grand view down the long straight reach of the Wye to Clifford. There has been much grubbing-up of hedges and felling of trees and all is mud and desolation, with no trace of the green lane that Kilvert knew or of the footpath which is still marked on the map. . . .

Here at the north-eastern end of the parish, the owner of Lower Cabalva is gradually swallowing up all the smaller farms and consolidating them into a single big estate. Cottages are falling into ruins, and hedges being swept away to clear the vast fields that appeal to modern farming techniques. The landscape is changing as it has not done for centuries, taking on some of the open rolling spaciousness of the Downs.

On the steep pitch above Whitty's Mill a big yellow ditch-digging tractor was clearing out the laneside ditches, the long arm groping jerkily and clumsily into the mud. Its driver and the three roadmen at the Bronith were the only people I met in all the walk; the countryside is much emptier now than in Kilvert's time.

Much; very much. The machines have taken over from the men. The whole vast class of agricultural labourers, far the biggest in the parish in Kilvert's time, has vanished almost entirely – the great bulk of the work is done by the farmers themselves with their wives and families, often teaming up with relatives and neighbours at times of pressure. By them and their machines, that is. The drift from the land to the higher wages and greater freedom of the towns was just, very slowly, gathering way in Kilvert's own time, thanks above all to the coming of the railway, and accelerated steadily thereafter. There are few farmers today in Clyro, where most farms are not bigger than 150 acres, who can consider employing labour. A hundred years ago such an acreage would probably have required the labour of three men. As it is, agricultural wages are too high for the small farmer at the same time as they are still unattractively low for the labourer, and the machines have appeared to fill the gap. Apart from the sound of them, the countryside is now empty, the paths untrodden.

1870 *28 February*. Home after midnight in wind and rain, cheered by the solitary light in Hay looking towards the Moors.

A four-mile walk home from Hardwick vicarage; it is almost a lost experience – who walks four miles home after midnight these days? Kilvert walked everywhere, unthinkingly. He never owned a horse, which was as much a luxury article then as a car before 1914; the Model T horse was never produced. And how dark those Victorian nights were! A 'solitary light in Hay' – where today the incandescent orange street-lamps blaze across the valley all night. I remember walking home from Ashburton during the war, the soft Devon darkness unbroken around me; but we have not seen dark nights since 1945.

1865 *2 March*. On this day Kilvert officiated in Clyro Church, as far as we know for the first time: it is the earliest appearance of his signature in the registers. Feeling strange enough, no doubt, and far away from Langley Burrell, where he had been helping his father since his ordination two years before; all those unfamiliar faces, his solitary lodgings, the austere vicar and his aging wife (for the first Mrs. Venables was still alive). On the day of his arrival, his gaze had fallen on the bough of an apple tree in the orchard that then lay opposite the vicarage, and he had told himself that on the day he left Clyro, he would look at it again. Was he doing what I did, on the day I first went to boarding-school, after my father said goodbye and left me? There were thirteen weeks of eternity ahead, and I scratched a hole in the ground, hid a stone in it, and promised myself to come back and find it on the last day of term: it was a guarantee, somehow, that eternity would have an end.

But Kilvert came to Clyro on the brink of spring, and delight waited for him only a very short distance ahead. It waited for me too; but further off.

1870 *3 March*. Bought two copies of *Alone in London* and took one down to Prissy Prosser's for Marianne Price. The child was out, her grandmother sent for her and she came running out of breath, and radiant with delight. Her lovely dark eyes lighted up at the thought of a new book and looked shyly up to thank me from under her long silky lashes.

A large element of that delight was the joy he found in the children of the village people he visited so diligently. I must find out some time what *Alone in London* was – an improving work, I have no doubt. Kilvert had a genius for relationships with children, especially perhaps the children of the poor and especially girls: the roots of it went deep in him, and have been the subject of much debate, but about the reality of the genius there is no doubt at all. They adored him, and some of them at least remembered him all their lives. As both their pastor and (no doubt) the only man of education that most of them knew, he had a great deal to give, and he found as much delight in giving as they in receiving it.

1970 *5 March*. I was supposed to be meeting M in Hay, but gave it up and went to meet C from school: just as I turned into Bridge Street, M came hurrying up from the bridge. She had come across the fields and run into the farmer of Tir Mynach, who had delighted her with friendly talk – why should he be told to restore all the stiles on the footpaths Kilvert used across his land, just so folks could go mooning over them thinking of Kilvert? The stiles had been taken out, and *he* wasn't going to put them back. Didn't think much of Kilvert anyway – too fond of the women, if you asked him – spending all his time running around having tea with the women here and making up to them there. And as for those old barns, they had nothing to do with Ashbrook in Kilvert's time – not unless he used to get larking around with the girls in there, that was; they were a disgrace to the village the way they were at present, and sooner or later children would get playing there and be hurt by falling slates or something, and then what? Mr. Price wanted to leave the outside walls as they were anyway, just make a nice garage, like, inside. Were we being able to do what we liked to Ashbrook, now? Then why shouldn't Mr. Price do what he liked to the barns? And so on, and so on, all in the most friendly way. This is all *à propos* of a planning enquiry that's to be held into Price (the garage)'s application to convert the old barns on the village street, that recently were the Ashbrook farm buildings, into a workshop – there's a good deal of local feeling along these lines, resenting busybodies (i.e. the Kilvert Society) sticking their nose in. Actually the Society are only one of several protesters against the proposal, but they seem to get most of the blame locally.

1970 *6 March*. Set off up the Cwm at 3.30 – bright sun, patches of dazzling snow but the southward-facing slopes already green. Found the path above Penllan that crosses the swirling brook by a concrete footbridge, and finally made out the remains of what must be Kilvert's 'Jacob's ladder', a path climbing steeply up the hillside above the stream along the edge of a wood. But Kilvert's woods have long since gone; the woods in the dingle now are only young and untidy fir plantations. The path itself was only discernible as a margin free of trees inside the fence bordering the wood, but a foot or more deep in crackling bracken, brambles, and dead branches – I had a fearful struggle to get up it to the ruined stile at the top, where the molehills each had a tiny drift of snow in their northern lee and there's a wonderful view down the dingle – the top of Clyro church tower rising from the trees at your feet, the road to Hay winding across the valley, the big hills behind, the silent lordly purity of the Black Mountain towering over them all. At its near end, the smooth sloping ramparts of Hay Bluff run back from its sharp brow like a bit of 17th century fortification, something of Vauban's: beyond the

Gospel Pass to the right the slopes are more concave and dramatic, vertically furrowed, and steepening to a series of frowning exposed horizontal strata at the crest.... On past Great Lloyney and the little stone cottage of Tre Waelod, where old William Griffiths the molecatcher lived in Kilvert's time, and out past a grove of dead firs on to the naked hilltop at 1,000 feet, just as a grey snow shower came over the valley like a sheet of dark glass, and snow fell thickly on the hilltop. It had been summer in the valley, but was winter up here all right. The snow stopped as I turned down the lane to the Homme – it died away in a final gentle drift of snowflakes falling in sunlight, catkins yellow in the bare roadside hedge. The Homme, where the poor mad Meredith woman lived, is a mean-looking little farmstead with a penumbra of corrugated iron and old tyres, its fields dotted with the melancholy rusty hulks of decaying cars like tanks on a battlefield....

The paths everywhere are falling out of use, and most of them would be forgotten entirely but for the right-of-way markings on the latest edition of the Ordnance Survey maps. A century ago they were the highways of the village. But the countryside is emptier now; and, what is more to the point, almost all the dwellers in isolated farms and cottages now own cars, so much so that even the buses which wrought such a revolution in rural transport in the 1920s have almost vanished from the roads (there are three a week now to Hereford, one a day to Hay). The revolution in the rural standards of living over a century implied by this is staggering: a world in which folk commonly walked to Hay market from Bryngwyn, five miles over the hills, as remote imaginatively as the Middle Ages. It is a change which even the nostalgic may find it hard to regret with a good conscience. The paths vanish, but paths are not in themselves beautiful, though they may lead to beautiful places, and they vanish because people do not want to use them; if they want to, they can. With difficulty; but one cannot decently ask that Ben Lloyd should have to carry his horse-collar home from Clyro to Bryngwyn, rather than pitching it into the back of the Land Rover, in order to make the climb up Jacob's ladder easier for you and me when we fancy a walk.

We drove to Clyro Court that evening for a whist drive in aid of the school funds. The big house, where Baskerville, the squire, lived, has been a secondary modern school for twenty years; if Kilvert read that, he would assume at once that England must have had its Revolution; the change of functions, to him, could have suggested nothing less catastrophic than the France of 1793. But no: the stealthy processes of Time and Economics do these things gently, but more firmly. The heir killed in the First World War, his sister struggling on till after the Second, the estate then broken up and the house sold; it would have seemed a fantastically improbable prediction to Kilvert, but to us it is so commonplace as to be tedious. The gentry garrisons have evacuated their decaying fortresses.

The house is mid-19th-century Jacobean, graceless and coarse and pretentious, but with a certain scale about it and some fine individual features. A high colonnaded entrance hall leads into the staircase hall, which is the full height of the house and lit by a glass dome in the roof: a pompous ceremonial staircase with massive cast iron balustrades sweeps up to the landings running round all four sides of the well. We played in the old drawing-room, which has elaborate and rather fine plaster decoration on the ceiling and a beautiful and striking iron and brass fireplace – worth £6,000, one of the girls from the school claimed – but is not otherwise attractive. And anyway it's used as a classroom and full of desks – though the building has been quite kindly treated and well maintained, it's a sad sterile shell of the house it was designed to be, the furniture all infinitely too slight and functional for the rooms. My fellow-gent at the table I landed at for half-time refreshments held forth vehemently on the pity of all the gentry leaving their houses and the decay of craftsmanship, also against black immigration etc. etc. M came across a charming chap who worked for the builders who did repairs in the house twelve or fifteen years ago; he told how, set to repair the wall at one end of the drawing-room, they found it was false, and taking it down, found behind it not only the great double doors that open into the neighbouring room, but the elaborate mouldings off the door-

frame, which had been carefully removed and tied together when some forgotten builder put up the false wall in the past. I'm pleased to say they put them back round the doors.

The Baskervilles lived here for a hundred years, and are gone for ever.

1970 *9 March.* The electrician came to have a look at the electrical work to be done in the house, and got talking over coffee in the kitchen – he has known the area for a long time. Electricity, he says, must have been installed here at the time it first came to the village, in 1948 (and what a change that must have been!). Interesting on the present state of the big houses – a good many still privately owned, but often only a fraction of the original house; at Maesllwch Castle and Garnons, two-thirds of the old houses have been demolished since the war. When one thinks of it, it's not a region of very big nor of very old country houses – Maesllwch, Clyro Court, Cae Mawr, Whitney Court, all built or rebuilt since 1800. Did the gentry come with the railways, drawn by the fishing perhaps? He was lamenting, too, the passing of the time before the first War, and between the wars, when there was little traffic and the country was still at its loveliest – though he recalled big Sentinel steam lorries thundering along the main road up the valley at a fearsome lick between the wars. Didn't like socialism – it made things

Opposite, top: Clyro Court: where the squire, young Herbert Baskerville, lived with his unmarried sisters. The Victorian country house is still in its glory in this old photograph, which must date from before 1914. Note the archery target in the porch, and the immaculate condition of the lawns; it was on these lawns, where Kilvert often played croquet, that the Kilvertians sat to hear William Plomer's readings from the Diary (see p. 126).

Opposite, bottom: The country gentry in their splendour, as Kilvert knew them. These are the Thomases of Llanthomas, at Llanigon, whom Kilvert knew well, posed in front of the porch of their family home – itself now long since gone. Mr. Thomas, a squire-parson like Mr. Venables, reigns in the midst of his extensive family; the girl standing in the middle of the group is Daisy Thomas, the object of the best-recorded of Kilvert's romances. But it might be any one of a dozen families – Bevans, Dews, Crichtons, Morrells – with whom Kilvert mixed familiarly: it is a picture of a state of society.

too easy for people. Talking of the depression in the
electrical (as in the building) trade at the moment – his
firm, which used to employ 20 men, now has only 7 or 8.
Selective Employment Tax is a crushing burden. The
E.T.U. too is militant and powerful, and employers – no
·doubt it's a trade of small employers – have to toe the line.

The passing of the time when the country was still at its loveliest
– when was that? As many answers as men, no doubt; what
you do seem to be able to rely on nowadays is a general agreement
that it was at some time in the past, and I do not think Kilvert felt
that. There is a case for saying that one of the happiest chances
about the Diary is that it was kept at a time when the English
countryside was precisely at the peak of its beauty. The peculiar
quality of the English agricultural landscape is its combination of
lushness and neatness, its effect of an estate landscaped and
brought to gradual perfection by the inherited toil of dozens of
generations; and in its pure form, it is hard to imagine that it can
ever have been seen to greater advantage than around 1870. The
great farming depression of the end of the nineteenth century was
on the doorstep, but its presence was not yet sensed. There had
been twenty or thirty years of agricultural prosperity, based on
the growing markets of the industrial cities. Farming techniques
had been improved, yields multiplied; the land was fruitful as
never before. Yet up to this point but hardly further, the great
shock wave of the Industrial Revolution and its consequences had
had little direct effect on rural life and manners. Here in
Radnorshire at any rate, the drift from the land had hardly
begun, the traditional village communities were still intact. The
machine as yet was hardly present – only the threshing-machine
and the slow little branch railway up the valley to Hereford
portended the shape of things to come. Local society moved at the
pace of the horse, and it was the horse too which cultivated the
land. It is our great good fortune that Kilvert brought to this
pre-industrial landscape a sensibility given acuteness by the
unconscious awareness of change to come; for that is, surely, the
essence of the Romantic reaction to the cultivated English landscape. We see that landscape clearly for the first time through the
eyes of the Romantics because their eyes were modern; like us,
they saw the old world in terms of contrast with a new. The

change was very close at hand – a labourer at Langley Burrell caught it for Kilvert once in a memorable piece of unconscious symbolism:

1875   William Ferris told me to-day his reminiscences of the first train that ever came down the Great Western Railway. 'I was foddering', he said, 'near the line. It was a hot day in May some 34 or 35 years ago, and I heard a roaring in the air. I looked up and thought there was a storm coming down from Christian Malford roaring in the tops of the trees, only the day was so fine and hot. . . .'

There is the arrival of the machine in Arcadia for you. A roaring in the air: a storm coming down from Christian Malford. Just so. But just when *did* the great change reach Clyro? And what is the meaning of this nostalgia that slips so easily between our eyes and the reality of that old landscape?

1870   *13 March.* As the sun set, a lovely rose tint stole over the snowy mountains, but paled and died leaving the mountain tops cold dim blue before I reached Clyro. The silent folk lying still in their winding sheets in the churchyard. . . .

There was a visionary in Kilvert somewhere; the touch here is something between Samuel Palmer and Stanley Spencer, and I think this capacity is the most truly original thing we are ever allowed to see in Kilvert, the deepest layer we ever reach. It flashes out only in a very occasional phrase. It has nothing to do with his religion, which lies much nearer the surface: for that reason perhaps, because it could not readily be made to fit into the formal commitment round which a diffident young man ordered his life, it was probably only vaguely sensed by Kilvert himself. Nevertheless it is my guess that it was some awareness of these as it were unsanctified powers stirring within him that led him to start the Diary, where they could find respectable expression. A man who could see the snow-covered mounds in the churchyard that way would need to say so somehow.

1870   *16 March.* Below Tybella a bird singing unseen reminded me how the words of a good man live after he is silent and

out of sight. . . . Also the scent of an unseen flower seemed
like the sweet and holy influence of a good kind deed which
cannot be concealed though the deed itself may be hidden.

Kilvert could be pretty bad, too, and as usual the bad is as
significant as the good. Beside his occasional visions, these trite
moralisms are sad stuff indeed, and the reason surely is because
they come from the formally religious level of his consciousness,
which was a shallow one; one can see in them an attempt to
reconcile his perception, which was native, and his creed, which
was imported, and the result is to destroy the quality of the
perception. Kilvert was a son of modest intelligence and little
self-confidence, but he had a sensibility capable of a true and
original vision of the world, especially the natural world. It was
his misfortune that he grew up passively under the dominance of
an authoritative father, and of a formalized, authoritarian,
socially compulsory Christianity. He accepted it, inevitably, and
did injustice to his sensibility in doing so. He was too obedient a
son of his father and his age ever to have second thoughts about
that commitment – on the contrary, he built his profession on it;
but it never provided an issue for what was truest in him, and
though he tried all his life to make his imaginings Christian or to
suppress them, the Diary is there to witness to the continuing
tension that he had set up within himself.

A religious commitment, to be worth much, must provide a
channel of expression for whatever is most fundamental in a man.
Like most of his contemporaries, Kilvert in practice adopted the
opposite view, that the value of commitment lies wholly in the
objective truth of the creed; and to my mind his own Diary proves
him wrong. The irony of it is that his own native vision *was* in
fact a religious one, fully capable of Christian expression; the
fault was in the inadequacy, for all its graces, of the form of
Christianity within which he grew up, which could find no proper
accommodation with the Romantic sensibility. It was the only
form of Christianity Kilvert knew; he settled for it, on the only
level at which he could settle for it, and sentenced himself to
partial outlawry for life.

'Eighty-seven, if I live till the 6th of old March,' said William
Williams of Crowther's Pool, when Kilvert asked him his age.
Kilvert delighted in these village patriarchs, and their memories

of the unplumbed village past: he could always find time to listen to them, and there are few things in the Diary more interesting than his record of their reminiscences. William Williams was still thinking in terms of the old calendar, abandoned in 1753, over thirty years before he was born; but old ways lingered long then, and presumably the old calendar was still in common use in Clyro at the end of the eighteenth century, when he was young.

1870 *17 March*. On leaving the school at 11, I went up to Cae Mawr to see Morrell and he proposed a walk to Aber Edw as the morning was so lovely.

He was a devoted and conscientious curate, but his life was one in which it was easy to take a day off on the spur of the moment for a walk over the hills – and, for that matter, to devote a couple of hours a day to keeping a diary. The sense of leisure, of unhurried time, fills the Diary – it is one of its attractions today, when the life of leisure, a life that is which does not have to be organized round several hours a day devoted to winning one's bread, is a virtually forgotten thing. In Victorian England, work for most people was incomparably harder than now, but there existed a complete class dedicated to leisured life, and Kilvert was fortunate enough to be on the fringe of them and to share some of the freedom with which they organized their time; for the duties that were expected of the parish clergy were not such as to require the whole of two men's time in a parish of only 850 souls. You could call it an early example of feather-bedding. But then the country clergy were *expected* to lead lives of moderate leisure; and, no question, Kilvert spent his leisure well. I suppose only the retired folk and the hippies lead a leisured life in Clyro today.

They walked over the hills to Aberedw, a place of magic to Kilvert. He walked there in May, 1865, in his first spring at Clyro, only two months after his arrival there, and the day seems to have cast an enchantment on him that extended to the whole Clyro countryside for ever after: it was here, I think, that the first premonition broke on Kilvert of what Clyro was to be to him. We know of the walk only from a short reference in the Diary years afterwards; but because of it, Aberedw was a place whose name could move him to lyrical rhapsodies, and he describes several later walks to it in the Diary. It is still a magnificent piece of romantic landscape, unaltered since Kilvert's day. The bare heathery upland of Llandeilo Hill breaks down suddenly in a series of dramatically riven and weathered limestone outcrops to the Wye at the point of its junction with the little Edw; and the rocky slopes are furry with woods. Every element of romantic landscape is present: no wonder if it excited a young man in May on his first job free from home.

To get to Aberedw, Kilvert and Morrell walked over the intervening range of the Begwns, that form the watershed between Clyro and the valley of the little stream called the Bach Howey, in which Painscastle lies. Just after fording the stream they had an encounter –

> looking through the hedge we saw a crazy girl with a coarse ugly face under an old bonnet in the field sitting on the grass singing to herself something like a hymn tune in a rich mellow voice, the words indistinguishable, perhaps there were none. When she saw us through the hedge she suddenly stopped singing and saluted us in a sharp abrupt tone. She is said to be the illegitimate daughter of a gentleman in Bath who pays the people of one of these farms to keep her. . . .

There is no word of surprise or condemnation; it was the custom.

> We went on till we came to a brow of a hill which fell away abruptly from our feet. Then we saw the Begwns behind us looking very near, much too near, and directly afterwards we spied a whitewashed church perched on a tump and shaded by a huge yew in the valley below. I took the Church to be Aber Edw Church, but coming to a shoemaker's house with a small farm yard we found it was Llandeilo, and we looked blankly at each other having completely lost our way. . . .

This is interesting, because it is an indication, by no means the only one, that Kilvert did not walk by the map – the mistake would be unthinkable if he did. Indeed, he hardly mentions maps, which is odd to the mind of a modern walker for whom the one-inch or two-and-a-half-inch Ordnance Survey maps are items of equipment only less essential than his boots; and this although the first edition of the one-inch map had already been on the market in Kilvert's time for forty years. There is no indication that Kilvert ever owned one.

I don't think this was just a matter of poverty; Morrell, one notices, the comfortably wealthy tenant of Cae Mawr, appears to be as mapless as Kilvert. It points rather, I think, to a change in the use of maps. The early Ordnance Survey maps were documents for the geographer, the surveyor, the landowner rather than the walker – were they even, I wonder, mounted in any easily walkable form? The tourist map had not yet been born, for the tourist was still in his infancy: probably the Ordnance Survey did not think of him much till the 1920s, when he began to appear, open-shirted and pipe-smoking, on the covers of their one-inch series.

Kilvert and his contemporaries walked not by map, but by local knowledge and by signpost and where those failed by question and answer. The walker's map is designed for the visitor, not the native; and though people walked in the 1870s far more than they do now, they walked for business rather than pleasure and for the most part on their own home ground. Intensively though Kilvert quartered his own parish on foot, his excursions outside it are only occasional – here, at Aberedw, he is on the edge of territory to him unknown. And what need of a map when all long journeys were done by train? One can tell that he is not using maps, not only by the readiness with which he loses his way, but by the vagaries of his spellings of local place-names, which often differ far from the Ordnance Survey spellings. Where place-names, especially farm names, were concerned, he was still in the pre-literate age; many of them he had probably never seen written, and some of them probably rarely had been. Consequently he spelt them by ear, which in an area of Welsh place-names but English-speaking and most English-pronouncing population had erratic results; the purists of the Ordnance Survey had largely reverted to the Welsh spellings, and no doubt fixed them by doing so.

I doubt if this is a mere trivial detail of social history; behind it lies a real difference in ways of apprehending landscape. Kilvert's world was more exciting and less explored than ours because any country that he had not actually seen was a land of pure imagination to him; he did not see it first, as we often tend to do, as an abstraction on a map which always thereafter lingers ghostly between ourselves and a direct apprehension of the landscape. I think he saw it more freshly, as I see colours more freshly when I take my glasses off; the difference may even have something to do with the descriptive powers of his prose.

In any case, in the fuller countryside of Kilvert's day it was easy enough to find guides. At Llandeilo (Llandeilo Graban, that is) they met a shoemaker, who came with them to show them the way, and guided them to Llewellyn's Cave in the rocks above Aberedw; his parents used to talk a great deal about Llewellyn, he said, but he had forgotten all the stories. The oral memories were already dwindling.

Those pleasant walks of Kilvert to Aberedw have had long-term results that he can scarcely have looked for ...

1971 The Kilvert Society are abroad this week-end, and a be-anoraked group was observed assembling outside the Baskerville at 11. They mounted their cars and moved off in convoy; we followed independently and found them encamped around the rocks at Pen-y-Graig on the edge of Llandeilo Hill, in seven or eight separate picnic clusters. We formed one of our own, and the attendance book was passed round for everybody to sign. Their cars, about a dozen of them, were ranked below – typical Kilvertian cars, Triumphs, Morris Oxfords, Cortinas, that sort of thing – no Minis, no 2000s. It was grey, but not cold; and when we got under way about 1 (on a delicate suggestion that the ladies should follow in five minutes time), and set off across the hill toward Aberedw in a long straggling caravan, blue sky and sun soon began to blow across from the west. M and the children came too and we were soon last in the line, but it was beautiful walking country, the open hill covered with acres of rusting bracken, still green and yellow in patches. Ahead, the secretary led the march, blazing the way at forks in the track with white handkerchiefs tied to saplings brought for the purpose, and distant prolonged blasts of the whistle betrayed where he was trying to keep his straggling flock together. The children bore up well, but we made pretty slow progress, and by the time we reached Aberedw rocks, we had lost sight of the Kilvertians altogether. The view across the Wye was all blurred with haze, but the rocks are grand romantic crags, jutting out from the turf like shattered bastions, twenty or thirty feet high, ivy and holly trees growing out of the deep fissures. We finally found the main party just as it was moving off again, some straggling back across the hill toward the cars, the keener plunging on down the hillside to visit Llewellyn's Cave. We divided, M going back to bring the car round to Aberedw, I shepherding the rest straight down the hill – a departure from the planned arrangements regarded with some apparent disfavour by one sternly orthodox Kilvertian ...

1870 *21 March.* Evans the schoolmaster very much interested and rather anxious about the Education Bill.

He might well be interested for this was something that was going to change the face of England; the roots of a good many of the differences between the Clyro of 1870 and the Clyro of 1970 lie here. This was Gladstone's Education Bill, which for the first time provided England with a publicly supported system of primary schools (though education was not to be compulsory for some years yet), and thereby laid down the far-reaching principle that it is the state's job to see to the education of its citizens.

Clyro, like most English rural parishes, by this time had a church school (Kilvert taught in it daily), teaching the three Rs and the catechism, and supported partly by fees, partly by voluntary subscriptions from the gentry, and partly by an annual government grant which varied according to the proficiency of the children when examined by the Inspectors on their periodic visitations – 'payment by results'. Practically every child in the parish between the ages of four and twelve attended the school, though some were very irregular. How far this represents a genuine desire for education on the part of parents, many of whom could never have attended school themselves, and how far the success of gentry and clergy in bringing pressure to bear on their social inferiors, is hard to say. The education provided was of course very modest, and it would be thirty years yet before any child from Clyro school would go on to a secondary school (the first to do so is still alive, and I have met him). Nevertheless it was the essential beginning, and such as it was it was inspired and directed by the Church – one of the many schools that had been founded over the last thirty years in the effort to preserve the principle that education was the prerogative of the established Church.

The attempt was forlorn, and we forget now that it was ever made; but though we do not know what it was that Mr. Evans was anxious about, it may well have been this, and if so perhaps his anxiety was not altogether misplaced. The Bill would make little difference to Clyro, since it already had a school and the great majority of the children of the parish already went to it; but Mr. Evans may have been far-sighted enough to see where the principle might lead. For the moment, the state was only entering into partnership with the Church; but the state was a perilously formidable partner, and in the long run people who would not subscribe voluntarily to support church schools would pay taxes to support state ones. Education has slipped further and further away from the Church, and become more and more entirely secular; and though Clyro school is still a church school, few people now take any notice of the difference or are even aware of it, so much have the church schools been swallowed up in the state system. Vaguely, Mr. Evans perhaps feared something of the kind and felt that there was something lacking in a purely secular education.

Yet Clyro school is still there: smaller, because the population of the village has shrunk; its curriculum greatly expanded; but still there, in the same building at the western end of the village, where the road from Hay joins the main road up the valley. And in one interesting respect it is a better reflection of the village community now than it was in 1870. It was then essentially a working-class school, and universally recognized as such: the more prosperous farmers sent their daughters to boarding-school, the gentry educated their daughters at home and their sons went to public schools when they were old enough. But today the school is classless, in a way that would have astonished Kilvert – or very nearly so. The wealthy – and anyway for the most part the wealthy only come to Clyro on holiday or in retirement – may still send their children to private schools from the start; but the less opulent middle classes, the modern equivalents of Kilvert himself, cheerfully send theirs to the village school, though they may look outside the state system for their secondary education. This is a change of my own lifetime: it would have been unthinkable for my parents to send me to a state primary school in the 1930s, but my own child races round the playground opposite the Cae Mawr drive with the rest of the village children, and it pleases me.

> Between Pen-y-Maes and Hay I heard loud and clear the solemn tone of the soul bell at Clyro booming across the valley and river from the sequestered unseen Church, and wondered who could be dead. No sooner had I crossed the bridge than the soul bell and funeral bell at Hay Church tolled out in answer.

Today, people die silently and secretly: death was frequent and familiar then, and public.

1870 *22 March*. The industrious blacksmith chinks away at his forge night and morning late and early, and the maidens and mothers go up and down the water steps with their pitchers continually.

A biblical society: it might be an illustration from the Old Testament.

1870 *26 March*. It was a delicious spring day upon Clyro Hill; Kilvert walked over, as he did so many times that spring, to call on old Mrs. Williams, of the Oaks cottage above Painscastle, where she was dying, and where they make cake decorations for export today; the visit a duty, the walk a delight. The visit done, he walked on to the Rhosgoch mill, where, according to Hannah Whitney in the village, the old miller used to see fairies dancing of nights on the mill floor – but that was long ago, folk no longer saw fairies, and even the mill already looked to Kilvert old-fashioned (though it is said to have worked till after the First World War). Next he came to the little Methodist chapel at the Rhosgoch – a rival establishment to Kilvert, for the currents of sectarian rivalry were still running strong. 'Sectarian', though? – he would not have accepted the word, which flows so naturally to the pen in the 1970s; for him, there was the Church on one side, the sects on the other, and the Church of England, *the* Church of England, was most emphatically not a sect; the very word implied schism, secession from that Church.

AFTER KILVERT

Kilvert was a kindly man and no bigot and he was remembered after his death for his unusual readiness to show courtesy and friendship to dissenters, but the prejudice is apparent in him nevertheless. When someone cuts down his favourite birches on the Cefn y Fedwas, it is 'a dissenter no doubt – probably a Baptist' who has done it; when an election campaign in Chippenham, near Langley Burrell, begins to look menacing for the Conservative interest (Kilvert showed little interest in politics, but was a Conservative by inherited instinct), it is because 'the dissenters are behaving badly'. And when he went into the Rhosgoch chapel that day, what he saw was a 'building which was very ugly, high and boxy-looking and of course whitewashed, the usual conventicle'. The curl of disgust comes clearly through the choice of words.

The Church of England is established yet, but it is little more than a name and a form; today it is a sect, or rather the dissenting sects are as much Churches as it is, and in effect it recognizes them as colleagues. The old enmities have been laid aside in the face of a public disaffiliation from all the Churches alike on so vast a scale that the enmities clearly could not be afforded and the old notion of the Establishment, in which Kilvert was bred, has been virtually forgotten. According to that notion, the Church was something as universal, as objective, as difficult to opt out of, as the state itself; to be English was to be Anglican. The very existence of the dissenting sects was an inconsistency, an intellectual scandal. It was because they could not logically be fitted into his scheme of things that the dissenters were inevitably objects of distrust to the Anglican, that Kilvert looked so askance at Griffiths of Portway, the farmer from Bryngwyn who officiated at Rhosgoch chapel and was sometimes called in to baptize their children by the folk up on Clyro Hill. A Radnorshire hill farmer, who claimed to exercise the functions of an ordained priest – it was hard to swallow.

As you can see in his lament for the birches of Cefn y Fedwas and in his reaction to the plainness of Rhosgoch chapel, Kilvert held ugliness against the dissenters as well; the word has for him some of the meaning that 'Philistine' had for Matthew Arnold. The reproaches do have something in common: different though the levels are, the lack of sweetness and light with which Arnold charged the dissenters has its root not far from Kilvert's complaint. A view of the world which made no place for the beauty of the eyes was impossibly inadequate to a man who responded to that beauty so acutely; and though none of the Churches have accommodated to it very easily yet, few have neglected it as completely as English dissent.

Kilvert's attitude to dissent was perhaps only possible because Radnorshire was not then, and is not now, part of nonconformist Wales. In the pattern of its religions, as in its language and to a large extent in its society, it is much more English than Welsh: dissent here was not Welsh Calvinism but English rural Methodism, the creed of a working-class minority who refused to accept the dominance of the Establishment. There was a chapel of the Primitive Methodists, the toughest and most radical branch of Methodism, in Clyro parish itself, along at the Bronith a mile out of the village, although Kilvert never mentions it; perhaps one may assume that he stayed out of the Methodists' way, and vice versa. But the general rule of the Anglican Establishment, the official position of Kilvert and Mr. Venables was never in doubt in Clyro, nor in consequence was Kilvert's view of dissent.

'But their love, and their hatred, and their envy, is now perished; neither have they any more a portion for ever in anything that is done under the sun.'

On the way home from the Rhosgoch, Kilvert called in at Cefn y Blaen, where he found old William Pritchard, one of the patriarchs of Clyro.

> He remembers the old house of Cefn y Blaen and the large famous room which he says was 20 *yards* long and was used for holding a Court of Justice in for the country round in the time of Charles I. I asked him if he had ever heard any talk of Charles I ever having been about in this country. 'Oh yes,' he said, 'I have a jug that the King once drunk out of at Blaen Cerdi. He had breakfast that day in Brecon, dined at Gwernyfed and slept at Harpton, passing through Newchurch. His army was with him and riding two and two in the narrow lanes the line reached from Pen Vaen in Newchurch, through the village up to Blaen Cerdi. At Blaen Cerdi all the farm people, boys and girls ran out to see the King pass. The King was afoot. He stopped opposite the house and asked my ancestress Mary Bayliss to give

him something to drink. She went to the house and fetched him milk and water in this jug which has been handed down with the tradition in my family. I have always heard that this Mary Bayliss was an extraordinarily fine beautiful woman. I never learnt that the King gave her anything in return for the draught ... Charles II was in hiding for some time in this country and went about in disguise as a lady's servant. Once when he was in the pantry with the butler of the house where they were staying he asked the butler if he would give him a glass of wine. The butler said in a meaning way "You, are able to command what you like."'

What a marvellously vivid and circumstantial bit of folk tradition! In Kilvert's Clyro, this kind of continuity of tradition, this sense of the closeness of the past, still persisted, but it would not do so for much longer, and to the best of my knowledge no such memories survive today: I suppose education, putting a book-learned past in the place of a traditional one, and the pace of change have killed them. These memories must have been two and a quarter centuries old when Kilvert heard them – if they were authentic, that is, and the Charles I one at least has all the appearance of authenticity. The occasion described must have been in August 1645, when Charles, defeated at Naseby, retreated into South Wales in a last desperate attempt to raise a new army, and from there finally struck northwards, deliberately travelling by obscure and mountainous roads to baffle pursuit. The route described through Newchurch – which has probably never seen another reigning monarch – would fit in perfectly with such an intention; and one might add that the distance from Pen Vaen to Blaen Cerdi, only about a mile, impressive though it may have seemed to William Pritchard, would be just about right for the depressed remnant of his army which was all that Charles still had with him. The tale of Charles II on his flight after the battle of Worcester – obviously the episode to which it refers – is less interesting: it is strikingly less specific, and in fact Charles never came nearer to the Clyro area than Bristol. It looks very much as though the origin of the story is an almost precisely similar one in Clarendon's narrative of the flight – a useful reminder of the very variable value of different fragments of what seems to be folk memory, whose hotchpotch nature is still more vividly illustrated by another passage that Kilvert recorded only two days later from another of these village patriarchs – I *think* from the 87-year-old William Williams of Crowther's Pool, but from the published Diary it is impossible to be sure:

1870 *28 March*. Williams says the petty chief great landlords were called 'Normandy Kings'. One of them lived at Cefn y Blaen, one at Llanshifr, another at Great Gwernfydden. The one who lived at Painscastle was a giant. This giant carried off to Painscastle 'screaming and noising' Miss Phillips of the Screen Farm near Erwood whom he found disporting herself with her lover Arthur on or at Bychllyn Pool. Arthur sent for help to Old Radnor Castle and Cefn y Blaen. At Cefn y Blaen there were then 40 men each 7 feet high. The giant on the other hand sent for succour to Court Evan Gwynne where there was an 'army', also to Hay Castle and Lord Clifford of Clifford Castle ...

'Normandy Kings' sounds like a memory of the land-owning aristocracy imported from Normandy at the Conquest – but it would have to be nearly eight hundred years old! – the castles mentioned are real, and the houses mentioned seem all to have been manor-houses in their time. But when it comes to Miss Phillips and the giants, I give up: it will take someone much more knowledgeable than me to riddle out the elements of history – of some mediaeval episode of Welsh border anarchy, probably – that I am sure are present in it from the mass of chaotically anachronistic detail. The urge to record, and the apparent lack of historical curiosity about the content, are both equally typical of Kilvert: in spite of his Oxford degree, he never thinks like a historian, never asks such questions as 'What really lies behind this?' or 'When did this happen?'

1870 *29 March*. Turned aside into the meadow to look at the great stone of Cross Ffordd ...

Cross Ffordd is Crossway, an unpretentious little farmhouse a mile up the hill from Clyro on the Newchurch road. James Gittos, a shoemaker, lived there in Kilvert's time with his wife and their widowed son, also James, a threshing-machine engineer. The steam threshing-machine, the first sign of the mechanization of agriculture, must have been the only artificial form of power in the parish then, I suppose: it is curious that the father of the present occupant, Trevor Harris, who also lived there, was likewise an agricultural contractor, hiring out threshing-machines and other equipment to the local farmers, though I know of no link between him and James Gittos. The Harrises are cousins of Kilvert's Gipsy Lizzie, and it was Trevor's wife who typed this book – an appropriate Kilvertian association.

But why does Kilvert call it Cross Ffordd, although the present name, Crossway, seems already to have been in use? The answer, I think, is that Kilvert was trying out his Welsh: 'ffordd' is Welsh for 'road', so the name is a rough equivalent. The Welsh place-names and Welsh past of Clyro intrigued Kilvert, and from time to time he plays with Welsh like this, translating local place-names, signing his poems with Welsh pen-names. It is another aspect of his wide-ranging curiosity about Clyro's past, and it must have been an unusual one in Radnorshire at that time: even today, for that matter, Clyro must be about as Anglicized a village as it is possible to find in the Principality. That this has been Welsh country in the past is testified by the place-names on the map, which hereabouts follow the existing English-Welsh border with remarkable exactness. Not only the natural features but the older farm-names and village surnames are almost all Welsh. But the English penetration was already of very long standing in Kilvert's time: he never heard Welsh spoken in Clyro, and indeed it seems then as now to have been extinct almost everywhere in Radnorshire, except in its far north-west corner (where Kilvert himself was later to be vicar of St. Harmon's for a short time, and must have made a closer acquaintance with the language while he was there). Even memories of the Welsh past were already very faint, though old Hannah Whitney could remember wearing a Welsh hat in her youth, at the beginning of the century. Since then, of course, the tide has turned: Welsh is coming back in, and Welsh names are fashionable again. But in Kilvert's time it was at dead low water, which makes his own interest all the more striking, though he would never have claimed to be more than a dabbler in the language.

As for the great stone, it is there still – speaking a little louder now to archaeologists than it did to Kilvert, as dumb as ever to the rest of us.

1870 *31 March.* At Llanthomas, Henry Thomas was up among the branches of an apple tree blown down, hard at work in his shirt sleeves chopping away the limbs, quite in a workmanlike style and surrounded by an admiring group of four sisters.

'Quite in a workmanlike style' – one hears the surprise, and realizes suddenly to how great an extent manual work in 1870 was a badge of servitude. Only workmen did work: in all the record of his time at Clyro, full and strenuous though it was in its way, the only mentions of Kilvert ever dirtying his hands are the occasions when he does it to help old and crippled parishioners – and that is more than most of his contemporaries of his own class would ever have done, for he was an unusually kindly and sympathetic man. There is still a social stigma attached to making a living by the work of one's hands, no doubt; but we all dirty them now.

1870 *5 April.* A cloudless spring morning after a sharp frost, and Kilvert walked over the Black Mountain with Morrell of Cae Mawr and another friend, Bridge from Pont Vaen outside Hay, up from Llanigon past Cilonw Farm and over the Gospel Pass. They were descending the far side of the pass when

> just where the lane hedges and enclosures begin we met a humble cavalcade coming up the mountain. There was an old basket maker leading a small bay pony, poor and thin, with a good deal of its hair rubbed off and loaded with the implements and materials of the trade. The old man led by the other hand a small stout rosy cheeked girl and the rear was brought up by an older thinner girl with dark eyes, she holding a chubby child upon a donkey. The old man said he was going to Talgarth, but he lived in Gloucestershire where he had eleven at home ...

A pure Wordsworthian encounter: there is more circumstantial detail than Dorothy Wordsworth would have given us, but otherwise it might well have come straight out of the pages of her

Journals. Kilvert's Diary brings home forcefully to its reader how broad a streak of the picaresque there was in Victorian society of the 1870s, as there had been in the Wordsworths' Grasmere of the early 1800s, and conversely how little there is of it today. Curiously at first sight, the picaresque seems to be a more natural accompaniment of a relatively rooted immobile society than of a footloose shifting one like the present. Most, though by no means all, of the wanderers that Kilvert encountered were either unemployed and on the tramp looking for work, or itinerant tradesmen like this basketmaker. Even after the coming of the railway, for the poor walking was often the only feasible means of travel; and not only the kaleidoscopic cities, but even the roads of quiet rural backwaters like Clyro were salted by these passing travellers. Kilvert often stopped to talk with them here, moved perhaps about equally by curiosity and kindness, and the stories he heard throw revealing and often pathetic shafts of light into the lower depths of his society – precisely as Wordsworth had done seventy years before. This encounter below the Gospel Pass could so easily have provided the material for a poem like *Michael* or a passage from *The Excursion*.

It is hardly too much to say that over the whole of Kilvert's Diary there looms the presence of Wordsworth, much as the Black Mountain itself looms over the valley of the Wye. It is a matter both of enthusiastic discipleship and of unspoken and possibly unconscious influence. Kilvert was a zealous Wordsworthian, with a constant interest in Wordsworth associations and Wordsworth anecdotes – of which there were a good many to be had in the neighbourhood of Clyro, for the Wordsworths had several times stayed at Whitney, only three miles away, with the Monkhouses, cousins of the poet's wife: the daughter of one of them was the wife of Henry Dew, the vicar of Whitney in Kilvert's time, and Kilvert knew the Dews well. Wordsworth is 'dear old Wordsworth' to Kilvert and he is mentioned in the Diary far more often than any other poet (there is one quotation from Keats but no mention of him, one mention of Byron, none at all of Shelley, only one even of Shakespeare – Kilvert's tastes in poetry seem to have been restricted and clearly defined). This is not surprising – Wordsworth after all was twenty years dead by 1870, a fully established and respectable figure of the canon of English poetry, indeed probably its latest fully accepted figure – just the sort of taste in fact that you might expect in a conventional young man with some feeling for poetry.

But Wordsworth's influence on Kilvert goes far deeper than this somewhat orthodox, if unusually intense, enthusiasm, and how far Kilvert himself was aware of it is an interesting question. The Diary itself says nothing about the particular qualities of Wordsworth that most attracted him, and very rarely quotes from him – there is, for instance, nothing in it to show that Kilvert knew *The Prelude*, which one might expect to have a particular appeal for him, though he surely must have been familiar with it. But Kilvert's whole awareness of the landscape and the rural poor seems saturated and moulded by the tradition of Wordsworth, and I cannot believe that this is coincidence: if one is looking for literary influences upon the Diary, this is overwhelmingly the most important, indeed the only one worth mentioning (though it *is* coincidence, as we have seen, that in all English literature the closest parallel to the Diary is Dorothy Wordsworth's *Journals*, for he cannot have known them). The influence of course may not necessarily have been direct, for the whole English literary and visual reaction to landscape had by 1870 been deeply affected by Wordsworth; and it is certainly not true that Kilvert's attitude is merely derivative, for there is abundant evidence in the Diary that his reactions are spontaneous and deeply felt – for instance, his *visual* awareness is noticeably more acute than Wordsworth's, who has no parallel to Kilvert's sense of colour. But the mysticism which underlies Kilvert's attitude to nature, coupled as it is with an orthodox Christianity, is profoundly Wordsworthian: the Wye valley landscape in which it is set is closely akin to Wordsworth's Lakeland landscape; and above all perhaps the figures of the rural poor are viewed with a sympathy, seen against the background and invested with the qualities of the landscape they inhabit, in a way that is at once natural to Kilvert and yet surely learned by him from Wordsworth. Whether he knew this when he recorded his encounters with them, whether he realized how much of Wordsworth had entered into him, I do not know, but it would surely have delighted him if he had. It is curious, I think, that his own verse makes so little attempt to imitate Wordsworthian models: that he never attempts a Michael, a Margaret, or an old Cumberland beggar. I do not think that the results would have been happy if he had; but he did write a good deal of verse, and I am surprised that he did not try.

But the object of Kilvert's walk with Morrell and Bridge that day lay further on, to examine the exotic happenings at Capel y Ffin, where the eccentric Father Ignatius was building his monastery. In the course of its long quiet history the neighbourhood of Hay has thrown up only three figures whom an educated man of the 1970s is in the least likely to have heard of, all of them in the last hundred years; and an oddly mixed lot of minor celebrities they are – Kilvert, the diarist: Ignatius, the eccentric: and Armstrong, the murderer. Armstrong, the Hay solicitor hanged for the murder of his wife in the early 1920s after one of the classic poisoning trials of the century, is still vigorously alive in local legend, and his house in Cusop, on the outskirts of the town, is still pointed out. Ignatius is a stranger figure, a bizarre religious enthusiast who attempted the revival of monasticism within the Church of England single-handed, on the basis of his own zeal, credulity, financial incompetence, and total lack of discretion. In 1870, after some disastrous preliminary attempts in East Anglia, he, together with a few ill-chosen fellows, established a community at Capel y Ffin in the deepest recesses of the Black Mountains, and set about building a monastery, financing the work out of the proceeds of his own evangelistic preaching tours.

One imagines that the impact on the neighbourhood of the news that monks had appeared at Capel y Ffin must have been comparable to that produced by the appearance of hippies a hundred years later. Any human species more exotic than a monk to the rural population of the mid-Wales border in the 1870s it is hard to conceive. The upper classes of the neighbourhood may have understood the notion better, but probably liked it less in an age when, only twenty years after the secession of Newman and his followers, anything that looked like a movement Romeward within the Church of England was regarded with the deepest distrust: and their doubts are unlikely to have been assuaged by the discovery that Ignatius – or Joseph Leycester Lyne, to give him his family name – had been refused priestly ordination. Given all this, it is unlikely that Kilvert and his two friends walked over to Capel y Ffin with any predisposition to admire what they found there; and the objectivity of Kilvert's account does great credit to his capacity for detached observation. He had doubts about their cleanliness and contrasted their 'morbid unnatural life' unfavourably with that of those 'living naturally in the world and taking their share of its work, cares and pleasures', a very standard Victorian middle-class reaction (and one hears very clearly echoes of today's comments on the hippies who squat here and there in ruinous cottages on the Black Mountain). But he reported fairly the respect expressed for the monks by the masons working on the building, as he later clearly respected the sincerity, devotion, and simple kindness of Ignatius himself, whom he met on another visit in September. Much of this is simply the intense objective curiosity that was so invaluable to him as a diarist, and his description of his visits to the monastery at Capel y Ffin are among his masterpieces in this respect; but perhaps there is a hint of something else too, of a sneaking, not fully admitted admiration for so ascetic a vocation, felt by one whose calling seemed to demand no such sacrifices and who could devote a fine spring day to a walk on the hills with his friends.

All this enterprise of Ignatius's ran swiftly into the sands, whatever that may prove; the community at Capel y Ffin, always tiny and always devoid of any flicker of life except that imparted to it by its founder, collapsed immediately after Ignatius's death in 1908; and the buildings today are almost as much a ruin, though much less visited, than the seven centuries older remains of Llanthony Priory, three miles further down the valley, to which Kilvert, Bridge, and Morrell walked on for lunch that day.

Then, as now, Llanthony was one of the most exquisite and romantic ruins in Britain, set in the deep narrow Vale of Ewyas with the vast flanks of the sheltering spurs of the Black Mountain towering through the naked arches of the ruined nave; then, as now, the western range of the old cloister was quaintly occupied by an inn; and already, in 1870, the tourist tide was lapping this far up this remote valley. Kilvert, who hated tourists with a venomous and slightly inexplicable hatred presumably proportionate to their rarity in his time, went into paroxysms of wrath at seeing how 'two tourists with staves and shoulder belts all complete postured away among the ruins in an attitude of admiration', though by the time he wrote his diary he was characteristically able to glimpse the comic side of his own anger. One needs to realize that the tourist of 1870 was a subtly different

phenomenon from the tourist of today. In Cornwall that August Kilvert met another group of the species and described them as 'insufferable snobs' – *snobs*: one blinks, and then realizes that this is a word that has stood on its head since the last century: the snob in 1870 was a member of the lower classes who showed less than the due amount of respect for his betters, and realizing that puts one on the track of the inflection that 'tourist' had for Kilvert's ears. He was not a member of the opulent middle classes on the trek, but one of the earliest swallows of popular affluence; the idea of the holiday was just taking shape. The traditional order of things was that there were those who worked and those who did not. For the leisured the spacious picnic, the scenic tour, were part of ordinary life. For the others there was six days' work – ten or twelve hours a day, probably, too – and Sunday at home, year in, year out, and that was that.

But by 1870, the railways were making popular travel possible for the first time in history, and the faint broadening-out of affluence downwards in society was enabling people who would never previously have dreamed of doing such a thing to take the occasional day off work. The true revolution that the railways brought to passenger travel was not in speed but in price; and by 1870 the railway excursion invented by Thomas Cook was in full swing. More likely than not, Kilvert's tourists were clerks or artisans; and their appearance at Llanthony, to admire the scenery that the upper classes had previously regarded as part of their own exclusive spiritual estate was indeed a token of social revolution, as Kilvert clearly felt. His distaste is both a nice example of Victorian social attitudes, and very typical of Kilvert's profoundly conservative instincts. He was, remember, in the position of a poor white in the southern States: a poor member of the lowest stratum of local genteel society, it was he who would feel first the rising pressure of social claims from below. It is lucky, too, that he cannot see Llanthony today.

Opposite: The inn in the ruins of Llanthony Abbey, seen in this marvellous period photograph as Kilvert must have known it, and hardly changed at all today. The central figure on the bench might well be the bullet-headed Somerset innkeeper whom Kilvert knew.

1970 *6 July*. A gruelling drive over the Mountain as I feared: the usual litter of parked cars, picnics, and pony-trekkers on the open turf below Hay Bluff, and in the narrow lane descending to Capel y Ffin a terrible jam of traffic. We found ourselves stuck in a convoy of about eight cars behind a silly woman in a Mini whose efforts to pull in to let other cars coming in the opposite direction pass usually ended with her stuck broadside across the road. A weary crawl down to Capel y Ffin and on to Llanthony, where most of the cars stopped – K's disgust would have been powerful. It was very warm there, the green hills seen through the ruined arches of the arcade as beautiful as ever: the immediate juxtaposition of the two so totally incongruous as to be thrilling, and a bit more, as though you couldn't quite bring them into the same focus. There's scaffolding up next to the tower, and three men were at work repointing the stone – one had climbed up into the passage that runs round the two surviving sides of the central tower at triforium level, probably the first man to set foot there for a couple of centuries or so. We had lunch sitting on the stone ledge of the chapter house, while minute scarlet spiders ran in hundreds over the sun-warmed stones, a busload of sightseers looked doubtfully round the ruins, and a long queue of stout matrons formed in front of the only women's toilet. We left the beautiful ruin at 2.30 and at Capel y Ffin turned aside to see Father Ignatius's monastery – the church is a roofless ruin, short though lofty, and the white-painted conventual buildings are a pony-trekking centre. . . .

But Kilvert and his friends *walked* home, completing a round trip of twenty-five miles over the Mountain, and were 'not extraordinarily tired' at the end of it – one can just catch the note of self-satisfaction in his words. He walked everywhere, for walking then was not a hobby, but for all but the rich the ordinary way of getting about if no railway served – as I suppose it will never be again.

1870 *7 April*. Lunch at 12 and to Hay by the fields to take the Savings Bank. Sat reading a Cheltenham paper and book of Religious Anecdotes for an hour and no one came. But after I had left the office, a nook behind the green baize curtains, and had sallied forth into the street I met a Llowes woman coming to deposit money very leisurely having understood from Tom Williams that Savings Bank office hours were from 2 till 4 instead of from 1 till 2 ...

This seems to have been a very average day's business at the Hay Savings Bank, to judge from the references to it in the Diary. Growing concern for the conditions of the poor – and no doubt for what the poor might do if nothing was done to improve those conditions – led to the formation of many local savings banks in the nineteenth century, designed to encourage thrift in the poor and to provide a safe investment for their savings; the justification of the Victorian economic system after all rested on the assumption that it was possible for any honest man to make a living for himself and to provide against his old age without recourse to the harsh resort of the Poor Law, and savings banks were a device to this end. They seem to have been moderately successful ones too, especially in rural areas, though one may well wonder how it was possible to make savings out of an agricultural labourer's wages in the 1870s. The Hay Savings Bank, though, seems to have been a modest concern: whether it was entirely run by the local clergy is not clear, but it appears to have been open only during the lunch hour, and Kilvert presided there every Thursday. On no recorded occasion did he have more than one piece of business to transact, so it seems unlikely that the institution made very much impact on the economy of the neighbourhood. Perhaps, though, the best days of the Bank were already behind it, for it had had to face the competition of the Post Office Savings Bank since 1861.

His labours at the Savings Bank completed, Kilvert went up to Hay Castle to call on his friends the Bevans, and heard from Mr. Bevan that Cambridge had won the previous day's Boat Race – 'I am very glad and I think most people will be, Oxford or not,' a remarkable display of broadmindedness for an Oxford man, even though Oxford had won for the previous nine years in succession.

Kilvert took a mild interest in rowing – he had been a member of the Boat Club at Wadham in his Oxford days, if only to the extent of failing to pay his subscription, and on at least one occasion on a later visit to Oxford he watched the summer eights.

But there is no sign that he was a sportsman (more than once he records scoring for the village cricket team at Langley Burrell, but it was his younger brother, Perch, who played), and sport leaves little mark on the Diary. He takes just sufficient interest in the great public occasions of the sporting year occasionally to record their results. But there were many fewer such occasions then than now: soccer had only acquired its code in 1863, and professional football and the F.A. Cup were still in the future; the first Test Match was not played till 1877; Kilvert himself records the arrival of tennis in 1874 as 'a capital game, but rather too hot for a summer's day'. Mass spectator sport was still unknown, awaiting the transport innovations, the leisure, and the mass circulation newspapers that made it feasible. In fact the only two sporting occasions that in 1870 attracted anything that can reasonably be called a mass attendance were precisely the two that Kilvert takes notice of – the Boat Race and the Derby, both events with a long tradition behind them and both close to London with its population of over three million. That one of them should be no more than a race between Oxford and Cambridge is a remarkable fact that has often been commented on, and a striking testimony to the dominance of those institutions in English society and to the theatrical function of the nineteenth-century upper classes. The events of their leisure and their domestic lives could be major incidents, causes of rejoicing and sorrow and excitement, for the millions of grey people beneath them. They can often be seen at this theatrical function in the pages of the Diary; Kilvert himself had a walking-on part.

When I looked out between 11 and 12 before going to bed I saw one of the magnificent sights of the world, the crescent moon setting.

When down the stormy crescent goes
A light before me swims,
Between dark stems the forest glows,
I hear a noise of hymns.

And the crescent moon was sinking low over the dingle behind the poplars.

The poplars are mentioned often in the Diary, and must have

been one of the chief features of the view from Kilvert's windows at Ashbrook in his day; but they are long since gone, and I cannot make out with any precision where they stood, another reminder of the hopelessness of ever seeing things quite as he saw them.

The quotation is from Tennyson, one of the only two poets apart from Wordsworth who (on the evidence of the Diary) seem to have made any significant impact on Kilvert (the other being the Dorset dialect poet William Barnes, to whom he once paid a memorable visit). Both were a generation older than Kilvert, but still they were his contemporaries, and a man's taste in contemporary poetry is often more revealing than his taste in the classics, for it is not dictated to him; though Tennyson in 1870 was already Poet Laureate and about as well established as a living poet can be, so it can scarcely be called an adventurous taste. Kilvert clearly knew his Tennyson pretty well – he is quoting here from *Sir Galahad*, and elsewhere there are several references to *In Memoriam* and the *Idylls of the King*, as well as to other poems that appeared with *Sir Galahad* in 1842. In terms of pure chronology, I suppose a rough parallel would be a 1970 enthusiasm for Dylan Thomas; but of course it flies to pieces in your face, for in 1870 there was still a mainstream poetic tradition readily accessible to the educated public, and in 1970 there isn't.

I have already argued that it was Wordsworth who did most to form Kilvert's sensibility; but the forms of his poetry, interestingly enough, are Tennysonian, or rather sub-Tennysonian, and sometimes very strongly derivative indeed to the point of pastiche. Undoubtedly he got better value from Wordsworth than from Tennyson, though this may reflect his own limitations more than the limitations of the poets – the Wordsworthian sensibility could be expressed in prose, which was Kilvert's strength, whereas Tennyson's strength lies in his ear, and can't. Is it perhaps true too that the rhythms of poetry are less stable, more superficial, more of the moment than whole structures of sensibility like Wordsworth's – so that Kilvert could feel comfortably at home within a seventy-year-old sensibility, whereas his ear demanded the moderner rhythms of a Tennyson? It would be a commonplace of criticism to add that in any case Tennyson had only his rhythms to give; for an autonomous way of seeing the world, Kilvert had no choice but to go back to Wordsworth.

1870 *8 April.* In the green lane between York and Cefn y Fedwas
I came upon Smith of Wernog hedging. He told me that a
child had arrived at Pen-y-Wyrlod and wanted to know if
something cannot be done to separate Stephen Davies and
Myra Rees. I said there was no law to prevent people living
in concubinage. People are very indignant about this affair
and think it a great scandal to the parish, and rightly so.
But what is to be done?

Something, apparently: at the end of May Stephen Davies's
landlord paid an unexpected visit to Pen-y-Wyrlod and, outraged
at the irregularity of the household, gave him notice; whereupon
the couple apparently yielded to *force majeure*, for when Richard
Chaloner, the census enumerator, called a year later, he found a
respectable enough household of Stephen living with a young
wife, presumably the same girl, and a one-year-old daughter, and
one assumes that Kilvert and village opinion were satisfied by
this happy result.

How much have moral attitudes changed in Clyro over a
century? It is not an easy question. Perhaps one's first reaction is
surprise that the moral laws could be so defiantly flouted in
mid-Victorian England; but we are dealing here with a peasant
morality, and it is doubtful if the Victorian proprieties ever
penetrated very far at that level of society. True, 'people are very
indignant' – how many people, I wonder, and which ones? Were
the sanctions of community disapproval less formidable in a
community of small hill-farmers than among the middle classes?
Interesting questions, but I don't know the answers. The sanctions in the end were apparently formidable enough anyway; and
here perhaps there is a difference today, for tenant farming is
nearly dead, and the particular form of pressure that may have
made Stephen Davies bow to the proprieties in the end is no
longer possible. But although Clyro is on the whole more tolerant
towards sexual peccadilloes these days, and the mothers of
illegitimate children certainly no longer contemplate drowning
themselves in the Wye, communal notions of right and wrong are
still firm, and households like Stephen Davies's seem if anything
rarer now than they were in Kilvert's time. There is more to this
than morality, though: perhaps the main explanation is simply
that it is no longer normal for unmarried girls to live as servants

in the same houses as men. There are always the hippies, of course, of whom anyone will believe anything, but they are not part of village society, and do not want to be.

1870 *9 April.* .... up the path by the quarries along the hillside to John Morgan's the old soldier's. He and Mary his wife were cosily at tea. And after the veteran had done and pocketed his clasp knife he covered his face with his hand and whispered his long grace audibly.

I cannot find the path, nor even the quarries, which I think must have been swallowed up by a plantation; no doubt they were one of the innumerable scratchings for building stone that dotted the hills so thickly then, when if a man intended to build a house near Clyro he was as likely as not to dig a hole in the nearest field and quarry the stone for it himself. Already in Kilvert's time the quarries were falling into disuse as the railway made the more tractable mass-produced materials, brick and slate, economically available, and the innumerable minute local enterprises gave place to the few big central ones, the process we have become accustomed to in so many fields since then.

John Morgan is one of Kilvert's patriarchs – he and Hannah Whitney in the village, perhaps, are the two figures who more than any others represented to Kilvert the quintessential qualities of respected age, wisdom, simplicity, memory, faith. John was younger than Hannah, eighty-three to her ninety, but whereas her life had apparently been spent in the Radnorshire hills within a few miles of Clyro, John had been out into the world, to fight in Wellington's army during the campaigns in Spain. A strange patch of memory it must have made, those violent public events in a dry alien land to which forces to him incomprehensible had taken him – he remembered secret parleys, when on picket duty at night, with French sentries who doubtless understood as little of it as he, and when it came to the Franco-Prussian War, he said he knew nothing of the Germans, the French were more natural to him, and he wished them well. And after that exotic interlude, back to the small world that Hannah Whitney had never left. There is no evidence that any of the other village folk had ever wandered so far from home; and Kilvert delighted in the old man's memories, of battles like

Vitoria and the Pyrenees as remote (and no more remote, one needs to remember) to Kilvert as the Somme is to us.

The old soldier, we note, had a simple, deep, unquestioning piety whose charm even to Kilvert perhaps already lay partly in its old fashion. He eats his tea with a clasp-knife – it would be a while yet before modern cutlery would reach the cottages of Clyro.

1870 *12 April. ...* These sudden deaths and short illnesses make one thoughtful and it is a solemn thought how absolutely unconscious one may be of carrying one's death warrant about in an unsuspected disease that may bring on the end at any moment.

It was a thought no Victorian of the 1870s could well afford to forget entirely, for sudden death – so great a rarity today as to be a scandal – struck frequently then, and was not even any great respecter of social distinctions. And in particular Kilvert could not afford to forget it; for he too had an early death within him.

1870 *16 April.* More and more people kept coming into the churchyard as they finished their day's work. The sun went down in glory behind the dingle. but still the work of love went on through the twilight and into the dusk until the moon rose full and splendid. The figures continued to move about among the graves and to bend over the green mounds in the calm clear moonlight and warm air of the balmy evening. ... As I walked down the churchyard alone the decked graves had a strange effect in the moonlight and looked as if the people had laid down to sleep for the night out of doors, ready dressed to rise early on Easter morning . . .

Easter is the only point of the year at which the Christian and the natural cycles perfectly coincide, marking for both the point of rebirth, and it is not an accident that Kilvert's description of the Easter of 1870 is one of the finest examples of the possibilities of his prose style: for once his sensibilities worked in precise harmony with his vocation. The experience of that Easter – 'the happiest, brightest, most beautiful Easter I have ever spent' –

takes on, as it is described in the Diary, the intensity of mysticism – the description, quoted above, of the village folk decking their family graves with flowers in the lingering twilight of Easter eve is an extraordinarily exact verbal equivalent of Samuel Palmer at his most visionary, though it is virtually certain that Kilvert had never heard of him. It is not at all a state of romantic excitement, of which there is plenty later in the Diary. It is figures, not people, who move among the graves; visual objects; the ritual is mysterious and impersonal. This is the true mystic's condition of communion: to some extent communion in a social ritual, but predominantly Wordsworthian communion with the felt processes of Nature.

1870 *17 April*. The morning was cloudless with a touch of frost, and Kilvert's first thought was 'Christ is Risen'. He was out of doors soon after 6 gathering primroses in the lane, now bisected by the by-pass, leading down past the shining mill pond, now dry, to the village mill, now a hollow shell – in the spring nowadays the bed of the old pond is blue with drifts of speedwell, and blackbirds nest in the loft of the ruined mill. He leaned over the wicket-gate into the meadow and heard the cuckoo for the first time that year, calling three times quickly near Peter's Pool. The morning was magical, and he was worshipping. Then he went home to Ashbrook, and tied up the primroses into bunches, to put on the grave of Peter Chaloner, the husband of his landlady who had been unable to dress the grave herself – a very typical touch of small kindness. They still put flowers on the graves at Clyro for Easter; though less than in Kilvert's time.

> There was a very large congregation at morning church, the largest I have seen for some time, attracted by Easter and the splendour of the day, for they have here an immense reverence for Easter Sunday.

That too still holds good: Easter Sunday is one of the three days of the year the parish goes to church nowadays, the other two being harvest festival and the Christmas carol service. Instead of the usual eight or nine of the faithful scattered down the nave, the church is suddenly full, and you realize what a depth of communal solidity still underlies the life of the village. I wonder what was a very large congregation in Kilvert's eyes? He says there were more communicants than usual, 29; but this must surely have been a small proportion of the whole. One suspects that at Clyro, as in so many other places, communion had been an almost unknown rite in the early nineteenth century, and that Mr. Venables and Kilvert were having an uphill struggle to revive it. Mr. Evans, the schoolmaster, led the choir in an Easter anthem, unaccompanied I think, for there is no indication that Clyro Church had either harmonium or orchestra in Kilvert's time. It has an organ now – played, strangely enough, by Mr. Evans, the schoolmaster.

1870 *19 April.* Set off with Spencer and Leonard Cowper at 2 o'clock for Mouse Castle. By the fields to Hay, then to Llydiart-y-Wain. It is years since I have seen this house and I had quite forgotten how prettily it is situated... Up a steep meadow to the left and by some quarries, over a stile in a wire fence and up a lovely winding path through the woods spangled with primroses and starred with wood anemones among trees and bushes thickening green. It was very hot in the shelter of the woods as we climbed up... One of the knolls overlooking the wooded side of the hill towards Hay was occupied by a wild group. A stout elderly man in a velveteen jacket with a walking stick sat or lay upon the dry turf. Beside him sat one or two young girls, while two or three more girls and boys climbed up and down an accessible point in the rampart like young wild goats... I could not make the party out at all. They were not poor, and they were certainly not rich... They were perfectly nondescript, seemed to have come from nowhere and to be going nowhere, but just to have fallen from the sky upon Mouse Castle, and to be just amusing themselves... They were full of fun and larks as wild as hawks, and presently began a great romp on the grass which ended in their rolling and tumbling head over heels and throwing water over each other and pouring some cautiously on their father's head. Then they scattered primroses over him. Next the four girls danced away down the path to a spring in the wood with a pitcher to draw more water, leaving a little girl and little boy with their father. We heard the girls shrieking with laughter and screaming with fun down below at the spring in the wood as they romped and, no doubt, threw water over each other and pushed each other into the spring. Presently they re-appeared on top with the pitcher, laughing and struggling, and again the romp began... I could not help envying the father of his children especially his troop of lithe, lissome, high-spirited, romping girls with their young supple limbs, their white round arms, white shoulders and brows, their rosy flushed cheeks, their dark and fair curls tangled, tossed and blown back by the wind, their bright wild saucy eyes, their red sweet full lips and white laughing teeth, their motions as quick, graceful and active as young antelopes or as fawns, and their clear sweet merry laughing voices ringing through the woods...

Some confusion of emotions there, perhaps.

... I cannot think who the wild party were. They were like no one whom I ever saw before. They seemed as if they wore the *genii loci* and always lived there. At all events I shall always connect them with Mouse Castle. And if I should ever visit the place again I shall certainly expect to find them there in full romp...

It was clearly a disorientating experience to meet a family who could not be readily placed in the firm social hierarchy of 1870; after all, what attitude should one adopt toward them? how should one address them if the occasion arose? But the description of the visit to Mouse Castle is one of Kilvert's finest *pièces d'occasion*, with its full, simple, direct rendering both of the scene and of his own reactions to it; and it is noteworthy that Kilvert's vision of people is not altogether blinkered by social categories. The encounter with the wild family is disconcerting, but exciting as well; is it too much to suggest that the sight of people living free and happy outside the ordinary social classifications made Kilvert sense that there could be freedom and happiness outside the social and psychological inhibitions imposed upon him by his upbringing? Like E. M. Forster's curate, Kilvert had met Pan and felt the enchantment. There are other indications in the Diary – initiates will remember Irish Mary – that encounters with the picaresque, with the folk who lived in the crannies of Victorian society rather than its rooms, sometimes brought Kilvert to the brink of forsaking convention; for a wild moment you wonder if we are about to transpose into the world of *The French Lieuten-ant's Woman.*

1970 *20 June* ... I stayed at home and wasted far too much of a wonderful day. Got a pie in the pub for lunch, watching a bit of the Test on their colour T.V. Then a long sleep, and I didn't really come alive till 4.30, when I drove into Hay, had a cup of tea at Hitchcox's café, and went on to Llydiart-y-Wain. A good many holidaymakers and cyclists in and around Clyro and Hay: one party was picknicking on one of the shingle banks that have appeared in the river below Hay Bridge.

Left the car, and set off up the path to Mouse Castle – I could set three or four tractors at once working away at the hay harvest, mowing, tossing, baling. The valley opened smiling below as I climbed up to the edge of the wood – a handsome mature oak wood, much like the woods above Holne Bridge. The path winds up narrowly between the trees; it was very cool and quiet, and the sun struck down through the canopy above in sudden pools and dapples of clear brilliant golden light. Half-way up I found the spring that K mentions, in a tiny cup of the hillside deep in the wood. The water trickles down a cleft at the back of it and out through a bit of old leaden gutter someone has stuck into the cleft; a shaft of light turned the little falling thread of water to silver and brought out the rich redness in the clay bank of the little dell. I crouched down by it. The buzz of a fly in my ear, the tiny falling trickle of water, a faint stir of wind in the leaves overhead, a bird trilling somewhere in the tree-tops. The path that the laughing girls ran down; and a hundred years, and the silence that has swallowed them.

Odd, by the way, that Kilvert shouldn't have seen Llydiart-y-Wain 'for years': it's barely half a mile beyond Hay. One realizes that, for all his intense quartering of his own parish, his excursions beyond it were very occasional, unsystematic affairs. But then, a hundred years later I *drove* to Llydiart-y-Wain: Kilvert, on foot, saw the country much more intensively, but he didn't see very much of it.

1870 *20 April*. Kilvert caught the morning train from Hay to Three Cocks, and thence by the Mid-Wales line (abandoned now, and part of it turned into a road) up the gloriously romantic valley of the upper Wye to Rhayader. He went to attend the laying of the foundation stone of a new mission chapel a few miles outside Rhayader, his host for the occasion – an old friend conceivably – being Middleton Evans of Llwynbarried Hall near Nantmel. He met Kilvert at Rhayader station and drove him home –

> ... a steep awkward pitch led up to the unlodged entrance gate of Llwynbarried which lies bosomed deep among woods so that one does not see it during the approach until the house is close and the road which had ascended, descends sharply upon it. It is a nice old fashioned Welsh country house whitewashed or stuccoed, and with gables. The house has been added to. Round the house stand some fine old oaks gnarled twisted weatherbeaten... Mrs. Evans was in the drawing room and received me very kindly and gave me some tea after which Mr. Evans took me out for a walk round the place, through the gardens and shrubberies and by the kennels...

All was in order. Three 'fine gentlemanly young fellows' were home from Radley for the Easter holidays; at dinner the talk was about Oxford, and afterwards they played Bezique. Next morning was fine, and Kilvert, lying in bed, heard the cuckoo, till the stable clock struck eight and the servant came to call him. He did a round of the gardens before breakfast with one of the boys, and saw a tame buzzard and a pump whose water smelt of sulphur, and the family asked him to read prayers for them. The Victorian genteel world was running smoothly in its groove.

1970 *6 September*. A Kilvert Society excursion to Llwynbarried where K stayed in 4/70. The Kilvertians assembled on the car park at Newbridge – the long grey house of Llysdinam, Mr. Venables' home, looks down on it from the far bank of the Wye – ten cars and 20-odd enthusiasts, I very sizeably the youngest there and my sex also in a smallish minority: the secretary briefed us by reading the relevant extract from the Diary, and we set off in a motorcade and in due course came to the almost overgrown entrance gate of Llwynbarried Hall... The drive is very rough now, and runs through what is almost a jungle of brushwood and low trees till it merges in the ragged parkland round the house, a small white Welsh manor house, very much as Kilvert described it, completely secluded in its little dell in the hills. The overgrown parkland is still thick with the gnarled crouching old oaks that K mentions. I liked the modest little place, though the back facade of the house is a rather ugly late nineteenth-century twin gable. I'm told the pump that smells of sulphur is still there, but the gardens have vanished and the clock has gone from the weatherboarded tower of the old stables and the back drive might as well be a Roman road, barely traceable under the rough grass that covers it. Apparently the Evanses sold the place about the time of the First World War. The cars were parked on the grass, and the Kilvertians, emerging, disinterred picnics from their boots and got down to lunch – some on folding tables and chairs beside their cars, some on fallen trees, two matrons sitting back to back on a tree stump... We had to hurry, for soon a blast on the secretary's whistle announced that the walk, following K's route to Abbey Cwm Hir, was about to begin: the party blossomed out into anoraks, caps, and thumbsticks, and we fell in. . . .

1870 *21 April.* The foundation stone of the mission church on Hysfa Common was duly laid, attended by a great crowd of holiday people (a startling statement indeed to anyone who has seen Hysfa Common, a featureless expanse of level boggy ground in what is in any case one of the remotest and least populated areas of central Wales; the mind contracts in vain when confronted with the question of how many people would be likely to attend the opening of a mission church there today), and Kilvert's description of the scene is one of his masterpieces of social comedy, one of the genres in which the Diary excels. The vicar's six-year-old daughter forgetting the invocation of the Trinity that she had been taught to recite for the occasion; the officiating clergy discomfited by a cloud of dust and lime kicked up by a group of restless boys; the unruly crowd demanding entrance to the tent in which a concert was to take place after the ceremony: all this is rendered in a precise loving straight-faced detail that brings it immediately to hilarious and vivid life. But the most distinctive trait of the writing, and the root of its excellence, is a subtler one: '. . . we with the offertory bags worked and squeezed our way through the crowd presenting the dreaded red velvet weapons at likely looking persons as who should say, "Your money or your life."' There is a nice irony about his own calling, but more than that, a pure objectivity which is the quality of the born observer. It is to be found in all the great scenes of social life in the Diary, the picnics, the dinners, the dances; even when he is in fact a participant, Kilvert sees everything, even his own actions, with the eye of a detached watcher – his diarist self is always looking on, unseen, sharp-eyed, with a gently ironic smile at the quaintness of the social comedy in which his curate self is at the same time an actor.

1870 *27 April*. Started after luncheon for Whitney Rectory, walking with my pack slung over my shoulders by the fields to Hay to catch the 1.50 train...

What a way to go! Whitney is four miles up the main road toward Hereford, the first village in England; to get there, Kilvert has to walk over a mile to Hay station and then take a train. It made good Victorian sense, of course – half an hour's journey instead of an hour's, perhaps – and one is reminded again of the extent to which Kilvert relies on steam and shoe-leather for his transport, of the way in which the railway dominated even local transport, and of its limitations for the purpose.

'Presently I saw Miss Dew in her black dress coming slowly up the green meadow...' Miss Dew, whose family then reigned at both Whitney Court (down by the river – abandoned and demolished, long since, in favour of a much grander house high up on the hill) and Whitney Rectory: seen, and rendered with Kilvert's usual sensitivity to colour, and so dressed in black still.

1870 *28 April*. Over at the Oaks, above Painscastle, old Mrs. Williams was dying, and though the afternoon was cold and grey,

AFTER KILVERT

Kilvert walked over the hill to visit her, as he did several times
that spring: up the dingle where the Morrell children were
picking flowers with their governess, up Jacob's Ladder, stopping
at the top for a chat with two Bryngwyn women on their way
home from Hay market with laden baskets, through the yard at
Great Lloyney, where a girl was searching for eggs, over the
hilltop, where an animal, a hare or a rabbit Kilvert thought, was
screaming with pain and terror among the larches: each commonplace incident duly celebrated. Commonplace, and yet how
infected by time! The children picking flowers with their governess – it could only be the nineteenth century; the market women
on their way home – any age, perhaps, since the thirteenth
century, but the curtain has come down on it now (when did
anyone last walk home from Hay market to Bryngwyn by Jacob's
Ladder, I wonder?); even the girl searching for eggs in the
farmyard – who keeps hens in that casual fashion nowadays?
Of all the incidents of that afternoon, the only one that might
be the same today is the rabbit screaming with pain on the hilltop.

On the way home, the late sun flared out gloriously, and for a
moment Kilvert was the pure visionary. 'Angels were going about
the hill in the waning light.' Not perhaps very orthodox angels;
and how characteristic was Kilvert's reflection afterwards, of
gladness that he had gone to the Oaks in spite of the grimness of
the afternoon – but not for the satisfaction of a pastoral duty
done. Rather 'Who could have imagined that so dull and dreary
an afternoon would end in such a beautiful glorious evening? The
walk has been lovely, happy, heavenly.' The journey is the end: it
is the contemplative, the nature mystic, not the pastor speaking.

When he came home, a new lodger was at the gate – I can see
the gate from the window as I write – a clerk from a solicitor's
office in Hay (fifty years later, Armstrong the poisoner was
arrested in that office). So there were two bachelor sub-
households in Ashbrook now, as well as old Mrs. Chaloner with
her daughter and maid – quiet isolated existences. Today the
children racket cheerfully everywhere; I wouldn't blame the
house if it feels an occasional twinge of nostalgia itself.

1870 *30 April*. Mr. Venables started in the Hay omnibus from

Clyro Vicarage for London for his two months' absence at
10.15.

Hay's apparently solitary horse-drawn omnibus was, one gathers
from other references in the Diary, a humble enough vehicle:
whether it plied on a regular route or went where it was required
I do not know, but I doubt if it normally took in Clyro on its route
– my guess is that it had made a detour to fetch Mr. Venables. For
that matter, I do not know what the chairman of the Radnorshire
County Bench was doing in so plebeian a vehicle, and why he did
not drive to the station in his own carriage as would have been
usual. I suspect though that it was something to do with the
confinement of his young wife, who was apparently already up at
Llysdinam, the Venables' country house, awaiting the birth of the
child who was born a month later: probably her husband had sent
Charlie Lacy, the vicarage coachman, and the horses up there
with her to enable her to have outings during her confinement –
upper-class pregnancies being elaborate affairs in Victorian
times, approached only on tiptoe.

The two months' absence was a regular event, and clearly
neither Mr. Venables nor Kilvert would have thought that it
required any explanation. Mr. Venables was a man of means who
could afford to pay a curate: indeed, on this occasion he had gone
further than that, finding another priest, a Mr. Welby, who came
to live in the vicarage and look after the parish for him in his
absence. Why he thought this necessary I do not know, for on
other occasions he left Kilvert in charge. The combination of the
lives of country gentleman and parson came easily to him, and
was taken as natural by his contemporaries: quarter sessions, the
routine of a country house at Llysdinam, periodic tours of
relatives and friends in London and the provinces, the care of his
parish at Clyro whether performed in person or by deputy: they
were all parts of a single pattern of life of the English establishment. I doubt if any conflict between his clerical and secular
duties ever occurred to him: both alike served to preserve the
settled order of a society approved both by God and time. To that
there is nowadays no equivalent at all.

1870 *3 May*. Kilvert started at noon to walk to Newchurch, by
Whitty's Mill and a path across the fields to the ruined house of

Whitehall, where he moralized, but stylishly –

> How all is changed, song and dance still, mirth fled away. Only the wind sighing through the broken roof and crazy doors, the quick feet, busy hands, saucy eyes, strong limbs all mouldered into dust, the laughing voices silent. There was a deathlike stillness about the place, except that I fancied once I heard a small voice singing and a bee was humming among the ivy green...

Well enough. The house has been repaired since Kilvert was there, and has fallen into ruin again, more completely this time; so completely that it has gone beyond even the thirst of the week-enders from Birmingham for repairable cottages.

> I went up the lane to Pant-y-ci speculating upon the probable site of the Coldbrook and the Black Ox which was the house of call on Clyro Hill for the drovers of the great herds of black cattle from Shire Carmarthen and Cardigan on their way down into England.

Odd that the site should already have been so hard to find, for the trade cannot have been twenty years dead. Here for once Kilvert *does* look back on a recently vanished order of things, of something on which the coming of the railways had already laid a touch of death. For generations the drovers had come this way with their herds of Welsh cattle bound for London, up from Painscastle where they had the cattle shod for the metalled roads on the English side of the border, over Clyro Hill and down to the Hereford road at the Rhydspence; and that was all finished with.

Kilvert went on to Newchurch, where he found the Vaughan girls, the vicar's daughters, teaching in the village school. He was a close family friend of the Vaughans, a family whose like it would not have been easy to find in England in 1870, even though England borders Newchurch across the county boundary, for David Vaughan, the vicar, was a working farmer, and Gilfach-y-rheol, the family home where Kilvert was so frequent and welcome a visitor, was, and is, a farmhouse. The Vaughans, in fact, represented the Welsh Anglican tradition of a peasant clergy, a tradition already dead in England, where the parochial clergy had been rising in social status perhaps ever since the Middle Ages, certainly since the seventeenth century: by the

1870s, witness Kilvert himself, they were firmly of the gentry, and readers of Macaulay (if there are any) will remember the scorn which pervades his description of their more proletarian predecessors of the 1680s. But in Wales things were different – on another visit to Newchurch three days later, he found two of the vicar's younger daughters at work castrating his lambs. It is not one's notion of the typical family activity of a Victorian vicarage, and it clearly was not Kilvert's, who displays a rather comic, and on this occasion quite unironic, fastidiousness at the scene: 'It was the first time I had seen clergyman's daughters helping to castrate lambs or witnessing that operation and it rather gave me a turn of disgust at first. But I made allowance for them and considered in how rough a way the poor children have been brought up, so that they thought no harm of it, and I forgave them' – decent of him! And who did he think *he* was? – 'I am glad however that Emmeline was not present, and Sarah was of course out of the way.' It is revealing of Victorian mores that Emmeline and Sarah were the *elder* daughters.

But there was nothing of that today: Emmeline (who was to die next year) was teaching in the school, and Janet and Matilda were in the class.

> Janet was doing simple division and said she had done five sums, whereupon I kissed her and she was nothing loth. Moreover I offered to give her a kiss for every sum, at which she laughed. As I stood by the window making notes of things in general in my pocket book Janet kept on interrupting her work to glance round at me shyly but saucily with her mischievous beautiful grey eyes. Shall I confess that I travelled ten miles today over the hills for a kiss, to kiss that child's sweet face. Ten miles for a kiss.

An interesting man, the curate of Clyro; more there than met the eye. It was not for nothing that he had known Lewis Carroll at Oxford.

1970 *3 May.* Suddenly a full summer's day, long and hot and lazy, and all the delayed impact of spring burst upon us like a bomb. Saw my first butterfly, a small tortoiseshell, only yesterday: today they were all over the place, peacocks and small whites too. I went to 8 o'clock communion and to matins. Strolled down the lane to the old mill before lunch. Flowers everywhere, celandines, dandelions, the little white cups of wood sorrel, and above all the blue speedwell in drifts under the trees of the old orchard beyond the stream. A green cornfield beyond, with a hint of blue in it. Found the site of K's wicket-gate, beside the mill-pond looking across the field; the view over the fields to the hazy ridge of the Black Mountain must be identical with the one K knew. No cuckoo calling today, but some of the village boys were looking round the mill and they called me to see a blackbird's nest they had found, just inside the eaves by the old loft door (the machinery has gone long since, but the roof and floors are still intact and you can see the beds for the millstones, though there are alarming holes in the floor). Four green eggs, and they had just put in a fifth they found under another nest, which was starting to hatch – there was a tiny hole in the shell, and you could see the little beak inside hammering away at it. The sleepy heat of summer lying over the green fields – down there at the end of the lane the road and the world seem miles away, and the 1870s could be very close...

1970 *8 May.* More and more humid, till a black thunderstorm built up across the valley about 3.30, and the rain started about 4. By 7 we were in the heart of it, a gloom like the last stages of the fall of the gods over everything, deluges of rain, tremendous thunder and lightning with the lights flickering off at every flash. In the midst of it, about 8, John and Prue arrived for the week-end with their very handsome two-month-old baby. Immediately afterwards the electricity failed altogether for two hours, so we got the candles out and had a cold meal out of tins.

Progress fails for a moment and you are driven back to Victorian ways of doing things – if you have the Victorian equipment. As a power black-out makes us realize, one of the chief meanings of progress is centralization; we rely on centrally provided services to a degree inconceivable in Victorian England. As a result, our society is richer, theirs tougher and less vulnerable. Kilvert's Clyro got its water from the brook, its light from oil lamps and candles, its heat from coal and wood; its ordure went back to the land, its scraps were fed to animals, what little inorganic rubbish it produced was burnt, buried, or lost. It had no public utilities at all, and even for its commodities it relied on the outside world to only a trivial extent: at a guess, 90% of its food for instance may have been produced locally, 10% imported, whereas today I imagine the figures are at least 75% – 25% the other way. It was consequently a self-reliant society, very little subject to hardships produced by perturbations in the outside world – in fact, there is never any mention in the Diary of the even tenor of the village's domestic life being affected by public events. Whereas our opulent and complex life is dependent in a dozen, or a hundred, ways on the smooth continuance of institutions and human agencies anonymous to us and quite outside our control; and sometimes they stop. That they might stop altogether sometime is one of the nightmares of the twentieth century; the return to self-reliance, the conservation movement, home baking and brewing, city dwellers moving out to crofts in the Highlands and hill farms in Wales, is becoming a mark of high sophistication. Whether progress, of the only recognized type, can be had on any other terms than centralization, I don't know, but it doesn't seem to have worn its benign face for long: it's much less than a century since most Englishmen voted with their feet on those techniques by abandoning them.

1870 *9 May*. On the way to see Mrs. Williams again.

The mountains burned blue in the hot afternoon and the air felt quite sultry as I climbed the hill. Coming back up the fallow from the Oaks to Wern Fawr I saw Richard Jones, the eldest son, sitting on the hedge bank with his boot off and a man standing by him, while the horses and polished plough gleaming like silver in the sunshine stood waiting at the beginning of another furrow. At first I thought he had had an accident and hurt his foot. But the bystanding man was a shoemaker and the young farmer was trying on a pair of new boots... The shoemaker had a benevolent face and as we walked on to Wern Fawr together he asked me if I knew him and when I said no, he said he went every Sunday morning to read the Bible to

Mrs. Williams, but he had been told that if I ever caught him there I should be very cross with him. I begged him not to believe any such nonsense and said that so far from my being cross with him he had my warmest thanks. He was a Painscastle man and I should think a good man. These are the misconceptions that are spread abroad about the clergy...

Horses and plough are within my memory, but not village shoemakers; here again mass production and the shop have taken over a job that in Kilvert's time was done by local craftsmen. Clyro's craftsmen today are the agricultural engineeer, today's form of the blacksmith, one or two small builders, and, more exotically, a potter – who however, does not work for a local market and perhaps hardly counts here; in 1870, beside two smiths, there were two millers, a saddler, a shoemaker, a tailor, two carpenters, and a threshing-machine driver. There were fewer shops in Hay, and the village did much more of its own work, and was that much more rounded and complete and shut-in a community; rounded and complete are good perhaps, shut-in less so.

The Painscastle shoemaker – we do not know his name – may stand as a type of the intelligent artisan, partly liberated by the nature of his calling from the despotism of his superiors' opinions, to whom English nonconformity has owed so much of its strength; he is in the tradition of John Bunyan. The suspicions still lay deep, clearly, between his congregational religion and the Church. Kilvert was more liberal than most; but his tone has the prejudice of one who expects prejudice in his opponents.

1870 *12 May*. On going to Sackville Thomas' yesterday, I found little Mary Thomas at home because the ground was wet and her boots full of holes. When she heard her grandmother telling me how it was that she could not go to school, she went away by herself crying quietly and bitterly. Poor child it was touching to see her trying to write on the floor with a bit of chalk, and working as well as she could by herself with an old broken piece of slate and torn leaf of a book trying to think she was at school.

There was a great deal of poverty in Kilvert's Clyro, and with it went a great deal of squalor and suffering. This may not be the end of the argument, though today there is a tendency to think that it is; but the truth of it must be faced and accepted before there is any possibility of an end to it, and a four-year-old girl in tears because her boots are so full of holes that she cannot go to school is a harsh enough image for the purpose. This does not happen now. It will not do to imagine Kilvert's Clyro as a place of trim clean cottages with flower gardens at the door and happy faces at the windows. Some of it *was* like that; but the Diary contains just as much evidence of squalid hovels – Kilvert himself often uses the word – sluttishly kept, with broken windows and holes in the roof, where disease spread unchecked and drunken fathers beat their children black and blue. I do not suppose Clyro housewives are by nature cleaner, or Clyro fathers gentler, than a hundred years ago; but the state is much more attentive now than it was then, and wealth is a great healer. There is much less suffering and much more comfort in the village now than in 1870. The questions about beauty, truth, and goodness may still remain, but only if you have the right to ask them.

1870 *14 May*. Over the great old fashioned house door of Court Evan Gwynne hung the sprigs of birch and wittan, the only remnants of the old custom I have noticed this May.

Court Evan Gwynne, a fine old house by all accounts, had already fallen from its former estate to that of a labourer's house; it was pulled down in the 1890s and replaced by a little square stone villa. Today it is a holiday house, like so many of the rest of them; trim, painted white, with bright orange dressings; a flagpole stuck on top of the little Norman motte beside it; a weathervane in the form of a large painted version of a family crest projecting from one end of the old timber-framed barn; renamed Castle Kinsey.

1870 *17 May*. Hay Fair today and tomorrow and I am right glad to escape the noise bustle dust drunkenness and the general upturn of the country.

1970 *15 May*. Drove into Hay with M and C in the morning to do the washing at the new little laundrette in Oxford Terrace.

– yes, well, no wonder we of the middle classes are subject to fits of nostalgia now that we have to do our own washing: imagine Kilvert at a laundrette.

> The first day of Hay Fair, which now seems to be purely a fun-fair, instead of a cattle-market and hiring-fair as in K's time. The little town full of great vans and power generators and stalls being erected – Oxford Road at the back of the castle entirely blocked by a huge dodgems rink and several other big mechanical shows. The men of the fair seem to wear a uniform of caked dirt – I've never seen anyone dirtier. . .

1970 *23 May*. The two Miss Clarks talking outside their back door to a man with a cardboard carton full of greenstuff.

> A swallow flew in through the open window of my study as I worked here this morning: I caught it, fluttering and trembling against the other window, and let it out. A lovely iridescent blue head and rusty cheeks. Nestling starlings squeaking continually from their nest inside the damaged roof of the verandah. Martins swooping and hawking at lightning speed in the dusk.

> A continual stream of traffic on the road this morning, but they're almost all cars bound for the holiday week-end, not heavy traffic for once.

The residents and the passers-by. The world's traffic flows down the road nowadays, and Clyro sits on the brink watching it go by. Monday to Saturday the heavy lorries thunder by; then at summer week-ends, from Easter onwards in a gradually thickening stream till the endless processions of August, they are supplanted by the holidaymakers' cars, cars piled high with luggage and children, cars towing caravans, cars towing boats on trailers. This is all new. Kilvert mentions tourists at Llanthony, but otherwise he never refers to them at Clyro at all. Probably a few of the gentry still came this way from time to time in search of the picturesque; but in general they had their own country houses for their holidays. For the rest, the spread of the railways had accustomed the middle classes to holidays by the sea, and at resorts all along the coasts the boarding-houses were going up; as for the lower classes, most of them never had any holidays at all.

MAY

The private and local life of Clyro flowed on, unperturbed by intrusions of the outer world.

1970 *24 May*. After lunch, we all went out for another voyage of discovery in the car, and it turned out even better than last week. We took the road below Mouse Castle which winds up to the top of Cusop Hill – across the valley we could see the road to Capel y Ffin winding steeply up the Black Mountain, a row of cars climbing up it shining like beetles in the sun. Even on our road there was no avoiding cars and holidaymakers, till we turned aside over Vagar Hill. The others went for a walk down a long overgrown green lane, while I soon returned and snoozed in the sun – a Land Rover showed signs of stopping and giving me first aid. Jenny had chosen to come out barefoot and wearing a blue maxi dress – the latest fashion – which had a very high Jane Austen waist and came almost down to her ankles, which given her height was a very long way – picking her way through the grass between the overgrown hazel hedges she was a most astonishing sight, most easily accounted for as having strayed out of the Idylls of the King.

We drove on to Snodhill, plunging down deeply into the Golden Valley, through narrow lanes where you couldn't pass another car but never met one – lanes with tufts of grass growing down the middle, running between high banks buried under a froth of hedge parsley and scattered thick with white stitchwort, more thinly with the deep pink campion, and here and there patches of cowslips, which grow best on verges, and deep blue, almost purple, bluebells which prefer the shade of trees: the trees which arch over the lane here and there and gather in little casual oases of deep shade and coolness at turns of the road. Every now and then a little grey cottage or farm sat deep in the greenery, and every now and then there was a sudden glimpse through a gap in the hedge of the land falling away to the rich pastures of the valley below. On the hills on its far side one big farmer has levelled all his hedges, and a wide stretch of the ridge looks strangely like the Downs, a great smoothly curving stretch of upland turf, unbroken except for isolated clumps of trees.

Just below Snodhill Castle, a bare fanged ruin on a tree-ringed motte where K had that noisy crowded picnic, we found a farm, deserted in the afternoon sun by all but a huge sow with a tribe of well-grown piglets and some calves, and opposite it a stream flowing across the road by a ford with a little footbridge. A pair of dippers were busy in the stream, bobbing most curiously at the knees – the first I've ever knowingly seen – and a swarm of gnats dancing above the water; C uttered a cry of 'Pooh sticks!' and in no time he and E were paddling in the stream and occasionally slipping over, with no very evil result, except that E had to be divested of her wet dress and pants, which we dried by driving along with one hung on each wing-mirror.

On the way home, we went to a farm which had a notice up advertising eggs for sale, and in no time found ourselves stroking the farm kittens and in warm conversation with the young farmer who works it alone with his even younger sister and the occasional help of his mother. A most friendly pair: we talked leaning on the wall and looking down from a great height, over 1,000 feet, on the little town far and bright in the valley below in the clear evening sunshine, with the great mountain behind it. He talked about his life, farming 200 acres, all but 30 of it pasture, in the farm he was born in, which his father bought at the break-up of the Clyro Court estate in 1950. He and his sister are hard at it up to 9 at night, and make enough to get by on and no more, but they like the work, they can arrange their own hours, they're their own masters, and what more can you want? And certainly both of them have a healthy happy look about them. Some of these people who complain most about the farm prices, he says, drive round in Jaguars and have never done a day's farming in their lives. On the other hand, it was true that though a farm might represent £50,000 worth of capital, there was precious little you could do with it; if you mortgaged, you had to pay 10% interest. They discovered who we were, wondering if we were some of the tycoons from Birmingham who have moved into the district to live in the last few years. They talked too about the time when one postman did all the local deliveries on foot – and you still got the post earlier than you do now, when there are three vans. And about the local habit of knowing people by their Christian name and their job, or farm – 'John Cefn-y-Blaen'. You also hear the surname and job, in the traditional Welsh fashion – 'Price the garage'. It's what comes of being short of surnames, no doubt, everyone being Price or Jones or Lewis, but it's odd that K never mentions the practice – it surely can't be new. The young farmer said too that until very recent years much of their land on the hilltop was rough open grazing – as both K and the early O.S. maps show – which he has now enclosed.

Much food for thought there. When Kilvert came to Clyro, the parish had a population of about 850 souls (it had reached a peak of nearly 1,000 in the 1840s, and had been falling slowly since then), who fitted clearly into three main social categories – the gentry, the farmers, and the labourers. The gentry comprised five families – the Baskervilles of Clyro Court, the Morrells of Cae Mawr, the Crichtons of Wye Cliff, the Venables at the vicarage, and the Colletts, or later the Hodgsons, at Lower Cabalva, and of these the Baskervilles stood out in a category of their own. Herbert Baskerville was the squire: he owned a large part of the land of the parish, and was gradually extending his hold, and his family had a longer-standing connection with Clyro than any of the others – indeed, I am not sure if any of the others were more than tenants. Nevertheless, in the census of 1871 which so conveniently illuminates the society of Clyro in Kilvert's time all these families clearly formed a single social group. They all employed seven or eight domestic servants; they were all ranked as 'of independent means'; they all lived in country houses, not farmhouses, approached by private drives and standing in their own grounds (the vicarage, of course, is a special case).

Below them came the farmers, the great bulk of them tenants, and farming areas varying from 350 acres in the case of the big farms in the valley bottom, the Court Farm, Boatside, and Upper Cabalva, to smallholdings of less than 50 acres up in the hills.

These differences obviously implied wide differences in the wealth and to some extent the social standing of the farmers; but again a broad similarity covers the whole group. The more prosperous among them might employ a full-time domestic servant, have a piano in the parlour, and send their daughters to boarding-schools – as Richard Jefferies observed them doing twenty years later – but all were distinguished above all by their working relationship with the land and by their role as providers of employment. Much of the labour was provided by their own children – it is common to find two or three unmarried sons in their twenties living at home, and it was among them no doubt that the drift to the towns would begin in the next decade, for it must often have been a grindingly frustrating position for a young man. There were also in most farms a number of living-in farm-servants, also young and unmarried, and very often including a girl or two to work in the house or the dairy.

It was, I think, among the farmers and their families that Kilvert spent many of his happiest hours at Clyro – hearing them talk about their memories of older days, being given tea and bread and butter (home made, for no bread nor butter was made anywhere else at Clyro in 1870) by the farmers' wives, playing with their children, and petting their dogs. Although he mixed freely and gaily with the gentry, it is easy to imagine that there must always have been an irksome sense of dependence there – always it had to be at *their* invitation, and always there must have been the inescapable implication that Kilvert, though socially of them, was economically far beneath them, £100 a year mingling probably with £2,000 or so. With the labourers the boot was on the other foot. Kilvert could sympathize with them, and may even have been popular among them, but the gulf of wealth, culture, and knowledge that stretched between him and them cripplingly limited communication; there was little lure in the frequent squalor of their cottages, and they could not well offer hospitality nor he decently accept it. But with many of the farmers he was on a rough economic equality – and economic equality is a good foundation for human contacts – while no doubt he was human enough to enjoy the touch of superior status that his education and his clerical rank conferred on him. The Walls at Chapel Farm, the Hills at the Upper Noyadd, the Merediths at Bryn-y-Garth – each of these homes, and many others like them, was an oasis where there was always a ready welcome, no social formalities, eager children, the sense of well-being that lays no obligations on a visitor.

Thirdly there were the labourers, much the largest class in the parish – the unmarried ones commonly living-in on the farms, the married in rented cottages. All were miserably poor – Kilvert does not often mention actual hunger, but the Diary gives plenty of evidence of wretched housing, ragged clothing, and blanketless beds. Among them too, the urge to move to better-paid jobs in the towns must have been strong indeed once the possibility of it was realized. The labourers and their families, though they appear often enough in the Diary, tend to appear marginally; they are never as fully reported as the gentry and the farmers because, as I have just said, although Kilvert was a faithful and diligent visitor, he could not enter into their lives as he did into those of their betters; and perhaps because of this, it is easy for readers of the Diary to emerge with a picture of Kilvert's Clyro that does not take sufficient account of the mass of irretrievable poverty and drudgery that lay at the bottom of it.

Beside each of these three main classes it is possible to identify a satellite class, roughly on an equality with it yet differently employed. Beside the labourers, there were the domestic servants of the gentry – though most of these doubtless fared better than the labourers and would have considered themselves a step above them. Beside the farmers, there were the village craftsmen – a considerable group, as we have already seen – and perhaps more doubtfully one might add such anomalous figures as the post-mistress, the policeman, and the innkeeper. And conceivably one might claim to detect, beside the gentry, the skeletal hint of an intelligentsia – though the intelligentsia have never bulked large in Clyro society, and it is hard to see who might be included in it from the 1871 census beyond Kilvert himself and the Morrells' governess, for nobody would have considered the schoolmaster on any kind of equality with the gentry.

It was a society which, except among the gentry, married late – rarely before twenty-five. For this there were obvious economic reasons. Farmers' sons usually could not contemplate marriage till their fathers died or retired, and they could take over the farm. With labourers, the main problem was probably housing. Kilvert makes no mention of new houses going up in the parish in his time, and till a cottage fell vacant a labourer was more or less condemned to live-in at a farm where there was no accommodation for married men.

For a society bound by these restraints, and in which contraception was presumably unknown, the standard of sexual morality seems to have been strikingly high – it is not obvious that the illegitimacy rate was much higher than it is today, when neither of these conditions applies. Families were large, but not as epically large as one is apt to think of Victorian families. The record in Clyro in 1870, or rather in 1871, appears to have been held by Farmer Williams of Great Lloyney (or Llainau, as Kilvert spelt it), who had ten children under fourteen living at home, though they were apparently the fruit of two marriages. Four or five was a commoner size – partly, no doubt, because of the frequent deaths of children. By 1871, virtually all these children went to the village school (or at least were described as 'scholar' by the census-taker) from the age of four or so till eleven or twelve, when they started work.

Another distinctive group, the old, is also discernible in the parish, including such patriarchal figures as Kilvert's two favourites, John Morgan the Peninsular War veteran and Hannah Whitney. They do not seem to have lived with their children as often as is commonly supposed. Many of them apparently went on living, alone or with their partners, in the cottages they had inhabited all their lives, old age weighing more and more harshly on them as they became progressively less able to care for themselves. Occasionally perhaps there might be a chance of an almshouse in Hay. Some of them inevitably depended on poor relief, though to do so meant a wounding loss of pride and prestige in the village; few of Kilvert's, and Mr. Venables', acts of kindness to the poor seem to have given more genuine pleasure than their success in extracting a pension for John Morgan from the War Office, and so freeing him from the necessity of 'living on the rates' – pensions of any sort, in any rank of society below the Court, being almost unknown in the 1870s. Otherwise, they struggled along as best they could, growing vegetables in their cottage gardens, helped out no doubt by families and neighbours, not always unhappy, not apparently much complaining; and when they couldn't, they died.

The change in the nature of village life over the last hundred years has been immense, and one's constantly asking oneself, when did the big change really come? Has it been an even process, or can you put your finger on a major watershed, a crucial decade perhaps, which essentially separates the old from the new? Mr. Walker maintains that the big change came when the market women bound for Hay on their donkeys on Thursday mornings started passing his door at 7 a.m. instead of 5, and he may be right – there must be a major easing of economic pressures behind a change of that sort. If one's looking for watersheds, there is no shortage of candidates in the field of public events – the two world wars, the Depression, the Labour Government of 1945? Yet I wonder if any of these has marked as great a change in the village as the break-up of the Clyro Court estate in 1950 (though indeed all four of those great public events probably contributed largely in their various ways to this local one). In one sense, I suppose, it meant the disintegration of the parish, the loss of one of its chief centres of unity, for the estate was a power in the place to which the great majority of its inhabitants must have owed a degree of subordination in one way or another, directly or indirectly, and nothing has replaced it in that role. On the most obvious level, all, or nearly all, the farmers were tenants in Kilvert's day – where will the rents come from? he asks himself when the season is bad – and today all, or nearly all, of them are freeholders, and in most cases this freedom dates from 1950, when they bought their farms. And the estate office where the rents used to be paid is now our children's playroom. The farmers are better off now than they were then, of course, but I imagine this has little to do with the fact that they now own their own land – probably most of them pay as much in interest on their mortgages as they formerly paid in rent – and comparatively they have certainly gained less in the last hundred years than have the descendants of the labourers of 1870. The change is more in mind and in attitude, in the sense which my young farmer mentioned of 'being your own master', of having no one above you to whom you are bound by the compulsion of self-interest to defer; and so far so very good.

But the break-up of the estate obviously reached further afield than the farmers. It meant that most of the residents in the village became house-owners for the first time (at prices that look ludicrous today: one of our neighbours has told me that buying the house in 1950 cost less than repairing the roof a year or two ago), also that a number of jobs disappeared; but more fundamentally than any of this, it meant a change in the social assumptions of Clyro. While the estate survived and there was still a squire at the Court, Clyro was still something of a monarchy: there was one man in the parish who cast his shadow over the others, and, if his word was not precisely law, still nothing much was likely to get done without his will and it would be best not to offend him if you could help it. Kilvert himself tasted village tyranny in his home at Langley Burrell; the Baskervilles seems to have reigned much more complaisantly in Clyro, but it was a monarchy still, and in 1950 it abdicated. Clyro today is something much more like a Jeffersonian republic – admittedly one in which many take no interest in the public thing, and which, if it no longer has to bow to a monarch, now finds itself bound by the decisions of the faceless They in Llandrindod Wells and Whitehall; but I think there is real gain here nevertheless in human independence and self-respect. Not that Clyro is any kind of image of the classless society. The gentry are still with us, farming, travelling, visiting London, rearing horses and worshipping them, and there is certainly more money in Clyro than ever before in its history, most of it concentrated in largish lumps. But the parish council and the rural district council are not gentry-dominated; and, what is perhaps more important, most of the parish is not dependent on them either as employees or as tenants. Clyro in practice probably owes its independence less to the institution of elective forms of local self-government than to the decay and final break-up of the Baskerville estate.

The gentry survive, not much reduced in numbers, but they are no longer readily defined by the appearance of their houses or the size of their domestic staffs. Some live in farms, some in cottages; the biggest of their ancient fortresses are gradually falling out of private hands altogether. As for the domestic staffs, no doubt the gentry still are roughly distinguished by having some kind of paid help in the house, but it is almost invariably part-time and very inconspicuous – the chief source of domestic employment in the village nowadays is the pub. The identity of the gentry does not rest on a landlord–tenant relationship, nor on the distinction between a life of work and a life of leisure, nor yet on a clear-cut distinction of wealth, though obviously there is a tendency that way. It is hard in fact to see any other foundation for it than education, mores, tradition, and force of habit. Most of the gentry owe their identity partly to descent from families who were undoubtedly gentry in the last century; but if one wanted a rule-of-thumb definition, it would be good enough to say that the gentry of Clyro in the 1970s are those who have had a private education and give sherry parties.

The labourers, meanwhile, have vanished. Below the level of the gentry, the entire population of the parish – only about 450 now – forms a single, though not very homogeneous, class. Farm-hands have been replaced by machines, owned or hired at need, and the farmers work the land themselves with the help of neighbours or of contractors at the peaks of the farming year – in a way, I suppose, it is a move back toward the co-operative farming of the open-field areas of lowland England in the Middle Ages. Most of the parish are self-employed; the largest employers of labour now are probably the agencies of local and central government, notably the county council roads and education departments. Of the old satellite classes, full-time domestic servants have virtually disappeared, the craftsmen have shrunk to the two or three men who work at the garage and one or two jobbing builders, and the intelligentsia, in the sense of school-teachers, have increased slightly.

But besides the gentry and the middle classes, Clyro now harbours a third group who cannot comfortably be identified with either: the aliens from outer space – the retired folk from the Midlands who live in new bungalows, and the week-enders, the hippies, and various other refugees from twentieth-century urban life, who tend to prefer old farmhouses and cottages. They fall into no single category of age, wealth, or class (though most could fairly be described as middle class). They bring with them exotic industries like potting and cake-decoration. They stand apart because very few of them are absorbed into the main stream of village life – they have come to Clyro late; many of them are only there occasionally; to hardly any of them is Clyro home in quite the same sense as it is to its primordial inhabitants. It is a group to which there was no equivalent in Kilvert's time, when the village was much more of an organic unity. Admittedly, Kilvert himself was a newcomer and an alien; but his function, as well as his nature, made him a part of village society in a sense in which few or none of these newer visitants are.

The classes pursue their own ways of life with mutual tolerance, but they interlock very little; and here the valuation of the
change that has taken place is more doubtful. The social divisions
of Kilvert's day were absolute, but in their daily activities people
of all classes worked in close and necessary co-operation and with
a good deal of personal contact; today the tendency is for the
classes to draw apart into circles of private friends. It is most
notable that where, at the northern end of the parish, a new
estate has been built up since 1950 based on Lower Cabalva that
in acreage must now rival the old Clyro Court estate, its economic
and social structure is totally different. The land is kept in hand
and farmed centrally and as efficiently as possible; isolated
farmhouses and cottages are abandoned and ruinous, hedges
flattened, and the total number of dependants on the estate in
any sense could be numbered on the fingers of two hands, if not
one. There is wealth here, but no approach to monarchy. There is
less subordination in Clyro, but also more privacy; community is
less strong, and the tendency is for people to draw apart, though
this process of suburbia is only in its early stages here.

1870 *28 May.* Kilvert was returning from a brief visit to his
home to greet his sister Emmie, just arrived from India.

> From Langley to Clyro by early express. Galloped through
> Hereford in a fly with a white horse and just caught the
> Hay train at Moorfields ...

The railways were still in their young and growing stages, and
the system was very untidy in its details. Consolidation had not
yet taken place to any great degree: there was a multiplicity of
local companies, and a corresponding multiplicity of stations.
Hereford had three: Barr's Court, the original terminus of the
Shrewsbury & Hereford line, which was the city's first public
railway; Barton, on the later Great Western-owned through line
to Newport; and Moorfields, the terminus of the independent
Hereford, Hay & Brecon company. Of these three stations only
Barr's Court, on the east side of the city, remains in use today,
Barton and Moorfields, which were comparatively close together
on its western outskirts, having vanished many years ago.
Kilvert's route to Clyro from Chippenham had been much simp-
lified by the opening of the Gloucester and Hereford branch of the

Great Western in 1869 – before that he would have had to go round through either Worcester or Newport – but it still involved changes at Swindon and Gloucester, and a change of stations in Hereford, where he arrived at Barr's Court and left from Moorfields. Since the lines were moreover owned by independent companies, connections were a chancy business, and Kilvert was for ever making frantic dashes across Hereford, a city which he did not love, and often missing trains at the end of them. Twenty years later the journey would have been easier; now it is of course impossible, the lines from Gloucester to Hereford and Hereford to Hay both having vanished within the last decade.

1870 *1 June*. Going out to the school at 10 found Mary Brookes, the Vicarage housemaid, at the door just going to ring. She had run down breathless with an open letter just received in her hand to announce that Mrs. Venables was confined of a nice little girl at 1.5 a.m. yesterday. Three cheers.

The news flew through the village like wildfire, and they were ringing the bells all day, and the village spoke of nothing else, and at night the Clyro Court gardener and the schoolmaster lit a tar-barrel bonfire in the Bron in honour of the baby – Kilvert saw the light upon his bedroom wall.

The vicar was very well up in middle age, and he had had no children by his first wife; so the arrival of this first child, at the family home at Llysdinam, was some reason for rejoicing. But again how it reminds one of royalty! Like the squire – and in this particular case perhaps even more than the squire – the vicar was a representative figure, a role that is almost extinct now; some shreds of it still cling to the monarchy itself, but they are wearing rapidly to nothing, and as they go the office starts to look purposeless. The representative role belongs with the hierarchical society: there is a sense in which the monarch personifies his people, and because of that his life cannot be private – what happens to him happens to them, and hence they have a legitimate interest in how things go with him and his family. As their place in society forbids them the full dignity of being individual, his makes him more than merely individual. And what could be more proper than that the vicar, on a lower level, should share this vicarious function? So there was great rejoicing at Clyro at the news that Mr. Venables had a daughter.

All this is unthinkable now. Who last bore something of this representative role in Clyro, I wonder? I see it as perishing long ago, perhaps at the time of the First World War – which made such havoc of the representative principle by involving everybody equally in the great affairs of the world; but it is a nuance of attitude that cannot be pinned down precisely, and no exact dating is possible.

1870 *2 June.* As I walked home down the Long Mills hill the brick-kiln glowed bright and red through the dusk.

A casual enough observation, but interesting in its implications when you think about it. Kilvert was walking home to Clyro along the Hay road from the Wye Cliff gate; the site of the brick-kiln was in the hollow on the left of the road. There is a bit of scrubby coppice there now; the soil is full of bits of broken brick and earthenware, round the ponds that fill the old clay-pits. It must have been a very small-scale affair, wiped out apparently within a few years of 1870, no doubt by the competition brought by the railways. But *brick* – this is not at all a brick part of the world, or at least it was not in Kilvert's time; as I have already said, the local stone was the universal building material. As in almost all the stone areas of England, one of the most immediate visual results of the coming of the railway was the rapid decline of the quarrying and use of stone and its replacement by bricks, which for the first time could be transported cheaply enough from the places where they were made (in the Midlands chiefly) to compete economically with the traditional material – often enough with disastrous aesthetic consequences, as notably in Clyro itself. It is noticeable that they were used first for door and window dressings and for angles in general, since they saved the skilled and laborious task of cutting stone to shape, stone still being used for the rest of the walling (the estate cottages of 1876 in the village street are an example); presumably at this date stone still worked out cheaper, except for these positions.

It is easy enough to understand that mass-produced imported bricks would knock a one-man local brick-kiln out of business in a very short time; but what were his bricks used for anyway? It isn't easy to find examples of pre-railway age brickwork in Clyro:

the chief exception would be the Court farm, a big square brick building of the earlier nineteenth century, very Herefordshire to look at. But at a guess the kiln may have been devoted to the production of pipes rather than bricks: the fragments in the soil on the spot seem to be largely of pipes, and there must have been a considerable demand for them for drainage.

1870 *3 June*. Sitting room windows open till very late. A group of people talking and laughing loud in the Swan porch and on the steps in the dusk. I was delighted to hear Teddy Evans proposing to some other children to play the old game of 'Fox a Dandley' ... I had no idea the old game was still played by the present generation of children. Teddy Evans was singing

> My Mother said that I never should
> Play with the gipsies in the wood &c.

Warm summer evenings. One of the qualities of Kilvert's observation is the sharpness of it; another is the width of its range. He notes so much partly because he has so few private concerns to demand his attention. Here he is sitting in his room, alone, with no family responsibilities to demand his first concentration, his work over for the day; a little bored perhaps, instincts and sensibilities *demanding* to be employed – no wonder the net of his observations and reflections is so wide.

1870 *6 June*. 'Letters from my mother and Dora', and he proceeds to set out at length incidents of family life from these letters as though he had witnessed them himself. No man itching to get back to his book keeps a diary this way, and indeed there is no sign that Kilvert was much of a reader; he writes rather as though time hung heavy on his hands. If so, he found the right use for it; one wonders again how he used to occupy himself before he started his diary.

1870 *7 June*. Up early and writing in my bedroom before breakfast. The swallows kept on dashing in at the open window and rustling round the room. The road sides are now deep in the dry withered wych blossom blowing and rustling about lightly and falling from the Churchyard wyches ...

How those tantalizing details bring the lost past back to life – the evocation of the small things that make the background of experience, as much as of the intentions that makes its foreground. The commonplace experiences of a commonplace man, and yes, in a sense so they are, and yet the result is one of the finest English examples of that strange literary form, the diary.

A commonplace man? No man who kept a diary like his could be altogether commonplace; yet, *but* for the Diary, Kilvert would long since have been forgotten as certainly and as absolutely as any man of his class and his generation. A country curate of third-rate intelligence who never had an original idea in his life, wrote feeble sentimental verse which failed to find a publisher, and died of appendicitis on the brink of middle age – you can hardly imagine a stronger candidate for oblivion, yet the description is true of Kilvert. No doubt there is more that could be said. A devoted pastor, a man of unusual charm and warmth of personality – yes, yes. These are qualities for which a man's contemporaries remember him, but they die with his generation; they win him no memory when his time isover. So yes, an obscure life – as Kilvert himself took for granted; a life of which, but for the Diary, nothing at all would be left today but an ugly tombstone in a Herefordshire churchyard, an entry in a few official documents, and, for a few individuals, an empty name on the farthest fringes of remembered family history. And for the last century or so, most men have left that much; total oblivion is becoming a hard and a rare thing to achieve.

Actually, it is the obscurity of the man that gives the Diary much of its appeal. The diary of a public man, of any man who has a reputation for something other than the diary itself, gives you only a new look into a past itself already public, a past already known and shop-soiled. Kilvert's Diary has the rare quality of opening a window on a past otherwise totally unknown, a past that everybody would have assumed to be gone and forgotten beyond recall. Figures known to history always have a strut about them; these people are so private, their actions so unselfconscious, so unaware of a reader. The everyday life and gossip, the transient appearances of the landscape in a small Welsh village a hundred years ago – again, can one imagine anything more completely lost and inaccessible to every faculty but the imagination? And then there the Diary is, and a small window opens on that lost landscape, and you see it, clear and minute and secret and frozen and alive, like a landscape in the background of a Flemish Renaissance painting, a Patinir or a Breughel. These are the dead – not brought back to life again, but still living; there we are back in the lost past at the moment when it all happened.

The Diary conveys that impression of the past recovered only because it was written by a man who saw it more intensely than those around him and whose skill at translating that vision into words has not often been equalled in English. Obscurity alone is not enough, of course. Heaven knows how many diaries of forgotten men lie unread and unreadable at the back of bureaux, in solicitors' tin boxes, on the top shelf of the cupboard in the attic. There are two other things needed, the two gifts which Kilvert did possess in very exceptional degree – an eye and a pen, a knack for precise observation and a gift for vivid description.

The other great obscure diarist is Parson Woodforde; Pepys and Dorothy Wordsworth mingled too much with the great, Gilbert White is too much the scientist. As far as observation of the life around him goes, Woodforde comes very close to Kilvert. Both have a true perception of the human comedy, of the infinite and intriguing varieties and curiosities of life and character. The difference is that Woodforde stops there; it is the quaintness of his diary that more than anything else attracts us. He has not Kilvert's ear for actual dialogue; still more (and here, perhaps, what we are up against is less a difference of individual characters than of modes of perception over a century) he has none of Kilvert's acute Romantic visual sense. Because he cannot, in this sense, *see* his own world, he cannot, like Kilvert, bring it before *our* eyes. What lies between the two men is Wordsworth, and the revelation that he brought. In Wordsworth's sister the visual perception is exquisitely present, but Dorothy, though purer, is thinner than Kilvert; she does not give us her world in anything like the same voluminous detail.

The Diary is attractive in another way too, but this is adventitious, not intrinsic. It happens to appeal particularly to our nostalgia because of the beauty, the middle-class prosperity, and the security of the England it describes; perhaps too because that England is just sufficiently close to us to be half familiar through the related memories of our parents and the recollections of our own childhoods – we have the illusion at least that we can imagine ourselves there. Kilvert's is the mythic pre-1914 England that to a middle-class sensibility so easily wears the look of Eden. Financial security, plenty of servants, international peace – not noble considerations, but they count. How cosy he looks, bedded snugly into a tranquillity that still had forty years to run, to us who hardly expect to die in our beds! Nothing is as secure as the past. And then too the beauty, which, though likewise adventitious, is not I think merely subjective. Kilvert had extraordinary luck: what he was given to describe was a wholly rural England which had been gardened to the pitch of visual perfection at the very moment before the wave of modern industrialism crashed down over it and left it strewn with bricks, cars, overhead wires, concrete blocks, and old prams.

1970 *7 June*. Out on the verandah at 9 or so, the light thickening only very slowly, and a blessed hush on everything. The roads as quiet as in K's time, not a thing moving on the by-pass, not a voice to be heard; only the rustle of the brook outside the kitchen, now as then, and the occasional plaintive mewing of a lamb from the fields across the by-pass.

1870 *7 June*. And this is the birthplace of Sarah Smith. Sarah of the Cwm. To me there seems to be a halo of glory round this place. Yet in what poor mean dwellings these wild rich natures, these mountain beauties, are born and reared. Many sweet and sacred memories hover about these hill homes and make the place wherever one stands holy ground.

Kilvert's romanticism runs easily into over-lushness. His literary merits are instinctive, which is their excellence; but he never shows much sign of a discriminating literary taste, and his writing suffers from a corresponding lack of pruning. There is, though, more than a literary weakness to be remarked on here. The sentimentality is characteristic of an age that put a green baize door between its emotions and its instincts, and particularly characteristic of Kilvert, whose culture, calling, and circumstances all alike forbade him to look below the sentimental level of his feelings. Indeed, in this instance as in a good many others in the Diary, neither Kilvert himself nor perhaps any of his contemporaries would have been aware that any other level existed, for Sarah Smith was nine, a pupil of his in the village school.

1870 *9 June*. In the night there came a cooler wind and fair showers out of the west. The falling white blossoms of the clematis drift in at the open window on the fresh morning breeze. In the garden there are red roses, and blue hills beyond. Last night the moon was shining in at my west window through the lacing boughs of the mountain ash – the moonbeams fell across the bed and I saw 'the gusty shadow sway' on the white bed curtain ...

What a gift the man had! I just don't know how this *could* be better done, yet it's entirely unselfconscious. 'In the garden there are red roses, and blue hills beyond' – where it matters most, the over-exuberant flow of adjectives disappears completely and there are the pure colours in all the absoluteness with which he saw them.

1970 *9 June*. Shrewsbury ... a fine session at the Lion, Cyril holding forth with great vehemence on the goodness of the old days and how tolerably off even the poor really were. All four of us, at bottom, hate the present; is it typical of our age, our class, or what?

Good question. As Cyril knows, I do not believe that the poor were tolerably off in the old days, though equally I know that there are no absolutes in tolerance: what is tolerable is what is tolerated, and that is all it is, except in a sense which makes all human societies the collection of vermin that Swift thought them. But to me, now, the lot of the Summerflowers and the Mrs. Corfields a hundred years ago does not look morally tolerable; and yet I don't quarrel with the accuracy of my own diary entry: I know I am rightly placed among the haters of their own time.

Why? What is it that makes four Englishmen in 1970 (ages, forty to seventy: upper middle class, professional and academic rather than commercial or industrial) quarrel with their present? The question is all the more pointed because Kilvert had no quarrel with his, nor would I expect our equivalents in his time to have had one.

There are two answers, and you take your choice for the amount of emphasis you put on each. You can argue that it is a subjective and purely selfish reaction, reflecting nothing but the declining comfort and prestige of the middle classes, in particular of the professional and academic middle classes as against the men of industry, of business, of the mass media and entertainment. It means only that, unlike Kilvert, we have to make our own beds and to do our own washing up, that we resent the encroachments on our pockets and our comforts made by the growing power of the organized working classes, or the isolation and helplessness that we feel in the face of the great brute corporations, government, business, trade unions, that now prowl like tyrannosaurs through the wreck of the Victorian garden. Perhaps; perhaps. Or you can take the other line, and say no, it is objective, and something has indeed gone wrong with the world; or at least its blacker possibilities, which the Victorians closed their eyes to, have again been thrust roughly upon us. The evidence is familiar enough to be tedious: two world wars, the political use of murder by the million, nuclear weapons, the threat to the environment: these are things that do not threaten a class, but all men equally, and a century ago they did not exist. It comes to two things really: radical insecurity on a global scale, and ugliness. And, maybe, the spectacle of human wickedness, but that is less novel.

You pay your money and take your choice. There is this, though, to be added: this hatred of the present is a local thing. I am not aware that it is characteristic of the Third World, nor of any but the middle classes at home; they are the only ones, perhaps, for whom things have ever been good enough in the past to tempt them to contrast it favourably with the present. Global insecurity is not much of a threat to those whose individual lives were never secure; nor ugliness, to those who had little or no chance of ever appreciating beauty. Fair enough, but again we are in the world of subjective reactions, and the insecurity and the ugliness are not in our minds but real, outside, there.

1970 *12 June*. M went to the dentist in Hay. He told her about some medical beanfeast he was at in London at which he got talking to an American who asked him where he lived.

He replied that he lived in the west of England near Hereford, thinking that was the nearest place an American was likely to have heard of. He hadn't, the only place he knew in the west of England was Clyro. He turned out to be the secretary of the Minneapolis (or something) branch of the Kilvert Society, and much shocked at our dentist's only possessing a copy of the abridged edition of the immortal work. If he's done nothing else, it seems, Kilvert has had some impact on the American awareness of English geography ...

1870 *15 June.* Evans brought John Williams of Paradise to me at the school on suspicion of the itch. I went to Paradise and spoke to his mother about it, recommended sulphur and hog's lard ...

A strange function for a curate! But then for many of the villagers he was, no doubt, their only contact with the world of learning, and hence the natural source of advice. There was a doctor in Hay, but I doubt if he often attended the labourers of Clyro, who probably still lived or died by grace of traditional remedies and the curate's advice. The parson bulked much larger and the doctor much smaller in the world then, when religion was knowledge and so much of medicine still guesswork.

1970 *16 June.* Cyril holding forth with immense vehemence on the iniquities of the Health Service, how much better it was in the old days when you had a direct financial relationship with your doctor, and refusing to be convinced that this was bought at the expense of far worse service for the poor.

Cyril no doubt had the 1930s rather than the 1870s in mind, and will probably point it out with emphasis when he reads this; but the reflection of his remark on Kilvert's world is interesting. Kilvert, no doubt, *was* in the position that Cyril recalls if he fell ill: he sent for Dr. Clouston in Hay, and he came, whereas today more often than not Kilvert would have to go to the nice new surgery in Hay and wait his turn with the others. The interesting change, though, is in the general attitude to disease. Kilvert and his social peers at Clyro were in effect living on the modern assumption that disease is curable, a remediable accident; his parishioners were still living on the opposite, immemorial assumption that both disease and its issue are matters of fate to be stoically endured. Doctors, hospitals, modern medicine, were just, but only just, beginning to creep over the fringes of their consciousness. Shift to today, and the change is complete: there is the clean modern surgery in Hay, dedicated to the proposition that illness can be controlled and cured, that this area of nature has been colonized, brought under human control. When it cannot, when the young die – as they died often in Kilvert's time – it is a scandal to us. The area of helplessness and submission, which pressed so straitly round the villages of 1870, shrinks and shrinks.

Individually, that is. The private fears diminish; the apocalyptic fears expand. They had disease and death within a stable historical order, where we have health within a total historical uncertainty. They assumed that things would go on as they were, and on, and on. We act on a similar assumption, because it is all you can act on, but we don't believe it, for it has become impossible to imagine our world a hundred years hence.

1970 *19 June.* The oak tree at the bottom of the lane to Penllan has its trunk covered with election notices and advertisements, and on the opposite bank the willow-herb is in flower, the first I've seen this year. It was very hot and airless climbing up between the high hedges: in the lane just above Court Evan Gwynn large skipper butterflies were dancing along the foxgloves. Turned into the lane to Wern y Pentre, which plunges most gratefully into a cool dark damp tunnel of trees just beyond the first of the Bird's Nest cottages, and discussed the state of the hay in scholarly fashion with a chap driving a tractor in one of the fields. Took the footpath below Wern y Pentre along the edge of an uncut hayfield, the margin thick with bracken and sorrel; past Little Gwenfythen and on across the fields toward Great Gwernfythen. The hay harvest is in full swing and in the last field they were mowing, the farmer's daughter driving the tractor. The farmer was watching from a corner of the field, and we had a long talk about the weather and the past of the village, where he grew up. He lamented the way the church had sold off the fine old vicarages of Clyro, Llowes, and Painscastle for much meaner houses, and told me that the present vicarage used to be the post office and was bought to replace the old vicarage sometime about the 1940s. There used to be three old cottages where the policeman's house now stands. I asked about the Baskerville estate. He told me that after Ralph Hopton Baskerville, the heir, was killed in the First World War, his widowed sister moved back to the Court, took over the estate, and resumed the name; but it was too much for her to manage, and it fell into a bad way. For a time it was let to Captain Mavrojanni, who did his best with it and was popular locally. Then in the late 30s, a Mr. Adams, Mrs. Baskerville's son, came to the Court, and vigorously set about putting things to rights – he put in fourteen new gates at one time on Great Gwernfythen alone – but after a year or two inherited an estate at Canon Frome and moved there, taking the name of Hopton with the estate ...

The concrete episodes of the narrative reveal as clearly as the pen of a barograph the shifting pressures of English social and economic history in this century. The farm run by family labour, the girl driving the tractor; the falling standard of life of the Anglican clergy; above all the decay of the landowning squirearchy, the heir gone in the great killing, the estate running down in the Slump: all that is missing here is the final chapter, the break-up of the estate, the end of the assumption on which the whole narrative, and so much of the story of English rural society, is based.

Mavrojanni is an odd exotic name for a tenant of Clyro Court; but in fact it is a memento of an odd exotic episode of British imperial history, the British occupation of the Ionian islands in the first half of the nineteenth century. The episode detached a few island families from their ancestral homes – among them the Mavrojannis – and made them British in the next generation, British enough for the tenant of Clyro Court to have been a captain in the British regular army.

1870 *21 June*. The day of the great picnic at Snodhill Castle, the Victorian country gentry in the full pomp of their leisure and pleasure; Kilvert, who was among them observing it all with a humorous and gently ironic eye, wrote an account of it which is one of his best pieces of social observation. It is the trivialities that his eye fixes on and makes into the material of comedy, the scramble up the mound and the amateur attempts to boil the potatoes. Kilvert was among the possessors, who do not commonly look for the cracks of their society but see it as hard surface, and it was the little irregularities of that surface that charmed him. It is a limitation, but as it is the way that most men see their society most of the time, it brings the scene more easily home to us and helps us to see it in the life. And the historically significant details are there, accidentally – the farm girls running out into the porches of 'the quaint picturesque old fashioned farm houses of the Golden Valley to see the string of horses and carriages, and the gay dresses of the ladies' – which unwittingly give us the remoteness of the valley in thos days and the theatrical role of the gentry, their function of providing a spectacle and a vicarious enjoyment for the narrow lives beneath them; the vast elaboration of Victorian picnics, the 'flowery wreaths and green and wild roses to adorn the dishes and table cloth', the catalogue of the food – 'the usual things' (the casual, give-away adjective!): cold chicken, ham and tongue, pies of different sorts, salads, jam and gooseberry tarts, bread and cheese, and 'splendid strawberries', and 'cup of various kinds, claret and hock, champagne, cider and sherry' – how much it reveals of easy money to spend, and of the substructure of servants that held them all up.

1970 *22 June.* The builders at last arrived and set to work at once ripping up the playroom floor, which has dry rot in the joists, and by the evening all the boards were up, the daylight falling for the first time for a hundred and twenty years or so into the dark old cellar beneath ... We moved to the downstairs kitchen, where M toiled all day and did wonders to get the place into cleanliness and order, a real semblance of the snug kitchen it must once have been.

– was in Kilvert's day: here, I presume, Mrs. Chaloner reigned. It opens on to a little yard, which has a gate on to the brook; in the bed of the brook a water-hole has been dug out, where no doubt Mrs. Chaloner, or more probably her maid, used to dip a pail for the house's water-supply. One of the builder's men found an old brass weight at the bottom of the water-hole – a Chaloner relic, perhaps? The ever-varying sound of the brook is perpetually in your ears in the front rooms of the house, a thing which has been familiar and surely dear to everyone who has ever lived here; Kilvert once wrote a poem about it, not a good one.

1970 *28 June.* A fine day for the Kilvert Commemoration service – by mid-morning the village was gradually filling up with perceptible Kilvertians, eyed doubtfully by the inhabitants; the Baskerville, I gather, was booked solid by a contingent from Birmingham. Miss Trice came to lunch; she faced the prospect of eating in the old kitchen with equanimity, and told us that, not approving of Kilvertians, she had taken care to lock her door before leaving. I left them at 2.30 to go to the Commemoration service, and was swept up in a most astonishing occasion, whose general atmosphere was startlingly reminiscent of Speech Day – the same gathering of hundreds of unknown, or dimly known, people from afar for a vaguely pious but not very precisely conceived purpose, the same sense of a local community swamped for a day by a multitude of aliens, the same hectic succession of functions, the same series of brief interviews with people you don't know who are interested in you because of what you do. What on earth would K have made of it all! – the thought of Clyro being swamped by this solemn pilgrimage in his honour! It would have seemed the wildest possible fantasy to him, surely, and a ludicrous one as well. But I suppose this is in the nature of published diaries – part of their attraction is the contrast between the privacy of their origin, their complete innocence of any intention of publicity, and the fact of their publication. (In which case this one, for some time now, hasn't been quite innocent.)

The village street was lined with cars parked head-to-tail, and although the service wasn't due to start till 3, the church was already packed, an amazing sight. In the end they had to bring in some chairs and the vicar reckoned there must have been over 350 there; overwhelmingly middle-class and middle-aged, I thought, and about two-thirds of them women, a solid, homogeneous congregation in K's church, with the sun bright on the churchyard outside. And what with the Warden of All Souls reading one lesson and William Plomer the other, and the Dean of Hereford preaching a sensible sermon, K was fairly respectably commemorated. We sang the hymns he liked (a pretty milk-and-water lot too), and performed an 'act of remembrance', and gave the church a wall alms box and some hymn-book shelves: a thorough job.

Afterwards everyone flowed out and across the road to the village hall for tea. It was a terrific jam, but I was seized and rather embarrassingly smuggled in round the back on to the high table on the platform. At the end, Lord Borwick took me off to the church tower to teach me the ropes of hoisting the flag on festivals, a job I'm taking over from him. It's an alarming ascent, up ladders over yawning gulfs, one of the ladders wormeaten at that, but there's a fine view from the tower: we could see the Kilvertians streaming along to Cae Mawr for the last act. I hurried home to collect the family and followed. When we arrived at Cae Mawr, everybody was already assembled on the lawns, listening to William Plomer reading some Diary passages relating to Cae Mawr, which he did superbly, with an exact judgement of the degrees of lightness and solemnity required, no vestige of idolatry, and a poet's precise estimation as to the place and length of his own comments and so on. Behind his back was an enormous cedar with children playing on the lower branches, and in the background one of the finest views I've ever seen of the Black Mountain, the whole grand unbroken sweep of the escarpment rising up dun green above the bright fertile green of the intervening valley, and changing lights and shadows moving across its face in another afternoon of the most perfect clarity of atmosphere. What an attractive house Cae Mawr is! The most interesting of Plomer's extracts was one that doesn't appear in the published Diary, a superb account of the dawn chorus of the birds as K heard it one May morning when he had been up all night at the vicarage with a sick horse of the vicar's. Plomer stood on the lower of the two splendid terraced lawns where K played croquet so often, and the Kilvertians sat on the grassy bank that divides them and on rugs on the upper lawn, listening with due devotion. E scampered around insinuating herself here and there, establishing herself between the knees of one middle-aged male admirer and adding occasional loud chanted comments, and C played on the cedar; and the Kilvertians somehow seemed a much more sympathetic body than they had in church. Their central enthusiasm isn't really religious at all, and there was no forced piety about this, rather the friendly sharing of a pleasure. It seemed too that a lot of village folk and farmers had come in who weren't at the church, and with them and the playing children the audience was no longer so forbiddingly monolithic. In the verandah of the house, set out on display, were the results of the annual Kilvert competition at the village school – each child writes a little thesis on the Kilvert associations of some particular house, preferably their own. A girl from the Upper Noyadd had won, which would surely have pleased K.

Surely: it was the home of the beautiful Florence Hill, who a hundred years ago was much about the age that this girl is now.

1870 *29 June*. . . . There was a dispute whether he was a gentleman or not, Mrs. and Miss Bridge saying he was. Bridge
asserting that he was not . . .

– how absolute the social categories were then!

1970 *2 July*. . . . To Staunton, to pick strawberries in a field
where you can pick your own at 1/– a pound. A grey dismal
morning, with showers of drizzle; a dozen or so pickers at
work in the field, bent anonymous figures in dirty raincoats, looking like ineffably dismal peasants out of a Hardy
novel. But we got 6 lbs. quite quickly . . .

Strawberries, like most fruit, cannot yet be picked mechanically – it is an islet of pre-industrial technique not yet overwhelmed by the tide of mechanization; hence it is expensive, and it is becoming common practice to open fields and let people pick their own.

A hundred years ago labour was cheap and used lavishly and wastefully, today it is very expensive and economized to the utmost. It is a simple economic change, but it bites deep into society; the gap between cheap-labour and dear-labour societies is one aspect of the great divide between the primitive and the modern, between the Third World and the other two, and it goes together with things like do-it-yourself kits, the rise of the trade unions, and motives for emigrating to Rhodesia or South Africa, as well as with the modes of strawberry-picking.

The remarkable thing, when you come to think of it, is that the change from a cheap-labour to a dear-labour situation has taken place at the same time as an unprecedented rise in population, which you might expect to have the opposite effect. A somewhat similar rise in the price of labour took place in the second half of the fourteenth century, with similarly far-reaching effects; but that was due to the Black Death and the consequent shortage of working men. In our time the opposite cause seems to have produced the same effect: in a hundred years the population has doubled, but the price of labour, allowing for inflation, has more like quadrupled. It is a tribute equally to the success of working men in winning a bigger share of the produce of their labour for themselves, through the exercise of their increasing economic and political power, and to the immense increases in productivity achieved by mechanization. Witness the farms of Clyro, which in 1870 employed something like one wage labourer for every 50 acres; today there is hardly a farmer's labourer in the parish.

Whatever the advances in productivity, I suppose a dear-labour economy is not likely to appeal to an employer much; a Victorian farmer did not have to invest capital in the men he employed, and a man is more adaptable than a machine. But obviously, except for the risk of unemployment it carries with it, it is more attractive to the working man. Dear-labour societies are likely to be relatively democratic and egalitarian ones, therefore, and we have moved a long way in that direction since Kilvert's time. None of the assumptions of his society is more alien to us than its assumption of the easy availability of cheap human beings to look after the necessities of your existence – to cook, to wash up, to clean the boots, to bring hot water to your bedroom. There were eight servants at Clyro Court, seven at Cae Mawr, six at the vicarage, six at Wye Cliff, seven at Lower Cabalva.

However, we can pick cheap strawberries.

1970 *3 July*. . . . among other things, he remembers Armstrong the murderer . . .

Armstrong, the little country solicitor, who in 1921 poisoned his wife with arsenic, which he said he bought to kill dandelions; the large ugly Victorian villa where it happened still stands in Cusop. It was one of the great murder trials of the century, Spilsbury and Curtis Bennett on show at Hereford assizes, in the old Grand Guignol Days of the death penalty. My goodness, what one would give to have had Kilvert's version of that! For the Hay of 1921, so anyone who knew it will emphasize, *was* essentially Kilvert's Hay, railway-dependent, horse-and-donkey, pre-bookshop Hay – and think, *think* of the impact of the arrest of the town solicitor for murder in that tight, slow-moving little community – murder in Llaregub! The town solicitor! – *that* must have shaken that cosy little society of the local gentry in which Kilvert floated so happily fifty years before, appalled its frilly little proprieties, drawn its attention to the comfortably forgotten depths beneath: Hay Bluff thrusting itself suddenly above the lower hills. And the talk in the pubs, in the shops, in the streets, in the trains; journalists prowling round the little town, hungry for news; police, as flabbergasted by the appearance of major crime as Walter de la Mare's vicar by the untimely sounding of the Last Trump just before his harvest festival. Hay in all the headlines, a piece of local gossip achieving the status of national news – O heady days! And in what glorious detail, with what shocked fascination it would have been recorded for us, if only it had happened fifty years earlier! Hay has never forgotten it. Kilvert brings more pilgrims to the area than Armstrong, but Armstrong provided much more delicious gossip; and the story is still good material for a newspaper article, come an anniversary of the murder.

1870 *4 July*. . . . We drove to call at Wye Cliff. We were shown upstairs into Mrs. Crichton's boudoir, of which she has herself painted the door panels, wainscot, etc. . . . The walls were hung with paintings of her own in oil and water colours. This room is holy ground.

The Crichtons were young, and Mrs. Crichton was pretty, and she raised a delicate flutter of innocent sentimentality in the curate's heart. There is nothing more fascinating in the Diary than the complicated chronicle of Kilvert's encounters with Eros that can be traced through its pages, a theme at the same time so eternal and so quaintly time-conditioned. Kilvert, remember, was a bachelor of twenty-nine, of acute sensibility if not of strong passion, but bound by the triply strong restraints of his poverty, the Victorian proprieties, and his cloth. It was a common Victorian situation: the intense creative energy that characterized so many men of the age may well have been erotic in origin, the product of instincts that, denied one outlet, would find another. In Kilvert's case, there is not much doubt that the intense sensuousness that is one of the chief distinctions of his Diary has this origin, as the imagery at times suggests. Not, of course, that Kilvert was frustrated by the lack of female company; the pressure of feeling in the Diary is so great precisely because he was in their company constantly, and it kept his senses alert in a constant flicker of romantic and sensuous excitement. Who has not had the experience, between sixteen and twenty-five or so, when there is a beautiful girl round every corner, and because of it we live on tiptoe, our senses more alert to the beauty of the world than they ever will be again? The difference with Kilvert is that it lasted longer, and that with his contemporaries he was not allowed to recognize his feelings for what they were; to a Victorian curate, Eros was scarcely recognizable within marriage, let alone without it. To live in a community full of intoxicating young beauty that you can neither touch nor even admit that you desire is a heady, frustrating, yet not necessarily unlucky experience; emotion squirts out in powerful jets at unpredictable angles, and so it did with Kilvert, often in the typically Victorian form of sentimentality, as with Mrs. Crichton, or with Emma Hockin, whom he was going to visit in Cornwall in a fortnight's time. With them, the high park walls of Victorian matrimony put an additional inhibition on Kilvert's emotions. The ground about them is holy, Kilvert can wipe a tear from his eye at parting; so much he could permit himself, sentimentality being respectable, even charming – but no more.

Or take another angle. A week later he can write:

> Often when I rise I look up to the white farm house of
> Penllan and think of the sweet gray eyes that have long
> been open and looking upon the pearly morning sky and
> the mists of the valley and the morning spread upon the
> mountains, and think of the young busy hands that have
> long been at work, milking or churning, with the sleeves
> rolled up the round arms as white and creamy as the milk
> itself, and the bright sweet morning face that the sunrise
> and the fresh early air have kissed into bloom and the
> sunny tresses ruffled by the mountain wind, and hope that
> the fatherless girl may ever be good, brave, pure and true.
> So help her God. The sun looks through her window which
> the great pear tree frames and lattices in green leaves and
> fruit, and the leaves move and flicker and throw a chequer-
> ing shadow upon the white bedroom wall, and on the white
> curtains of the bed. And before the sun has touched the
> sleeping village in the shade below or has ever even struck
> the weathercock into a golden gleam, or has crept down the
> steep green slope of the lower or upper Bron, he has stolen
> into her bedroom and crept along the wall from chair to
> chair till he has reached the bed, and has kissed the fair
> hand and arm that lies upon the coverlet and the white
> bosom that heaves half uncovered after the restlessness of
> the sultry night, and has kissed her mouth whose scarlet
> lips, just parting in a smile and pouting like rosebuds to be
> kissed, show the pearly gleam of the white teeth, and has
> kissed the sweet face of the blue veined silky lashed eyelids
> and the white brow and the soft bright tangled hair, till she
> has unclosed the sweetest eyes that ever opened to the
> dawn, and risen and unfastened the casement and stood
> awhile breathing the fresh fragrant mountain air as it
> blows cool upon her flushed cheek and her half veiled
> bosom, and lifts and ruffles her bright hair which still
> keeps the kiss of the sun. Then when she has dressed and
> prayed towards the east, she goes out to draw water from
> the holy spring St. Mary's Well. After which she goes about
> her honest holy work, all day long, with a light heart and a
> pure conscience.

Samuel Butler would have had something to say about that, and the obvious twentieth-century, deflating comment rises like a bubble to the surface of the mind, but the passage deserves a more careful analysing. The girl described is one of the Williams sisters of Penllan, Lucretia, who was eighteen, or Mary, who was sixteen, farmer's daughters living with their mother and stepfather, and this breathless rapturous entry comes as near to actual eroticism as Kilvert ever gets; but it wears veils that are still thick enough to conceal its nature from its author. The sun creeping into the bedroom to kiss and fondle the sleeping girl – a mere charming fancy, nothing more. Even so, in this voyeuristic passage Kilvert has crept alarmingly close to a dangerous discovery of something within himself; and so, surely, the sudden withdrawal to the freshness of the mountain air, to the shelter of prayer and holiness. There is no other passage in the Diary which better illustrates how the very acuteness of Kilvert's rendering of the seen world around him can provide an issue for a deeply dis-trusted instinct within: if sentimentality is one of his escapes, sensitivity to beauty is another. One may doubt, perhaps, whether Kilvert would have allowed his imagination so much liberty with Mrs. Crichton; but the Williams sisters were unmar-ried, while on the other hand they were a full social rung (or more) below him – the imagination could have more liberty just because no liaison was conceivable.

There was also another escape, and it is the one that has attracted most comment. Two days before his rhapsody about the girl at Penllan, Kilvert was climbing up the lane in the Bird's Nest dingle, and it too had associations for him:

> Sometimes my darling child Gipsy comes down to school this way, but more often she comes down Sunny Bank when the days are fine, and then over the stile by Little Wern-y-Pentre. Yet often and often must those tiny feet have trodden this stony narrow green-arched lane, and those sweet blue eyes have looked down this vista to the blue mountains and those little hands have gathered flowers along these banks. O my child if you did but know. If you only knew that this lane and this dingle and these fields are sweet to me and holy ground for your sweet sake. But you can never know, and if you should ever guess or

read the secret, it will be but a dim misty suspicion of the truth. Ah Gipsy.

She lived at Pen y Cae, higher up the hill. In the more formal language of the census records of 1871, she appears as Elizabeth S. Jones, scholar, granddaughter of John Harris, the farmer of Pen y Cae; aged ten. It was, apparently, Kilvert who christened her Gipsy, because of her looks; she had just been put into the reading class at the village school, and she bewitched him as girls of this age often did, the Vaughan daughters at Newchurch, Boosie Evans the schoolmaster's daughter, Carrie Britton at Langley Burrell, and many others. He rhapsodized about them, he kissed them, he romped with them in the farmhouse kitchens; and nothing causes deeper divisions of opinion among present-day readers of the Diary or more clearly marks the passage of time between his century and our own. Freud has destroyed our innocence, and no curate these days could do these things; or if he did, it would certainly arouse the gravest suspicions among the girls' parents, and word would deviously reach the vicar and the bishop. I think we can be sure enough that this did not happen in Kilvert's case, or some echo of it must have reached the Diary. As it is, the Diary entries exude the candour of a perfect innocence: their very raptures make it clear that it has never crossed the writer's mind that Eros also frequents the Bird's Nest dingle, that 'the truth' that Gipsy would never know might itself be only a veil for a darker truth that lay deeper down. So might a Victorian schoolmaster rhapsodize equally innocently about his boys. You cannot do these things nowadays: nobody could write such diary entries with an unshadowed mind.

Nymphomania was a Victorian addiction: Ruskin and Lewis Carroll jump immediately into the mind, Carroll especially, whose girls were the same age as Kilvert's, and whom Kilvert apparently knew at Oxford. In a pre-Freudian age so bent on the divorce of sex from sentiment, it was an easy way out for the timid, the idealistic, the easily inhibited – categories in which it is not hard to place Kilvert. 'If he hadn't been such a good young man, he could have been a very wicked one' – that was said of Kilvert sixty years after his death by a woman who had known him in her youth, and, tantalizingly gnomic though it is, it is not hard to guess at the interpretation. He was attractive to women,

and attracted by them – that much could be deduced easily
enough from the pages of the Diary. But this was the 1870s, he
was the product of a vicarage upbringing and education at the
hands of a sternly moralistic father, he was a country curate, all
his life he accepted the conventions. He *was* a good young man.
There are times in the Diary when a transposition into Ernest
Pontifex's story from *The Way of All Flesh* seems close at hand,
but in the absence of a Samuel Butler one knows it will never
happen. The daughters of the country houses flit through the
pages of the Diary, charming, tantalizing, unthinkable –
unthinkable, that is without recognizing the presence of Eros
(which must not be recognized, and if his presence *was* recognized, unthinkable except in the context of marriage; and how
could a penniless curate aspire to that?). But with Gipsy Lizzie or
Boosie Evans or Marianne Price, the case was different. They
were children, they lived on the other side of an unbridgeable
social chasm, most of them were his parishioners; he could permit
himself liberties with them without ever dreaming that Eros had
anything to do with the case, as he could never have done with
the daughters of the local gentry. At that, the liberties both of
action and of imagination were slight and innocent enough – a
'romp' in a farmhouse kitchen, the vision of the morning sun
creeping into the girl's room at Penllan.

The age of innocence is past, and the passages read oddly to us
today; among the Kilvert cognoscenti, they are the subject of
bitter debate between those who find them charming and those
who think that Freud would have had something to say about it.
The answer, surely, is both. To suppose that there is no erotic
element present in Kilvert's raptures about Gipsy Lizzie and the
rest of them is to rack credulity to death; but equally, to suppose
that Kilvert was conscious of its presence and deliberately
exploited what was obviously a remarkable capacity for friendship with children for this purpose is an anachronism; it imports
a twentieth-century consciousness into a nineteenth century
where it is quite alien, and it makes nonsense of the Diary, which
after all is virtually the only evidence for Kilvert that we have.
Kilvert's passions for children were erotic in origin and innocent
in fact, and there the matter may well rest. Without them, his life
at Clyro would have been a far flatter and poorer thing. The Clyro
he sees and reports is viewed through the delicately refracting

medium of a romantic excitement to which they were the chief stimulus; like the 'tender haze' which he so often described veiling those hills and making them more beautiful, as it still does.

1870 *6 July*. Archery at Wye Cliff in the summer afternoon.

> It was a pretty sight to see the group of ladies with their fresh light dresses moving up and down the long green meadow between the targets, and the arrows flitting and glancing white to and fro against the bank of dark green trees.

How nearly this is a picture! – a Renoir, perhaps? He resolves the scene into sheer colour and composition, in a way very unfashionable in his time. Although there is no indication that he ever thought of trying a brush rather than a pen, there is a great deal of the painter in Kilvert. The odd thing is that it appears in passages like these, and not at all in the records of his eager annual visits to the Royal Academy, where he sees with a very different and much more conventional eye which evaluates pictures in terms of their moral, emotional, and erotic significance, instead of the quasi-Impressionist values that he brings to the archers in the meadow. In this, too, it seems, there were in him the springs of a deeper originality than he could, or cared to, recognize, and he yielded too readily to the ruling conventions.

1970 *6 July*. On the summit of the Gospel Pass, I got out to walk home, and struck up along the edge of the escarpment to Hay Bluff. A stiffish climb of a few hundred feet, and at once you're lifted high above the tourist world, watching the cars crawl along the road five hundred feet below; I didn't see a soul on the escarpment, though a pony-track runs along it. The top of the Mountain is a flat, featureless upland with a thick growth of whortleberry and black peaty soil broken occasionally by little pools; but on the left hand, what a view! The sun was blazing in the sky, and even at over 2,000 feet it was very hot; and the air was full of shooting swifts, darting, turning, and tumbling, at incredible speed, cutting the air with a sudden 'wheww-wheww' as they swept by. Below, the hillside fell away in two giant steps, a thousand feet at each tread, to the valley floor, and from Hay Bluff the horizon lay twenty or thirty miles before you through a full 180°, from the Brecon Beacons round over the Begwns, Clee Hill dimly seen, and the Herefordshire plain, to somewhere far south of Hereford. On the prow of the Bluff you reigned over it all lonely as a king. Far below, two obedient files of pony-trekkers were making their way up to the Bwlch, a giant's toys but for the exquisite perfection that told you they weren't toys, but true midgets. There were the little farmsteads of the lower slopes, the huge sweep of smooth yellow-green turf, the slightly more verdant green blocks of the bracken neatly cut up by narrow sheep-tracks like a gigantic jigsaw, the wooded cleft of the Dulas gorge, the bare summit of Cusop Hill where we were yesterday, further to the right the great dark angular slabs of the Forestry Commission plantations spreading over the hills like a disease, and last of all the secret head of the Craswall valley, which you never see from the road; the air very pure, and the wind blowing sweet and fresh from the west. I began to scramble down the eastern edge of the escarpment, and as I fell below the edge, suddenly I was simultaneously out of sight of the road and out of the wind, in a complete sunny stillness broken only by the distant baaing of the sheep. The huge grassy slope at my feet was sown all over with the white specks of sheep and with grazing horses, mares and long-legged foals with creamy coats and long sweeping tails; there wasn't a car, a house, or a human being in sight, and you suddenly had the illusion of a world from which men had vanished and which had been handed over to the peaceful pastoral beasts.

A chestnut falcon with crescent wings – a kestrel? – glided by, and I scrambled hectically down the steep escarpment, past the horses, over the road, along the length of the grassy plateau, and down a beautiful tangled overgrown farm-track past the old farmstead of Cadwgan – lately abandoned, locked and silent, the yard full of grass and the garden of nettles – with fine views down into the valley. K thought it the best way on to the mountain, and I agree with him – there's pleasure in finding his judgements still true ...

The escarpment and the outline of the hills; the whortleberry, the swifts, the kestrel; the farmsteads, the grazing beasts, the track past Cadwgan. Three scales of time before Kilvert, one since: the cars, the pony-trekkers, the Forestry Commission.

1870 *12 July.* The day of the big party at Clifford Priory.

Walked to Clifford Priory across the fields with Crichton and Barton ... A crowd in the drawing room drinking claret cup iced and eating enormous strawberries ... the usual set that one meets and knows so well. Dews, Thomases, Webbs, Wyatts, Bridges, Oswalds, Trumpers, etc. ... Everyone about here is so pleasant and friendly that we meet almost like brothers and sisters. Great fun on the lawn, 6 cross games of croquet and balls flying in all directions. High tea at 7.30 ... After tea we all strolled out into the garden and stood on the high terrace to see the eclipse ... It was very strange and solemn ... The ladies' light dresses looked ghostly in the dark and at a little distance it was almost impossible to tell which was a lady in a white dress and which was a clump of tall white lilies. ... We wandered up into the twilit garden and there among the strawberries fastened to a little kennel by a collar and light chain to keep the birds away was a most dear delightful white pussy ...

1970 *9 July.* Set off for the site of Clifford Priory, and just beyond Peter's Pool a big Post Office Telephones van picked me up and gave me a lift into Hay (N.B. the assumption that walking is *abnormal*). Walked out a mile along the Whitney road and then took what may be the footpath K took to the Priory on 12/7/70. It's marked on the map as a right of way, but in fact there's no trace of a path, and the first three fields were waist-deep in growing corn; I decided to assert my rights and waded boldly through them, but saw nobody. Up through a field of green lissom wheat, swaying sinuously in every contradictory direction as the fresh wind ran a hand over it, then one of much riper barley with heavy dry heads, the stalks making a harsh rattling as I passed through. Not now a good way to walk to an evening party. Emerged on the road close to the entrance to the Priory. The old drive still leads to a cottage in the stable yard, but the big house, which K thought so comfortable, was destroyed by fire in the 1930s and is now a job for the archaeologist, mere heaps of grass-grown rubble covered with thick undergrowth. But the remains of the terraced lawns are there, where K played croquet and watched the moon go into shadow that July evening; festooned with brambles now but still with a magnificent view, over the grey Priory farmhouse below and straight up the valley with the Brecon Beacons perfectly placed in the centre of the horizon, and on the left Mouse Castle, and Hay Bluff just showing its snout over the nearer hills. And in the house's finest days the view can never have been lovelier than today, that silvery sky and the light so clear on the hills. Behind, there is a high stone wall that I suppose once formed one side of the garden where the white cat kept guard over the strawberries – but now there's only an abandoned orchard and a dense jungle of trees.

Of the country houses that were the centres of gravity of the countryside in Kilvert's time, a good many have gone, burnt down or demolished in the last forty years – Clifford Priory, the Moor, Whitney Old Court, Wye Cliff, Llanthomas. After 1914, they felt the pinch of straitening circumstances – left empty for long periods, run only by skeleton staffs, their fire-fighting appliances old-fashioned, they were apt to burn. The gentry themselves survive, but they live in smaller houses; their social circle is strict, and in wealth and status they are an upper class still, but the country is no longer organized round them.

1970 *12 July.* Went over to the hotel and had an agreeable half-pint there with two local men – one of them the retired postmaster of Hay who was responsible for getting the 'on-Wye' put into the name about twenty years ago (being fed up with letters going astray to Hoy in the Orkneys or Hay in Australia – probably not much of a problem in K's time).

1870 *16 July*. Henry Dew brought the news that war had been declared by France against Prussia, the wickedest, most unjust most unreasonable war that ever was entered into to gratify the ambition of one man. I side with the Prussian and devoutly hope the French may never push France to the Rhine. Perhaps the war was a dire necessity to the Emperor to save himself and his dynasty. At all events the war is universally fearfully popular in France, and the French are in the wildest fever to go to the Rhine.

The party at Pont Vaen divided itself into croquet and archery ...

History since then has usually taken a different view of the origins of the Franco-Prussian War, the Prussian victory which came as such a happy surprise to the curate of Clyro that summer and autumn having come to wear a very different appearance in retrospect; all victorious causes having a knack of turning out very much otherwise than their supporters expect. It was the first crash of a thunderstorm that was to rumble round the horizon for three-quarters of a century, and to contribute largely to the destruction of the society that Kilvert knew; and children and grandchildren of the guests at Pont Vaen that evening would die in it. But none of this could reasonably have been foreseen. To Englishmen in 1870, war on the Rhine was mere news, a distant excitement. They lived in an age and a place in which the public and private worlds seemed to lie so securely apart from each other that the storms of the one were no threat to the peace of the other; the tides never rose high enough to trouble the tranquil waters of this rock pool. They did not know that the tides would rise higher soon.

The distinction between the real private worlds in which we live and love and sleep and the abstract public world of the newspaper headlines and the things the history books talk about is very, very old, and in the last thousand years it has grown much sharper; but the invasions of the private world by the public are sporadic and hard to predict. Men may live quiet lives for generations, careless of the great affairs of the world, and then war breaks out, or famine or revolution comes, the public world swamps the private, and there is no time to be John Smith, but only to be an Englishman, a sansculotte, or just a victim. But in

1870, in England, there was abundant time to be Francis Kilvert; indeed, he had never known any other state of affairs, though little more than twenty years before his time the public world could still loom frighteningly over the private even in England. Now the two were comfortably remote: there was war on the Rhine, but, the titillation of that news having subsided, they could turn back to the croquet and archery at Pont Vaen. But on 3 September 1939, when my aunts came up the garden path at Maryland and told us that we were at war, I burst into tears because I was frightened. And rightly; for in August 1914 the public world invaded the private world again in western Europe, and has never since evacuated it; if it does not always conscript us, our liberty is always on sufferance, and because we know it and feel it, the headlines make us afraid.

Because they are real, private worlds are very much more important than public ones. But it does not follow that the irruptions of the public world are always unwelcome: sometimes they are exhilarating. When life has been private and small for a long time, people start yearning for the heady experience of being caught up in a great public wave – as they welcomed war in 1914. It is only because we have had our fill of public gales and forecasts of them that the prospect of hearing of war on the Rhine and then turning unworried back to the croquet seems so alluring.

1970 *18 July*. The mason has found a lot of bits of old tombstones built into the end of the wall that he's repairing outside the garage, and at our request has left the lettering exposed – the name Elizabeth Prosser, a bit of doggerel epitaph:

> My marriage-bed is in the dust,
> Christ is my rock, in him I trust.

Did she, I wonder? The words have a sour fitness for Kilvert, too, who died at Bredwardine, ten miles away, three weeks after returning from his honeymoon in 1879.

1970 *24 July*. C's birthday party, and the whole day centred hectically round it. Belinda Jones, the policeman's 14-year-old daughter, came in to help get ready, while I went into Hay to shop. After lunch things got more and more hectic, getting the tea-table ready down in the old kitchen, blowing up balloons, getting the children dressed, etc. As usual, we weren't quite ready when the guests started arriving, but all went well. C originally wanted to ask most of the school, but we eventually whittled it down to nine, and two of those didn't come. As usual with C, mostly girls, some of them much older than himself – Linda Price from Penllan, Carol, Sally Anne, and Ian Powell from Lower House, Isobel Edwards from the petrol station, Jeremy Councell, and Deborah Price from the council houses. A bit slow to warm up, but M had prepared a huge tea – sausages proved the favourite item – and afterwards we played very merry games on the lawn: oranges and lemons, with E taking a shy but delighted part, 'What's the time, Mr. Wolf?', and blind-man's bluff, with me in the lead part lunging about the lawn. All this in full view of passers-by in the village street, who were amused. Then they all flocked downstairs to eat the rest of the tea, after which we went upstairs for a riotous treasure-hunt after presents which M had distributed liberally round all the rooms on the first floor. They all enjoyed themselves, I think – certainly when they went at 6, M and I were thoroughly exhausted ...

And then?

1871 *12 February*. This is Boosie Evans' birthday and at 6.30 eight of the children came to tea at my rooms, for I had arranged my yearly children's party to-day to celebrate the event.

There were Gussena Anthony, Mary Eleanor Williams the clerk's daughter, who came from Cusop on purpose to attend the party, Sarah Cooper, Mary Jane and Boosie Evans, Lizzie Jones of the Harbour, and Louie and Tillie Jones of the Clogau.

The children were a little shy when they first came in, and were standing together at the opposite side of the room. 'Come round here and warm yourselves. You needn't be afraid of me.' 'No, Sir,' replied Sena Anthony quickly and frankly, 'we're too fond of you to be afraid of you.' How easy it is to amuse children and make them happy. They were overwhelmed with admiration of one of the attar of rose bottles which Emmie had brought from Hyderabad. Then they were seized with awe at the sight of a lock of hair which I cut from the mane of the great lion at the Clifton Zoological Gardens when he was asleep, in August 1865. But one of the things which amused and interested them most was an old letter lock off my hat box.

I offered a sovereign to whoever could open it. They tried a long time, but the reward was not claimed. They were very indignant and angry with themselves when I told them the cabalistic word was 'pat'. 'And you were patting your pussy all the while, if we had only thought about it and noticed it,' said one of the children, alluding to my tabby cat who was lying in my arm chair beside me. First came buns, bread and butter, and tea poured out by Boosie amid great fun. Crackers and looking at picture books. They played bagatelle and the Race Game. Then came a grand fiery snap dragon. And lastly I told them tales till midnight, the story of Faithful Eric and the wolves, and the story of the fright Emmie had in the night at Hyderabad. Dear children, what a pleasure it is to have them. I am never so happy as when I have these children about me. And they behave so nicely, like little gentlewomen, much better than most young ladies. I should be very sorry to spend six hours in the company of many young ladies of my acquaintance, whereas to-night I was as sorry when 12 o'clock came as the children, and missed them sadly when all the bright faces trooped out into the dark night together to their homes in the village with Good-night and thanks and courtesies, and left me alone in my silent room.

Midnight! – it must have been much too late for the Jones girls from the Harbour and the Cloggau to go home, seven or eight miles away over the hills on a February night, perhaps too late for the clerk's daughter too. No doubt they stayed with relatives in the village.

1970 *27 July*. . . .the boat was filled, if not to capacity, still sufficiently like a pigsty – every seat taken in the upper lounges and on deck, piles of bags mixed with sprawling bodies all over the hallways, the bar crowded with people seeing how much cheap liquor they could drink in six hours, underfoot a gathering silt of dirty paper cups, discarded newspapers, raincoats, spilt tea, and vomit half-soaked up by sprinklings of sawdust – all the filth of democracy at sea. Not that I suppose anyone liked it; but at present if you design cross-Channel ships for the multitude, that's what you get. Crowds of boy scouts running everywhere, groups of scruffy hostile long-haired youths – an alien nation – and the middle-middle classes in invincible strength: the gentry with their polished children fly these days.

1870 *18 May*. Found the first train going down was an Excursion train and took a ticket for it. The carriage was nearly full. In the Box tunnel as there was no lamp, the people began to strike foul brimstone matches and hand them to each other all down the carriage. All the time we were in the tunnel these lighted matches were travelling from hand to hand in the darkness. Each match lasted the length of the carriage and the red ember was thrown out of the opposite window, by which time another lighted match was seen travelling down the carriage. The carriage was chock full of brimstone fumes, the windows both nearly shut, and by the time we got out of the tunnel I was almost suffocated. Then a gentleman tore a lady's pocket handkerchief in two, seized one fragment, blew his nose with it, and put the rag in his pocket. She then seized his hat from his head, while another lady said that the dogs of Wootton Basset were much more sociable than the people.

The excursion train in 1870 occupied socially much the same position as the Channel Islands steamer in 1970: the people who went to the Bath Flower Show for an outing then, go to the Channel Islands for holidays now, and the unopulent intelligentsia who travel with them apparently regarded democracy on the rail with much the same shade of disgust as democracy at sea now. No doubt there was more excuse for Kilvert, since in 1870 the class system was taken for granted, and it was a novelty, born of the railways, that the populace should travel by public transport at all. It is true though, that democracy is not an excuse for squalor, and that it seems permissible to hope that by 2070 it will travel without it.

Kilvert took his summer holiday in Cornwall this year, staying with friends near Falmouth. There were boating parties on the Fal, trips by waggonette to the Lizard and St. Ives and Land's End – at Land's End they encountered a 'noisy rabble of tourists', who justified Kilvert's opinion of the race by 'insulting the ladies', but it seems to have been their only meeting with tourists. They were the sign of things to come, but the age of the caravan parks was yet far out of sight; Cornwall was still a county of working tin-mines, which Kilvert noted from the train, and St. Ives was still dominated by its fish market. The Englishman's summer holiday was a barely perceptible social phenomenon; Kilvert's private visit to friends was something quite different and much older, a social custom of the gentry with a long pedigree behind it. To that extent he was right to recognize the tourists as a different race from himself.

The Lizard, Land's End, Gurnard's Head – one notes that they apparently preferred cliffs to beaches. They never bathed, as far as the record goes, though Kilvert did so on other occasions – presumably in 1870 it was not decorous enough for a country house party, or unthinkable for mixed company in an age when men commonly bathed, if at all, naked. But there were picnics – picnics everywhere, sherry in the waggonette, midnight suppers on 'hot roast fowl' after long days afield. In the virgin Cornwall of 1870, it was the sort of bachelor holiday that might well lend itself to a golden nostalgia afterwards.

1870 *5 August.* H. and I struck across the down to see the British Church buried in the sand ... Within the memory of persons still living the altar was standing, but the place has got into the hands of a dissenting farmer who keeps the place for a cattle yard and sheep fold and what more need be said. I do wish that some people of influence in the neighbourhood would bestir themselves and rescue from utter destruction and oblivion this most interesting relic of the earliest British Christianity, that which came to us direct from the East. Probably there was a Christian Church at Gwythian before St. Augustine landed in England to bring us the Roman version of Christianity.

Although it is not the central purpose of the passage, between the dissenting farmer and St. Augustine one can get about as exact a notion of Kilvert's churchmanship from this extract as from any in the Diary. He was an extremely moderate churchman, but his position was at least clearly enough defined for him to repudiate both extremes with strong feeling. We have already seen that he had little use for Dissent, especially the kind of militant anti-Establishment Dissent that apparently motivated the farmer at Gwythian and which is nowadays almost forgotten; but he shared equally the strong contemporary antipathy to all things Roman, fuelled as it was by aversion to Irish immigrants, horror at the spectacle of John Henry Newman and many other educated university-bred Englishmen turning back to an obscurantist mediaeval superstition in the 1840s, and memories of Pius IX's apostasy from the Liberal cause in 1848. He shared the conventional bigotries; but beneath them it is just about possible to discern a very moderate High Churchmanship, most likely inherited from his father, who must have felt Newman's influence at Oriel in his Anglican days. He did believe in a historical Church; and interestingly, one can read in this passage vestiges of the view so dear to the Oxford Movement in its Anglican phase, that the Church of England traced its authority from the Christianity imported into Britain in Roman times, by Joseph of Arimathea according to legend, and that the Roman connection later introduced by St. Augustine was a corruption.

1970 *9 August*. In Jersey.

> Writing this diary before going to Vauxhall, at the desk in the boys' old room – outside C and E sitting side by side on the nursery verandah, blowing bubbles, talking away to each other. 'I've sended off some of my flying servants,' says C, who's just learnt the word 'servants' – what a lovely bit of unconscious poetry!

1870 *4 August*. Sad music.

Auld Robin Gray

> 'I darena think on Jamie for that would be a sin.
>
>   And auld Robin Gray is a good man to me.'

No more she could weep, her tears were a' spent.
Despair it was come and she thought it *content*,
She thought it content, but her cheek it grew pale
And she dropped like a lily broke down by the hail.

Children's voices.

It had been a romantically happy holiday, but you pay a price for romance; and Kilvert's writing is rarely so evocative of a mood as it is in these last days at Tullimaar, when the prose itself breaks up into interjections and sudden disconnected jottings under the pressure of sentiment. For there was more to it than a carefree bachelor holiday: there was an intensity born of a romantic might-have-been: there was Mrs. Hockin. Two days later, on his way home, it all broke out with full force.

1870 *6 August.* Left Tullimaar, dear Tullimaar, and the happy days. The drooping of the transplanted flowers and the withering of tendrils torn from their clasp. Well. Well. Friends? Yes, I think. Yes, I believe. And for ever.

The desolate misery, the acute agony of those first four terrible hours, and the cold heavy dull pain of the rest of the long nine hours' journey as we flew through all the length of the Three Western Shires ... All through the journey my eyes were perpetually seeking for the one familiar face and form which had been so constantly before them for the last three weeks, seeking, seeking, baffled, longing, all in vain ... I thought – was it so – that there were tears in those blue eyes when we parted. I know there were tears in mine. Forget me not, oh, forget me not.

The Hockins were former Chippenham neighbours of the Kilverts, and Emma Hockin had clearly more than fluttered Kilvert's susceptible heart. No diary exists for the period of their former acquaintance, so what it may have amounted to is all surmise; but there is no indication that he had known her before her marriage, and if that is so, knowing our Kilvert, I think we can be fairly certain that it remained in the realm of sentiment. Clearly, though, at the time it went deep. If she was a woman of ordinary awareness, one assumes she probably had some notion of his feelings – but as to whether there really were tears in those blue eyes, no evidence remains. Kilvert seemingly liked and respected her husband; but a wistful sentiment clings round every mention he makes of her in his record of that Cornish summer. It was all a little conventional too perhaps, a little too neatly in the well-worn patterns of the hopeless chivalric love, but sincerely felt for all that. Hence the appeal of sad music: hence the lines of 'Robin Gray' he chose to remember: hence the associations of children's voices.

1870 *11 August.* Kilvert was back at home at Langley Burrell vicarage for a few days, before returning to Clyro. 'Old John Bryant told my Father to-day as they were talking about the War' – that far-away affair in Lorraine, where the French were falling back on Metz and the first small shadow of the power of Germany was beginning to creep across Europe – 'that he remembered the news coming that the King of France's head had been cut off. He was a boy at the time, 13 years old, helping to drain a field near Bull's Copse at Tytherton, and he heard the men with whom he was working talking about the news that had just come.'

What a memory! What a picture! The portentously public comes into contact with the minutely specific private, and how the accidental echoes ring. The tidal wave spreads outwards from the Place de la Révolution, and one last faint ripple washes up on Bull's Copse at Tytherton.

It would be tempting to make it a text for a sermon on the total detachment of the public world from the private. Here is Louis XVI's execution, a chapter heading for a history book, and what has it been for John Bryant, wresting his ninety-year living out of the fields of Wiltshire? News; mere news; a story from far away that provided matter for gossip one day a lifetime ago. The real world is the individual one solely, and past it history rides chattering by aloof and irrelevant. It is the distinction of good diaries, of Kilvert's most notably, that they remind us of the fact; that in them for once it is John Bryant we are asked to consider, not all that public clamour in the Place de la Révolution.

It is a text, one suspects, dear to Kilvert's own heart; but it will not quite do. To John Bryant, true, it *was* only a story; but it was one, nevertheless, which had affected his life, little though he probably realized it, and it would affect the lives of his grandsons and great-grandsons very much more. The thing is unprovable, but it is at least likely that because there had been a revolution in

France and the king's head had been cut off – the sense of shock at the violence of the affront to the traditional order can still be heard in the choice of words, which is probably John Bryant's own – life was a little easier for him than it would have been otherwise; that his masters felt it wise to think a little more of his interests and his preferences; that the law lay a little less heavily on him; that there was more talk of his rights, and that his great-grandchildren would go to school. Little though he knew it, too, the state was beginning to take an interest in him: one day it would uproot his descendants from the fields altogether, take them to its cities, and kill them in its wars; and the French Revolution has something to do with that, too. The public events may seem to ride chattering by; but some of them cast a cold glance, sometimes, over the man in the fields from the corner of their eye, and have their purposes for him.

1970 *17 August.* Driving home from Weymouth.

Saw the first reapers out in the cornfields on the chalk downs above Dorchester.

It might be a Kilvert entry, dated 1870; but they're machines, not men.

1870 *19 August.* Ben Lloyd of the Cwm Bryngwyn reeling up the steep fields above Jacob's Ladder carrying a horse collar and butter tub. Just as I came up the drunken man fell sprawling on his back. He got up looking foolish and astonished, and I gave him some good advice which he took in good part at first; but when I said how his wife would be vexed and grieved to see him come rolling home, I found I had touched a tender point. He became savage at once, cursed and swore and threatened violence. Then he began to roar after me, but he could only stagger very slowly so I left him behind reeling and roaring, cursing parsons and shouting what he would do if he were younger, and that if a man did not get drunk he wasn't a man and of no good to himself or the public houses, an argument so exquisite that I left it to answer itself.

How redolent of its period this is! Butter-tubs, horse collars, the labourer going home by the field path, licensing laws that enabled drunkenness in mid-afternoon – history has swallowed the lot of them. The clergy in those days, too, could afford to patronize where today they would deprecate; you can hear in Kilvert's tone the authority of class and the priggishness of breeding. One might guess too, from other passages as well as this, that Kilvert was not at his ease nor at his best with village prodigals.

1970 *19 August.* The enquiry must have permitted demolition of the Ashbrook barns, for most of them are already down in piles of stone and rubble ...

1870 *22 August.* . . . so much of my heart is still in this bachelor life ...

– though he looked enviously on fathers playing with their children, and though he did get married within two years of at last acquiring a parish of his own and with it the financial security that made marriage possible, yet Kilvert too in his time was one of the lucky bachelors. What more satisfying life is there than a young man's in his twenties, with his freedom and a job that he loves? and, for Kilvert, the ultimate security of the family home in the background as well? Domestic life did not demand his energies, they flowed out exuberantly into the leisured, full, and demanding life dictated by his calling. Between them, the endless variety of human contact with his parishioners and their children, the beauty of the surrounding landscape, the balls and the picnics and the croquet parties, the services of the church, the verse and the diary gave him the means of expression, the chance to discharge himself, which makes a young bachelor's life the dizzy, exhilarating thing it can be. It is later, when a man approaches thirty-five, that the slower heavier pull of domesticity will have its way. There is an isolation about Kilvert as vicar of Bredwardine, eight years later, that makes marriage natural; but in his Clyro days, his life flows so eagerly out through dozens of channels to mingle with the lives of others that there seems little left to give in marriage.

Living here a hundred years after him, I am a married man,

and I know the gulf that makes between him and me. This house,
Ashbrook, looms far larger to me than it did to him, for I own it
and it is my home, whereas to him it was only his rented lodgings.
To him it was the place from which you set out, to me the place to
which you come back. He was footloose, I committed.

1970 *23 August.* Went to 8 o'clock communion with M. . . . A
stranger middle-aged couple with a young man there; M
accosted them afterwards, thinking they were the people
from the little white cottage by the churchyard gate. They
weren't, but turned out, remarkably, to be Kilverts, grandchildren of Perch [Perch was Kilvert's brother] and now
the only descendants . . . They're staying for a couple of
nights at Fforest Cwm. Because he *was* here, they *are*.
Insoluble.

Later it came out a morning of warm hazy sunshine: I
strolled through the churchyard, taking photos of the Gore
tombstones, and through the ruins of the Ashbrook barns –
now just a great waste of mud with only the shell of the
buildings along the village street standing. Chatted with
Bob Price, from the garage opposite, about his plans for
them. He told me that his present cramped building was
the village smithy till he took it over from the last smith,
Thomas, in 1960 – though it had then been virtually out of
use for some time. He gave me permission to take as many
of the old stone slates from the Ashbrook barns as I wanted
in the evening, and I picked up three barrowloads of them –
they're lying loose among the rubble in the yard. They're
beautiful things, exactly shaped (though now mostly
broken), most eloquent of the craftsmanship that went into
them – I want to put them down on the garden paths.

The use of the old stone slates, once universal in Clyro, was going
out precisely in Kilvert's time, as the newly arrived railway
enabled the ubiquitous Welsh slates to undercut them. Ashbrook
itself, built in the 1850s, is roofed with Welsh slates – but perhaps
had stone slates originally? Or was it already worth carting
Welsh slates from a railhead at Hereford, or somewhere?

Tom Watkins from the cottages came up to talk to me –
he's interesting, for he's known the village for a longish

time, and he knows his Kilvert. Told me that the barns and the land used to go with the hotel, not with Ashbrook, apparently till the 1940s: then Mrs. Baskerville found she couldn't let Ashbrook as it stood, so put the barns and the land with it. Also that she used to have a private electrical generator where the petrol pumps now stand.

1970 *24 August*. After lunch we all packed into the car and set off for Worcester to put the Oddies on the train ...

Very Victorian, though we would have put them on the train at Hay then, even the old branch-line train to Hereford being faster than a horse-drawn coach. It's curious that whereas in general we tend to rely much more on public facilities than the Victorians did, in this one particular of land transport, the position is reversed: it was they who tended to travel public, we to travel private.

1970 *28 August*. The electricians reappeared, when we had almost given up hope, and connected up the immersion heater, so we have hot water, not only in the bathroom but in our bedroom for the first time since the house was built. A great luxury. Various exciting bits of electrical equipment arrived too – a dishwasher, a washing machine – though they're not working yet.

Mechanization coming to the house, which was designed to be worked by hand. In Kilvert's day there was apparently one servant, no doubt living in the attics, and she was dishwasher, washing machine, supplier of hot water to the bedrooms, and a great many other things combined. I don't imagine the house had a bathroom; certainly Kilvert never mentions it. He himself used to take a dip in a hip bath full of cold water in his bedroom every morning; on occasions it froze. The maid would doubtless have carried the water for that too, and it would be interesting to know whether the house had water laid on at all. A farmhouse wouldn't in the 1850s, a gentleman's house would, and Ashbrook's intermediate status leaves the matter in doubt. The dipping hole in the bed of the stream outside the kitchen door rather suggests that this was the only source of supply – water was still something you picked, not something that comes out of pipes. On the other hand, Mrs. Chaloner's lodgings were considered fit for Kilvert and his parents – does this imply at least the presence of a water-closet? Perhaps the dark windowless hole on the ground floor that filled this function when we bought Ashbrook was as old as the house. Perhaps it was one of Peter Chaloner's aspirations above his station that so infuriated the Squire.

1870 *29 August*. The long-talked-of Hardwick Bazaar for the Home Missions ... We got to Hardwick Vicarage at 3.30. The Bazaar was in full swing, the tent very hot and crowded. Everybody was buying everything at once. The Hay Volunteer Band banged and blasted away. Persons ran about in all directions with large pictures and other articles, bags, rugs, cushions, smoking caps, asking everyone they met to join in raffling for them. There was a series of water colour sketches of Alpine scenery, Monte Rosa, the Matterhorn, etc. beautifully executed by Mrs. Webb, 10/- each. I got up a raffle of ten people 1/- each for a beautiful drawing of the Schreckhorn one of the series. Mrs. Powell of Dorstone drew the prize. Everybody was there, from all the country round, the day lovely and the scene bright and pretty. I bought for 3/6 at the stall of Helen of Troy a walnut paper knife with a deer carved on the handle by Walwyn Trumper, his first attempt and very nicely done. The entrance to the field over a bridge across the sunk fence from the lawn cost 1/-. At 5 o'clock there was universal tea, cake, and bread and butter in a tent with long tables and forms. A pretty dark eyed merry maid waited on us. No teaspoons and I stirred my tea and cut the bread and butter slices with my newly acquired paper

1970 *29 August*. We drove into Hay for the church fête at the Castle – on the hundredth anniversary of K's bazaar at Hardwick. It was a perfect afternoon for it, and when we arrived it was going fine. The stalls and sideshows were all round the lawn, a skittles alley, a game in which you were supplied with a fishing-rod with a rubber ring in place of the hook and had to try to get it over the neck of a mineral bottle on the ground and pull it over (much harder than it sounds), a raffle, a vegetable stall, a cake stall that was sold out before we arrived, and so on. The women with their bright decorous dresses moved round, examining things on the trestle tables, and over them towered up the great dignified trees that ring the lawn, chestnut, oak, sycamore, and so on – from the size of them, they might well have been planted by the Bevans – while the children dashed about in the middle of the lawn on the beautiful velvety green. In front of the house – a quiet dignified Jacobean place built into the old curtain walls; one end of it is itself a shell, burnt out twenty years ago we were told – a loudspeaker dispensed noisy pop music, and by the old gatehouse and ruined Norman keep they were serving tea. Glancing through the ground-floor windows, there seemed to be books everywhere – perhaps overflow from the book-shop. We all had our spoils – E a little notebook, C a drink, M a lot of vegetables and some handkerchiefs, I a railway tea-towel – and I secretively scaled the ruined gatehouse and took a picture looking down on the town ...

Almost interchangeable at first sight; and yet on inspection the one-directional flow of time is clear enough. The Volunteer Band; the smoking caps; the price of Mrs. Webb's watercolours; pop music; perhaps even the notion that tea-towels might be a suitable commodity for a fête; the tricks of usage in the diary entries themselves: all of them, like fallen leaves on a seemingly motionless stream, show the direction of the current.

1970 *30 August*. In the afternoon we drove out to Bredwardine to pick blackberries in the same place as last week. This time we drove up the pretty avenue of youngish beeches that leads up to the churchyard, left the car there, and walked over the old castle mound to the blackberry bushes. The simple dignified white vicarage where K died lies just over the churchyard wall, adjacent to the castle mound; and he must have known well the steep scrubby bank above the river where the blackberry bushes grow. There are some noble trees, both on the mound and further along the bank, that he must have known – four huge sweet chestnuts, covered in green spiky fruit at present, and further on, at the top of the bank above the river, a real fairy knoll where we had our picnic – a small grassy mound shaded by three great ancient riven oaks and an elm. The blackberries weren't as plentiful as last week – other folk have been there, and indeed two family parties went by picking while we were there. But we got three pounds or so, while M did mending on the knoll in the warm hazy afternoon; then had our picnic, and the children insisted on playing blind man's buff and hide and seek. It was after 6 when we returned to the car, the sun gone behind clouds, the evening grey: we went through the churchyard and had a look at the strange, interesting, crooked old church, and then at K's grave – a plain, ugly white cross on the north side of the church, under the shade of a great beech. Our grubby little pair of urchins, E with a wicked grin and a great stain of blackberry juice all over her face, sat down on the steps of the cross, and surely K would take pleasure in that ...

1970 *4 September*. A bright morning after rain. I returned the parish registers to the vicar in the church, and went searching in the long grass and brambles on the south side of the churchyard for Peter Chaloner's memorial, stumbling over the forgotten mounds of the people that K new, among the leaning flaking headstones.

Oblivion comes easily in Clyro: the local sandstone, which all but the gentry used for their monuments in the last century, when cut thin usually shales away after fifty years or so, so that after two generations even the stones are dumb; which is proper enough.

Found a crop of delicious blackberries growing within the little railed enclosures round the monument of the Hamars of Boatside and the Venables' tombs. The enclosure round the latter is a fair-sized affair of massive but very rusty iron railings, and I was leaning far out over them to pick some succulent specimens when the section I was leaning on suddenly gave way and I came down with a crash on the tomb of Mr. Venables' old mother, bringing the railings with me and filling my hand with blackberry prickles. Not at all a reverent proceeding, and K wouldn't have approved. I pulled myself painfully to my feet and wedged the railing back in place as best I could.

Kilvert often came here. One fine March afternoon

1871 I spent a happy half hour wandering about Clyro church-yard among the graves. I visited the new heavy and ambitious erection which Mrs. Chaloner has put up to the memory of her husband Peter Chaloner. I also visited Maria Lake's grave close by the head stone of Joseph Cadwallader. Then I compared my watch with the sundial and they agreed almost entirely. I sat awhile on the old Catholic tomb of the 'Relict of Thomas Bridgewater' under the S. church wall, near the chancel door. This is my favourite tomb. I love it better than all the tombs in the churchyard with its kindly 'Requiescat in pace', the prayer so full of peace, with its solemn reminder 'Tendimus huc omnes' and the simple Latin cross at the head of the inscription ... A small and irreverent spider came running swiftly towards me across the flat tombstone and scuttling over the sacred words and memories with most indecent haste and levity. Here it was very quiet and peaceful, nothing to disturb the stillness but the subdued village voices and the cawing of the rooks nesting and brooding in the tops of the high trees in the Castle Clump [their descendants have moved to the trees up the Cae Mawr drive] ... somewhere near at hand I heard the innkeeper's voice behind the church and across the brook giving orders to a workman about planting some quick and privet. Near the old yew I found the flat tombstone of 'Eustace Whitney 1669' ...

1970 *4 September*. This is the wildest corner of the churchyard, and there were crowds of pink and white cyclamens and rosebay willow-herb springing up among the brambles; and among them close beside a row of Wall memorials, the monument to Peter Chaloner that K thought ambitious, though it hardly seems so now, half-obscured by grass and weeds; too ambitious for the Chaloners' station in life was what Kilvert meant, no doubt. I was able to put together a

good family tree of the Chaloners with its help. The vicar
showed me the stone outside the chancel where K sat that
still sunny spring afternoon: much of it is now buried in the
edge of the path, and the surface has almost entirely flaked
away, but there's just enough of the lettering left to
identify it., What puzzled me was why K called it 'Catholic'
– it's a fine strong early 18th century script, and you can
still read the date 1711 – but no doubt he was referring to
the idea of praying for the soul of the dead (which must
indeed be unusual at that date – perhaps Bridgewater's
widow *was* a Catholic?). Treading very closely in K's
footsteps this morning. I compared the church with his
sister's drawing of it on the Kilvert Society Christmas
card; and unmistakably it *is* the same building, though the
tower has been heightened, whereas I had thought the
rebuilding was *after* K's time. This makes the story of the
great window in Ashbrook coming from the church when it
was rebuilt a good deal more likely. I brooded in the
churchyard for a bit, the low morning sun falling slant
across the stones so that shadow lay in the lettering and
the names stood out clearly, the old familiar village names
– Thomas the blacksmith, with two tiny stones for dead
children beside him. And after a bit of searching I found
the flat stone of 1669 to Eustance (*sic*) Whitney, which K
mentions – fine strong simple lettering; I thought it had
gone. It must be the earliest stone in the churchyard.

> William Dewy, Tranter Reuben, Farmer Ledlow late
> at plough,
> Robert's kin, and John's, and Ned's,
> And the Squire, and Lady Susan, lie in Mellstock
> churchyard now.

They are all there, the vicar and his churchwarden, Walls and
Vaughans and Dykes, Hamar of Boatside who 'supposed he had
had the measles', with blackberries growing over his tomb, the
'Relict of Thomas Bridgewater' with her dubious orthodoxy,
Eustance Whitney the local pioneer of churchyard memorials,
Thomas the blacksmith with his two little children beside him,
the row of stones marking the places of Gore, the miller of Whitty's
Mill, and his fine daughters all dead of consumption in their

bloom, Miss Beynon of Pentwyn, who is reputed to have quarrel-
led with one of Mr. Venables' successors and built the little
Congregational chapel across the brook behind the church, lying
under a Gothic tomb-chest close beside the tower. There, too, lie
the Baskervilles – a military row of crosses against the west wall
of the churchyard commemorate the squire's numerous sisters,
and in front of them a towering stone cross, overtopping every
other monument in the churchyard except the war memorial by
the gate, was presumably designed to commemorate the succes-
sive heads of the family. Four tomb-chests radiate from its foot,
with ample room for inscriptions – things were expected to go on
for a long time. But of the four, three are blank.

Something, it seems, went wrong. The war came; the heir (the
son of Kilvert's squire) was killed – as was proper, gentlemen
being there to be shot at; other men from the village, sons of men
that Kilvert knew as boys, were killed too as the centuries-old
sea-wall broke and the tides of the great world rushed over the
little life of Clyro. Their names are on the memorial by the gate,
Ralph Baskerville's at the head of them in the society of death as
in the society of life. And after the war the world was changed. No
other male Baskerville ruled at the Court, and no other names
were ever inscribed on the tomb which was meant to commemorate a dynasty.

1870 *6 September*. Rode the elephant to Llowes after school to
ask Williams to drive me to the Three Cocks on my way to
Llysdinam on Friday evening. Poor elephant, his best days
are over, and his knees show the Cornish Coat of Arms
from a recent fall, but he is a noble gallant old fellow.

The 'elephant' was one of the vicar's horses; the Cornish coat of
arms, I believe, consists of a number of scarlet roundels – a
memory, perhaps, of that nostalgic summer holiday in Cornwall.
Kilvert normally walked everywhere, and took it for granted that
he should. On social occasions, he often got lifts in other people's
carriages, and the vicar was always prepared to let him have his
coachman and one of the vicarage vehicles when it was a matter
of catching a train; but only when he was in charge of the parish
in the vicar's absence does he seem to have had the occasional use
of a horse. What references there are suggest that Kilvert enjoyed

riding; but it was an expensive luxury, far outside the narrow range of his pocket. Once again he was reminded that, though of the middle classes socially, he was below them economically.

The car is an infinitely more plebeian means of travel than the horse was; and even in rural Radnorshire has been so since the 1950s at latest. Kilvert was in the position of the odd man out without a car who depends on other people for lifts; but that position was far more economically revealing then than now, for a man's reasons for not owning a car today are probably more likely to be inability to drive or personal whim than inability to afford it. It would be difficult to find anyone in employment in Clyro today who does not own a car, and what an astonishing social revolution that is! Who owned horses in the village in Kilvert's time? The vicar, the Baskervilles, the Crichtons at Wye Cliff, and the Morrells at Cae Mawr all undoubtedly had horses and carriages; there is no evidence and I think not much probability that anybody else did, except perhaps the Collets and later the Hodgsons at Cabalva, who never figure much in the Diary. The farms of course had working horses, and a relatively wealthy tenant farmer like Mr. Partridge at the Court farm may well have kept a riding horse too; but that would be all. Everybody else walked, as they had always done. The roads, as well as the footpaths, were essentially walking ways, dusty, unmetalled, narrow, and winding: a carriage was a rarity, a sure token of membership of the ruling few.

1870 *21 September*. Went to the Bronith.

BRONYDD the huge new roadside signs shout at you as you pass the little hamlet today, a mile short of Clyro as you approach it from Hereford-wards along the callous asphalt slash of the A458. Kilvert spelt it in English, because although almost all the old

---

Opposite, top: Lower House. A Clyro farmhouse, typical of the many farmhouses of the parish in which Kilvert was always confident of a warm welcome. This one, with its adjacent farm buildings, is probably almost exactly as Kilvert knew it. Lower House was the home of Lewis Williams (the poetry enthusiast – see p. 208) and his middle-aged parents; it was down the slope in the foreground that the blood was running to the road at the time of Kilvert's visit.

Opposite, bottom: The Gores of Whitty's Mill.

place-names of Clyro are Welsh, and the family names too, spoken Welsh had already long been dead in the area in his time. Of the Celtic nationalisms, only the Irish was conspicuously alive in the 1870s. Further into Wales, the traditional Welsh culture and language must still have been largely intact; but between these areas and England, Radnorshire formed part of a broad border-land where the one nation faded gradually into the other. It is the self-conscious nationalism of today that puts roadside signs back into the Welsh spellings that hereabouts have been obsolete for centuries and compels Miss Tong the postmistress to keep Welsh language application forms that nobody in Clyro will ever want for the renewal of driving licences. Boundaries acquire a mystical status, and up on the Little Mountain even the signposts marking the new Offa's Dyke Path, duly bilingual in Radnorshire, sud-denly and absurdly lapse into monolingual English when the path ducks into Herefordshire for half a mile.

> People at work in the orchard gathering up the windfall apples for early cider. The smell of the apples very strong. Beyond the orchards the lone aspen was rustling loud and mournfully a lament for the departure of summer. Called on the old soldier. He was with his wife in the garden digging and gathering red potatoes which turned up very large and sound, no disease, and no second growth, an unusual thing this year. The great red round potatoes lay thick, fresh and clean on the dark newly turned mould. I sat down on the stones by the spring and the old soldier came and sat down on the stones by me while his wife went on picking up the red potatoes. We talked about the war and the loss of the *Captain*. Mary Morgan brought me some apples, Sam's Crabs and Quinin's. The spring trickled and tinkled behind us and a boy from the keeper's cottage came to draw water in a blue and white jug [how like Kilvert to note the colour of the jug!].
>
> It was very quiet and peaceful in the old soldier's garden as we sat by the spring while the sun grew low and gilded the apples in the trees which he had planted, and the keeper's wife moved about in the garden below, and we heard the distant shots at partridges.

The life of the countryside going on in a fine September afternoon, wrapped in the profound peace that had lain for ages on Clyro.

1970 *26 February*. A hard white frost. Walked along the road to the Bronith at 11, and about a dozen big trucks passed me on the way, appalling monsters thundering by about a yard from my shoulder. No wonder you never see anyone walking on the road – it's not far unlike standing on the edge of a station platform as an express goes through. A lovely morning though, with a keen cutting east wind and bright sun. Noticed the details of the country properly as I went along, as you never can from a car. The road-widening has reached the Clyro side of the Bronith now – three men were at work cutting down the hedge on the north side of the road to the ground and burning it. All trampled mud and mess, and the Bronith now is almost a village on its own. The farmhouse itself must be new since K's day, and so also one cottage on that side of the road; on the other side there are two new bungalows, orange brick and plate glass windows, all very clean and trim and inappropriate.

The verge of the bottom part of the lane up to the Bronith cottages all mud, where the road-wideners have levelled the hedges. Climbed up the lane between the little farmhouse with the lopsided facade and the cottage that I think must have been the gamekeeper's in K's time. And there, immediately above it, I found at once what I knew must be old John Morgan's cottage, that K so often visited. Or the remains of it, for all that's left is one end wall with a chimney – you can see where the fireplaces have been on the two floors. All else is tumbled stones and mere ruin, and the end of the garden under the lane, where the old soldier grew his potatoes, is full of old rubbish that somebody has tipped there – broken bottles, a tin bath, the frame of an old pram, the rim of a steak-and-kidney pie tin with the bottom rusted out, a horrible mess of rusty iron and broken glass. Yet it must have been a snug little place, the cottage standing in one corner of a square terrace of ground levelled out of the steep hillside: it faces south across the wide valley, which was shining with pools in the morning sun, and behind the house a larch plantation –

which must be new, of course – hangs over the ruined gable and the space that used to be the garden. There was nobody about, and only the occasional rumble of a passing truck on the road below. I stood in the garden, where there's not a sign of cultivation left, but one or two clumps of snowdrops, and to my surprise the little purple ground-ivy (that Hannah Whitney told K was called 'bloody butcher') actually in flower. Somewhere here K once helped the old soldier to dig his potatoes; but you're left in no doubt that that was a hundred years ago.

Many of the cottages that Kilvert knew have gone, like John Morgan's, some of them vanished without trace except for a small patch of mounds and hollows in a field – roughly built in the first place, they crumbled fast once they were abandoned and the roofs began to let in the weather. For a hundred years past, the population of Clyro has been shrinking continually, almost exactly since Kilvert's time in fact – in this respect too he was here precisely on the watershed. The growth of urban industry and its offer of relatively well-paid jobs was the ultimate cause no doubt, the coming of the railway, the spread of education, and perhaps the agricultural depression at the end of the nineteenth century the proximate ones; and in this century the mechanization of agriculture came to round the story off. Generation after generation, the young have tended to move away to the towns, and one by one the old labourers' cottages have fallen empty. The process was accelerated by the housing revolution brought about by the coming of the council house from the 1920s onward, which soon meant that nobody was prepared to tolerate the conditions that most of the village had previously taken for granted – damp floors, dark rooms, leaky roofs, no sanitation but an earth closet in the garden, no running water, no electricity. The emigration from Clyro and the abandonment of the old cottages touched bottom, I suppose, in the 1950s; since then, the tide has begun to turn, as the affluent society breeds its week-enders, its hippies, its holidaymakers, all with their eyes on a cottage in the country, and the horizons of the retiring Birmingham businessman begin to extend as far afield as Radnorshire. The retiring businessmen build lavish, suburban-looking bungalows; the holidaymakers and week-enders, with their comfort in town behind them, go for the tradition, the contact with the long past, that nothing in their ordinary lives offers. This new, middle-class invasion has in the last ten years swept up most of the old cottages that had not already gone beyond repair and renovated them, so long neglected by their landlords, with a freshet of middle-class money. After life had been slipping away from Clyro for a century, life of a kind is coming back to it. Life of a kind: middle-aged life, week-end life, neither of them mingling much with those who have always lived and laboured here and make it their own by doing so. Your home is where you worked and raised your children, and to the newcomers Clyro is not that. Perhaps even that may come, though: perhaps the hippies, those wistful, footloose vagrants of our society, perhaps the Chinaman who lives at Pen-y-rheol, are the real hope for Clyro's future, since what they are looking for is an alternative to the cities and the money that started drawing the young out of Clyro a century ago, an alternative to them, and not merely a refuge from them. Perhaps the tide is really starting to come in again.

1970 *22 September*. After lunch caught the 2.53 en route for a gaudy at Oxford – a grey day, but the sun gradually forcing its way through the mist. Changed at Wolverhampton and Birmingham – for all its newness, a dismal hole of a station. The nostalgia began there, for I boarded a Paddington train which found its way down a goods spur to rejoin the old G.W.R. main line just short of Small Heath, and there was that once-familiar line, now buried under a load of newer memories and itself far gone from the dignity of its old estate. The relief tracks have been taken up, and the suburban stations all have the air of decay – some closed, with the debris of their buildings piled on their platforms, some with a new station name-board or some other odd sign of use and modernity incongruous among the general shabbiness like a green shoot on a dying tree, some dirty and faded but otherwise unchanged images of themselves as they were when life still flowed down the line, survivals of what one already recognizes as a vanished age.

As we cleared the suburbs, the hazy afternoon sun shone

in rich mellow gold on the gentle midland landscape, the chequerboard of pastures showing so clearly the ridge-and-furrow under the grass and surrounded by hedgerows set with full-grown elms, the roads running between broad grass verges, the few buildings all of brick – the landscape of late enclosure. All here was as it always was in my memory: this was the same sunlight that always shone on these fields. A much purer countryside, felt much more immediately, than that you see from the Euston line; I suppose the truth is that that runs up the industrial axis of England, and that the country along it has all felt the withering touch of the factory and the city, whereas this line runs through an agricultural backwater – no doubt the reason for its decay.

I changed at Banbury, as of old, and caught a diesel set to Oxford. Along the Oxford line, several of the neat lime-stone stations are closed and derelict – and Oxford itself, where we arrived at 6.15, was a shambles. The station, at very long last, is being reconstructed – the upside build-ings are being flattened entirely, only the skeleton of the platform awning and the office chimney-stacks still stand-ing, the platform piled high with timber and rubble. Outside, the old L.M.S. station has almost entirely gone, most of the space occupied by a car park ... We live among ruins.

I caught a bus, noticing at once the number of black faces to be seen, and got carried too far down the High to Queen's, as always used to happen. I walked back to college through Radcliffe Square, where I was struck and delighted by the change effected by the cleaning of almost all the buildings – the sun was down but in the Square the air was lit most beautifully by the glow of the honey-coloured stone, and so even more strikingly within the Bodleian quadrangle. I walked up Brasenose Lane to the college in the cool of the evening, the streets everywhere almost empty at this time of the year and day.

Inside college, everything looked familiar except the greater spaciousness of the back quad since the new building went up; and people with familiar faces, whose names I couldn't remember, were chatting in groups. My room was beside the back gate on the second floor, looking across to Trinity – not far from the room of my first year. A decent bed-sitter, and I leaned out of the window and luxuriated in the cool and quietness of the twilight, the shops shut, the colleges lifeless, little moving in the Broad, all the beauty and age and tranquillity of Oxford. I should have gone to New College cloister.

I had a bath (there was a bathroom on the landing now, if you please!) and changed into my dinner-jacket, and at 7.30 we had sherry in the J.C.R. followed by dinner, where I was surprised but undaunted to find myself on high table. The company was good and the meal first-class, and what a place! The lamps on the three long tables running down the hall shone on half-remembered faces, the scouts and the women (several of them now) moved between trim in white jackets; above, the walls soared up to the high timbered roof in half darkness, and at the far end of the hall the baroque extravagances of the crest of the screen stood out black against the illuminated white wall behind. There was the sober opulence of dinner-jackets, black ties, and polished black oak tables, the gleam of silver candlesticks; and from the walls all those who had been there before us looked down, those from whom we had inherited the regiment and the order. It was a proud strong thought that – the aristo-cratic pride and strength, that should make you able to stand against the current, and that say you must. I was very proud to be of them, loving ancient orders as I do, perhaps the more because I know I am never quite one of the porphyrogeniti, always the odd one, the maverick; and I wished this could have been fifty years ago, when the ancient orders still stood, when we would have had no shame of being a ruling few and would have felt the responsibilities of it, whereas now it is dwindling, to our great loss, to a quaintness and a luxury. I read 'On the Marble Cliffs' last week.

We went to the S.C.R. for whisky, and I talked to people, and soon after midnight I had had enough, so I left them still hard at it and went to bed, only slightly dizzy – looking out of the window last thing to watch the traffic-lights changing meaninglessly at the end of the empty Broad, as I

used to in my old room at the top of No. 12 staircase in
'48–9. But they've altered the cycle, and they only change
now when a car comes. A pity.

Hmm. A right old nostalgic wallow, in fact, and the weaknesses
in it stick out like bulges in a balloon that's perished. I suppose
when you look at it, there are two themes there – change in
familiar things, the railway stations, the newly cleaned stone,
the bathroom, the traffic-lights; and nostalgia for a vanished
state of society that the diarist (that's me – or *a* me at any rate)
never knew. I doubt if these are purely individual themes, though
individual they certainly are; they are also characteristic of their
age. Certainly there is nothing of either in Kilvert's diary
recordings of his revisits to Oxford – college gaudies had not been
invented in his day, but he went back more than once to visit an
old Oxford friend who was now a fellow of Corpus. Once again I
note that his Diary, which so powerfully feeds the nostalgia of
others, is itself remarkably free of it (as the facile romanticism of
his verse is not). Oxford merely interests and delights him: the
Diary swells out beyond its normal dimensions with snapshot
after snapshot of Oxford life precisely observed and caught, the
Professor of Mathematics indignant at the neglect of his University Sermons, the choir-boys of St. Mary's beating the bounds of
the parish – even a great tribal occasion like the summer eights
is simply observed, not made the occasion for lamenting times
gone. I think his is the better way of seeing, but I think the
difference is between 1870 and 1970 as well as between Kilvert
and Le Quesne, though the point is hard to prove. It is true, for
instance, that Kilvert in 1870 was ten years younger than me in
1970, and those ten years make a lot of difference to the way men
see their pasts; yet up to the time of his death, there is little sign
in the Diary of the two themes that are so obsessive in this Oxford
entry of mine, change in familiar things and nostalgia for an
imagined *ancien régime*. The difference is partly of fact, partly of
mood. To a man of Kilvert's generation, living where he lived, the
world of visible things *did* change more slowly than it does for
me. The first industrial age in Britain was fully established, and
the landscape, scenic and social, was apparently settling down as
the grass and the primroses and the campion grew over the scars
of the new railway earthworks; and the middle classes, clergy,

squires, and businessmen alike, felt no need to look backwards to a world they had lost when their lot in the world of the present and the foreseen future seemed secure and prosperous enough. Nostalgia was already abroad in the 1870s, but it was the very few who felt it – a literary few mostly, the Tennysons and the Matthew Arnolds. One of Kilvert's great strengths is his *naïveté:* he does not dream of himself in an imagined past, nor for that matter stand back to analyse his own diary. The perspectives of course would probably be very different if two Clyro diaries had been kept, one in the 1870s, the other in the 1970s, by inhabitants not of Ashbrook but of one of the village cottages.

1870 *26 September*. Magistrates' meeting at noon ... An unsuccessful attempt by Samuel Evans' daughter and wife of the Bird's Nest to father the daughter's base child upon Edward Morgan of Cwmpelved Green. It came out that Mrs. Evans had been shameless enough to let the young man sit up at night with Emily after she and her husband had gone to bed. Mrs. V. most properly reprimanded her publicly and turned her out of the Club. Such conduct ought to be strongly marked and disapproved ...

Kilvert in his occasional role of Jehovah: the old authoritarian morality at work, and obviously the vicar's wife and the curate were natural incarnations for it. We have got squeamish about using social sanctions to enforce morality, being unsure about the difference between right and wrong; the 1870s had no doubt at all, or at least the gentry had none and probably most of the village agreed with them on this. The tribe still ruled with a strong hand over the individual.

1870 *2 October*. After lunch I found a letter lying on my table from my Father ...

Capital F, you notice: the fifth commandment still reigning strong in that deferential society and that deferential soul.

Ashbrook did not have a letter-box till we gave it one a hundred years later; in the 1850s, when the house was built, letters were not expected and they were still comparative rarities to Kilvert in the 1870s. When every letter had to be written by hand, they were not composed without good reason, and he never experienced anything like the flood of superfluous paper written in any script but a human one that pours through our letter-boxes today. The 1*d*. that it would have cost his father to send it was roughly the equivalent in value of the 3p stamp of the early 1970s; but in 1870 you got a Sunday delivery for the money.

1970 *2 October*. A stormy night and morning, a buffeting wind blowing shivery down the valley, gleams of sunlight lying naked and bright on the Bron as I took C to school. Harvest Festival, which seems to be held on a week-day everywhere hereabouts – as in K's time. The church prettily, not elaborately, decorated; but at 9.30 communion there was nobody there but the Vicar's wife and us from Ashbrook. We sat in the stalls, with the great empty nave staring at us: an old dried-up river bed, with a few shallow pools here and there.

At 6.30, heard the church bell going for harvest evensong, and on the spur of the moment decided to go. Found nobody else in the church at all: the lights weren't on, except for the little lighted window in the door to the ringing chamber, the building cold and gloomy with twilight. However, it turned out that the service was at 7, and we were having a full half-hour of the bells. Soon other people began to arrive and fill up the nave from the back, as the most occasional church-goers always do – I, six rows from the front, eventually found myself the most advanced outpost. The Vicar came in and turned on the heaters, bless him, and the lights, which at once turned the twilight outside to night, and the decorations were brilliant in the light, the polished apples on the capitals, the beautiful display of flowers and fruits, all yellows and reds, on the altar. A tribe of Sunday School children came in, and settled, whispering and giggling, into the choir stalls on the cantoris side, supervised by the Vicar's wife. People latterly fairly poured into the church till there must have been 50 or 60 there, farm folk of all ages, a very different picture from the morning; after all, Clyro is a good village which still holds together, and clearly it still recognizes Harvest as one of its festivals ...

Harvest festival was already a big occasion in Clyro in 1870, when Kilvert records a whole day spent, in company with the schoolchildren, the gentry, and their servants, in decorating the church, apparently a good deal more lavishly than was normal by 1970. Unfortunately his description of the festival itself is lost, so there is no evidence how full the church was then; but, to judge from his description of harvest festivals in neighbouring parishes, one would imagine that then as now it was one of the best-supported church occasions of the year. This is interesting, for the festival can hardly have been very old at Clyro. The harvest festival, as distinct from the harvest home, was a Victorian innovation, though it seems already to have been well established in the Clyro area by 1870: presumably it owed its rapid success to its natural appeal to a farming community, and in fact it may well simply have taken over the older, unhallowed harvest home celebrations that went back goodness knows how far into pre-Christian times. Is this why harvest festival is a weekday occasion? In 1871 Kilvert describes a visit to Whitney harvest festival, which included parish games and a parish feast in the open air, which certainly does sound as though the Church had made a successful takeover bid for a previously independent festivity. Did the zeal of the gentry and their dependants in decorating the church in 1870 itself owe something to the need to emphasize the Christianization of a festival whose pagan past was still remembered?

Certainly the festival keeps its popularity in Clyro: as I have already said, it is one of the three occasions in the year, the others being Christmas and Easter, when the village still goes to church in something like strength. There is not much logic in it – Christmas and Easter are two of the three major Christian festivals, but the third of them, Whitsun, falls dead as a stone, whereas harvest is a church occasion only by very belated courtesy – but in a farming community, harvest is still one of the poles on which the year turns, when a man is forced to reckon up the sum of his dealings with the uncontrollable that is bigger than him. It is the farmers who make up the bulk of the congregation: whether they will still come when we have learned to control the weather, I would not care to say.

1870 *4 October*. To-day I sent my first post cards, to my Mother, Thersie, Emmie and Perch. They are capital things, simple, useful and handy. A happy invention.

It was not picture postcards, which were some way ahead yet, but the first stamped postcards which evoked this spasm of euphoria in Kilvert – Locksley Hall in a very minor key. It is the face that invention bore to Kilvert's generation. When Tennyson wrote his first 'Locksley Hall' thirty years earlier, the model of innovation was that grand, explosive, Frankenstein thing, the railway, which could be welcomed only by an act of faith; by 1870, innovation had become domesticated, the producer of 'simple, useful, handy' things, a force to be welcomed without fear or reservation because it offered no threat to the stability of the world: a touch of onshore breeze without which the day might have been enervating.

1970 *4 October*. We drove up to Bettws and had a look at the harvest decorations in the chapel. It was modestly but attractively done. I like the plain brave little building out in the middle of the field, its tiny intimate interior, the faith of the little group of people who still keep it alive and tidy; I don't wonder K liked preaching there – it would be like talking to a group of friends. I'd like to know the origin of it – it's clearly not 19th century, perhaps 17th century or even mediaeval. K and the Walls and the Dykes seemed very close at hand up there this grey afternoon. Under the low cloud ceiling, the air was clear and the view over the valley splendid. We drove on down the Rhydspence lane as far as the entrance to Lower Bettws; there we left the car, and took a track across a field to the Old House. This was new ground and most interesting, for the track must have been something considerable at one time: it has a regular stone surface, and crosses the wooded Chapel Dingle by an imposing stone bridge, a good 25 feet high, with ample curving abutments. Just beyond, the Old House is abandoned and hollow in a ploughed field – a neat little stone labourer's cottage, not very long empty, and sad. M went back for the car, but I went down the slope with E along the edge of the dingle; the clouds held in the intense greenness of the valley, and it seemed to swim in a green light of its

> own. We found an old terraceway that slants down to
> Upper Cabalva, and there M met us in the car.

This is at the north-eastern end of the parish, occupied by the
Cabalva estate which is fast becoming a single great ranch; and
the Old House – so called by contrast with what newer house, I
wonder? – where Thomas Watkins with his wife Catherine and
their four young children lived in Kilvert's time, no doubt with
poverty enough, stands empty in the midst of it, and in a year or
two it will be gone. As for the old track, this must be the
'highway, 1100 yards long, from the turnpike road at or near
Cabalva ... and passing through the Cabalva estate until it joins
the main parish highway from Rhydspence to the confines of the
parishes of Clirow and Brilley', which the parish vestry (Farmer
Partridge of Clyro Court Farm, Farmer Hamar of Boatside,
William Dyke, William Wall, William Phillips ...) decided to
abandon at a meeting in August 1866, at the request of the
owner of Cabalva. Kilvert was already in Clyro then; but he
never had anything to do with the vestry, where the landowners
of the parish ruled unchallenged. Now the lower course of the old
road is about to be engulfed in a vast new road construction,
where the A458 is being improved by a monstrous slash across
the hillside from Lower Cabalva to Cabalva Dingle, burying alike
the picturesque old stone bridge that carried the valley road over
the dingle in Kilvert's days and the newer one just below it
opened by Mrs. Baskerville in the 1920s – also an improvement in
its time, in the first age of the car. Roads take less account of
landowners' preferences now than they did in the 1860s.

1870 *5 October.* At the Bronith spring a woman crippled with
rheumatism and crying with pain, had filled her tin pail
and was trying to crawl home with it. So I carried the pail
to her house.

The harshness of nineteenth-century rural life, and Kilvert at his
best, for many of his clerical brethren would have thought it
beneath them to carry a pail, and apparently he does not even
know the woman's name. Mains water came to the village
between the wars, but few houses were connected to it till after
1945: even now it does not reach far off the main road, and few
farms or cottages can have had any sort of water in the house
before the 1920s.

1870 *7 October*. Kilvert took the sacrament to old Edward Evans in the village – the cottage, I think, stood somewhere on the site now occupied by the row built in 1876.

> Poor Edward very ill. What a scene it was, the one small room up in the roof of the hovel, almost dark, in which I could not stand upright, the shattered window, almost empty of glass, the squalid bed, the close horrid smell, the continual crying and wailing of the children below, the pattering of the rain on the tiles close overhead, the ceaseless moaning of the sick man with his face bound about with a napkin. 'Lord have mercy. Lord have mercy upon me,' he moaned. I was almost exhausted crouching down at the little dirty window to catch the light of the gloomy rainy afternoon.

Objectively, a perfect piece of social realism – what a text for a discourse on the iniquities that nineteenth-century society inflicted on its working classes! – made all the more powerful by the total absence of any such intention in the writer's mind. What scope, too, for a ferociously realistic painting that no painter of Kilvert's generation on this side of the Channel had the guts to undertake! Or for the novel of social protest that, once again, no Englishman felt moved to write between 1850 and 1900. In France, Courbet and Zola, in England – what? Millais and Dickens?

One notes again the security, the complacency of Kilvert's generation, after the tumults of the 1840s, and I at least dither between several reactions. Is one to be simply appalled at the consciousness that can contemplate conditions like this and be content to live quietly on? Or is one in some way to admire a community whose sense of corporate being is so strong that individual hardships just become insignificant to it? Or is the apt comment just that in Clyro things had always been like this, or worse, and that it occurred to nobody that much could be done to change them? Certainly this seems to be Kilvert's attitude: he knew that some of the poor lived like this, and he was sorry for them, but that was all. He probably went further than most of his contemporaries in sometimes asking himself the troubling question of why he in particular should be born to comfort and they to poverty. The squalor they lived in disgusted him – one can sense the disgust in every precisely chosen detail of the scene in the hovel, and it must have effectively blocked the chances of serious communication between him and them. Still, when it was his duty, he visited them; and curiously the aversion of the diary entry is more powerful now than any indignation of his could be. Moral attitudes on the printed page, when they do not repel, are apt to make the reader feel exempt from the duty of sharing them, whereas the conditions that Kilvert describes appal us just because he himself feels nothing more than disgust at them.

Wholly unvarnished Victorian cottage interiors are rare enough for this one to be very valuable; but, before we make it a stick to beat the whole of that society with, it should be said that Edward Evans's household was in several respects exceptional, as the census return of the next year makes sufficiently clear in its stark statistics. In it Edward Evans appears as an agricultural labourer of sixty-nine – he survived his illness of 1870, apparently, but whether he was able to bring in a regular wage there is no saying. He had a wife thirty years younger than himself, who is described as a 'charwoman' which may suggest that it was she who had to earn the family's bread, and three children aged between one and seven – I suspect that the wife was out working at the time of Kilvert's visit, and that the children had been left to look after themselves, while their old father lay ill in bed upstairs. Edward Evans, in other words, had launched out on a family perilously late in life, and the squalor in which Kilvert found him was in part a comment on that. Kilvert and his peers probably thought him imprudent, and that the hardships in which the family lived were of their own making; which is as it may be, but certainly the family was an unusual one, and very possibly their housing conditions also.

After leaving Edward Evans, Kilvert went up the village to Sacred Cottage (still there, by the lane up to the old walled garden behind Cae Mawr: it is one of the oldest houses in the village, and is said to be so called from having once been the vicarage) to call on Esther Rogers, a widow in her sixties who lived there with two grown sons. She talked to him about her brother, a heavy dragoon who was killed at Waterloo – thrust through by a French lancer as he lay on his face on the ground, shamming dead: she had a recollection of him (she cannot have been more than ten at the time of his death) as a fine tall man in a scarlet uniform on a black horse with white hoofs. The Napoleonic wars, remember, were just as close to Kilvert as the First World War is to us: Waterloo for his contemporaries must have had something of the echo that the Somme has now, with the same family memories of never-known or half-forgotten relatives who died there. And there would be differences too: the fact that Waterloo was remembered as a glorious victory, not an appalling botched-up slaughter; that, although there may have been as many British dead in the French wars as in 1914–18, relative to the size of population, they were spread out over twenty-two years, not packed into four; that in 1815 war was still fought overwhelmingly by the inarticulate, and did not leave a literature of horror and disillusionment to make it an abomination in the mythology of later generations. The differences are one of the reasons why Kilvert's generation could contemplate both their past and their present more contentedly than we can.

1870 *10 October*. All the evening a crowd of excited people swarming about the Swan door and steps, laughing, talking loud, swearing and quarrelling in the quiet moonlight.

Here come a fresh drove of men from the fair, half tipsy, at the quarrelsome stage judging by the noise they make, all talking at once loud fast and angry, humming and buzzing like a swarm of angry bees. Their blood is on fire. It is like a gunpowder magazine. There will be an explosion in a minute. It only wants one word, a spark. Here it is. Someone had said something. A sudden blaze of passion, a retort, a word and a blow, a rush, a scuffle, a Babel of voices, a tumult, the furious voices of the combatants rising high and furious above the din. Now the bystanders have come between them, are holding them back, soothing them, explaining that no insult was intended at first and persuading them not to fight ... Meanwhile the swarm and bustle and hum goes on, some singing, some shouting, some quarrelling and wrangling, the World and the Flesh reeling about arm in arm and Apollyon straddling the whole breadth of the way ...

Ashbrook is just across the road from the village pub – Peter Chaloner, who built it, seems at one time to have been the publican among his numerous other avocations – and Kilvert's sitting-room, with his bedroom above it, occupies the corner of the house immediately opposite its entrance; so goings-on at the pub must have impressed themselves forcefully upon his awareness as he sat there in the evenings. It is a tribute to the way Mr. Price conducted his house that they figure so rarely in the Diary: one gathers that it had not always been so under his predecessors. This evening was exceptional: it was the day of the autumn cattle fair at Hay, prices had been poor, and the farmers were on their way home with little money in their pocket but a lot of anxiety to drink away. The present tense and the vivid staccato reporting suggest strongly that Kilvert was recording it live – sitting at his table by the window, following the scene outside by ear, and writing it down as it happened, his attention fixed on the object and not on his own reaction to it as with all good observers.

Kilvert did not much disapprove of the Swan (so he almost, not quite always calls it, though in 1870 it had already been rechristened by its present name, the Baskerville Arms – the reign of the Baskervilles having started in Clyro only twenty or thirty years before) and accepted it as an inevitable feature of the village scene – as he did not accept (in both instances, one suspects, following the strong lead of the vicar) the village's second pub, the New Inn, which to the satisfaction of them both lost its licence in 1871. The New Inn, rechristened the New House, still stands, a tall white three-storeyed building that looks down the village street from its extreme northern end, showing now no sign of its alcoholic past, except perhaps the difficulty of imagining any other origin for a building of such size. One pub, they presumably thought, was enough in a village – and the New Inn was a mere alehouse, probably patronized mostly by labourers, while the farmers, their employers, went to the Baskerville. It was one thing for the farmers to drink, but quite another to put temptation in the way of their labourers, for they could not afford it, and it was their wives and children who would pay the price – such was the characteristic respectable view of the matter, which Mr. Venables and Kilvert doubtless shared, and indeed the Diary itself provides examples of it happening.

Drinking a hundred years ago was a very different phenomenon from today, and in particular there was a very clear demarcation between the drinking of the rich and the drinking of

the poor. Those who could afford it drank at home – at Clyro, the gentry would have had wine on their tables, the farmers home-made cider, and only the poor water. If a poor man wanted to drink, he went to the pub; and the pub was distinctly disreputable and disapproved of, not only because it was the resort of the poor, but because it led them out of the peculiarly strait and narrow way that was all that Victorian respectability permitted them. The enemy was not intoxication, which was socially tolerable, but improvidence. To that extent at least, there was no hypocrisy in the attitude: it was true that the rich could afford it, but the poor couldn't. Kilvert himself, being a relatively poor man, may not have drunk much at Ashbrook – it is most unlikely that he could afford wine, and beer and cider might be socially unacceptable as table drinks – but at the vicarage, at Cae Mawr, or at Clyro Court, wine would have been taken for granted, and there is never any hint that Kilvert saw anything wrong in drinking as such or did anything but enjoy wine himself when he had the chance. Strong though the teetotal movement was in Victorian England, it did not derive much support from the Anglican country clergy.

In so far, therefore, as the Swan was a respectable house, serv-ing beer for the most part to farmers who could afford it, Kilvert had no case against it, except the noise that very occasionally spilled out from it to disturb his evenings. But neither he nor any of the local gentry would ever have dreamed of being seen inside it. A gentleman drank at home; and he did not in any case mingle socially with the lower classes.

How much of a social centre was the Swan in Kilvert's time? Except for the vastly successful periodical Penny Readings (which certainly demonstrated the demand that existed for a cheap popular entertainment), it was of course the only organized

---

Opposite, top: The village blacksmith at work, about the time of the First World War. The wych-elms in the churchyard are still standing, and the roof of the 'Ashbrook barns' is just visible behind them.

Opposite, bottom: The village as Kilvert knew it. Ashbrook is just off the picture on the left, the Baskerville Arms on the right. Almost nothing has changed in this scene since the date when the photograph was taken, perhaps about 1890. Yet the sense of the passage of time is overwhelming – if only through the remoteness of an age when it was safe to pose a group of children in the middle of the main road from Hereford to Brecon.

kind of diversion which existed in Clyro; yet on the whole I doubt whether it was as socially effective as it is today. This is a guess, for no direct evidence exists, but I suspect that its patrons came from a much narrower band of Clyro society than they do now: certainly not the gentry, nor probably the wealthier and more respectable farmers – I doubt if Mr. Wall, the churchwarden, or Hamar of Boatside were to be seen there – nor the poorest of the provident labourers; which leaves only the smaller farmers, the rest of the labourers, and the village craftsmen. Again, there is no indication that the Swan normally offered accommodation or served meals; and there are suggestions that for most of its publicans until recent years, it was only a part-time occupation. It was a modest village pub, and nothing more; and it seems likely that the church was a more effective focus of village society than it, though here no doubt much allowance has to be made for Kilvert's peculiar angle of vision.

All this is very much changed. The Baskerville Arms (its old name is now quite forgotten) has been transformed within the last ten years by a very enterprising proprietor. It must have one of the best bar trades for many miles round, as a glimpse at the village street on a Friday night will immediately demonstrate: the car parking has long since overflowed the old inn yard, and slops up both sides of the street for a hundred yards in each direction, and the long spur of land between the street and the by-pass which used to be the Ashbrook orchard is now being made into a new car park. In the inn itself, the bar has been vastly enlarged and a flourishing hotel business built up, including the construction of a new wing of bedrooms connecting the inn itself with the old stables, which gives the Baskerville these days the look of an embryonic motel – for which function indeed its position just on the Welsh border by one of the major holiday arteries into the Principality admirably suits it. Kilvert would be very much surprised if he could see it today; though it is still a well-conducted house, and his sleep would probably be no more disturbed than it was in his own time here.

But besides the physical transformation of the building, there has been an even greater transformation of society and its drinking habits. The sight of those cars in the village street is itself enough, of course, to indicate one social revolution – the, to Kilvert unthinkable, revolution of affluence that has brought a car to almost every household in Clyro. This affluence has also destroyed the notion of Kilvert's class that for most Clyro folk drinking is an impermissible extravagance: there cannot now be very many people in the parish who never take their pint, or whatever, in the bar of the Baskerville, and – another revolution – that would go for women as well as men. (When *did* Clyro society begin to tolerate women drinking in pubs? I must ask somebody.) One factor involved here, certainly, is that as far as I know there is not a farmer left in the parish who still makes his own cider, or would dream of doing so, as would have been the near-universal practice in Kilvert's time. The ancient gnarled ruins of the cider orchards are still to be seen beside many farmhouses, and there is still mistletoe to be found on them, but I suppose the practice died out somewhere around the time of the Second World War; and with it, alas, went the practice of drinking cider, which must have been the drink of this part of the country for centuries, but is now the perquisite of the ladies and the nostalgic middle classes. Most of the cider made nowadays is fit for little else, anyway.

The farmers, therefore, drink less at home than they used to do and more in the pub; but almost equally important is its invasion by the middle classes. The English pub has become not merely respectable, but chic, as its decoration all too often testifies. I suppose the practice of *boasting* of the pub as one of the distinctive institutions of this country took its rise around the time of the First World War – one thinks vaguely, or at least I do, of Georgian poets, more Chesterbelloc, and (in the next generation) J. B. Priestley – and it presumably indicates the point at which the middle classes moved in on what had been a wholly working-class institution. The phenomenon obviously indicates in general the blurring of class distinction that has taken place in the last century – especially perhaps the growth of a middle class that, risen largely from below, forms its own patterns of behaviour or brings them with it from the working classes, and makes no attempt to conform to the patterns of the older aristocratic or professional classes. The pub itself, of course, has responded – architecturally by the evolution of the lounge bar, which the Baskerville too possesses: the social distinction between the habitués of it and of the public bar is subtle and far from clear-cut, but unmistakable nevertheless. Class consciousness, which no longer insists on separate buildings, draws the line at sharing the same room.

The result of all this has been an immense extension of the clientele and the social significance of the pub in Clyro. This probably owes something to the decline of other communities – the farm *community*, with its cluster of labourers and farm servants; the country house; the church. Because people are more alone nowadays at home and in their daily work, they seek society elsewhere in the evenings. There can be no question that the Baskerville nowadays is far the most vital centre and sounding-board of Clyro society; almost everyone goes there, often or rarely, and it is there that village opinion is formed. Nothing quite like this, and nothing so republican, existed in Kilvert's time. The tavern has swelled, the temple has shrunk – not a change that would be likely to commend itself to him.

1970 *10 October*. Talking with old Mr. Pritchard outside the shop – he's full of sly nods and winks at any mention of K, whom he says his father and aunt knew. If what he says has anything in it, it at least looks as if the parish had the worst suspicions about his relationships with his girls. He used to go chasing up to Newchurch in one direction and Llanthony in the other after them, according to Mr. P: died at 39 because he was worn out, Mr. P reckoned.

The trouble with Kilvert folklore in Clyro is that you never know whether you're dealing with genuine traditions, or with impressions based on reading the Diary since its publication in 1939. It is a fact, as I have said before, that the village on the whole is not very enthusiastic about Kilvert, but that may be as much due to his devotees as to any true memory of him – after all, you don't expect much to be remembered about a not obviously remarkable man who was curate for seven years a century ago. In this case, it looks as though genuine tradition is possible; but even then, it's as well to remember that what Kilvert did may be one thing, and what the village thought of it very much another. The Diary is incomparably the best, as it is very nearly the only, evidence of the kind of man that Kilvert was.

1870 *13 October*. The wind of the night tore down the clematis from the western corner of the house and left the huge bush hanging helpless and dragging from its hold on the mountain ash.

The clematis and the mountain ash had both gone without trace when we came to the house. We planted them again, for the sake of auld lang syne – the clematis much where it must have been before, by the steps into the estate office, the mountain ash round the back of the house. I like to do what little one can to restore the breaches of time.

1870 *14 October*. The children are many of them still busy picking acorns which they can sell to the farmers at 2/- and 2/4 a bushel. Acorns are so valuable this year that the farmers are jealous of them and exclude everyone from their fields. So the poor people are obliged to confine themselves to the road under the oaks ...

School attendance was not yet compulsory, and any point of the farming year which involved a sudden need for unskilled labour left Mr. Evans facing a lot of empty desks. Probably to many Clyro villagers the chief function of the school was as a child-minding centre, to keep their parents' hands free till the children were old enough to earn a wage; and if after a windy night even a seven-year-old could earn a few pennies by gathering acorns, love of learning and the admonitions of the curate were unlikely to be sufficient counter-inducement. In 1870 it had been a long hot summer, and a passage like this shows how the traditional rural economy of a village like Clyro, still yoked closely to the natural order, balanced precariously on the edge of the seasons. It was normal then to harvest acorns at Clyro: gathered by the children for sale to the farmers, they provided a welcome addition to the exiguous wages of the labourers (which are unlikely to have been as much as ten shillings a week), and hence the acorn harvest was always one of the seasons of the year when absenteeism at the village school was at its peak. This year though prices were unusually good: because of the drought, crops were scant and farmers were at their wits' end how to pay their rent, and marginal crops like acorns (for pig feed, I presume) took on unaccustomed importance. Again it's impossible to avoid reflecting that the life of the poor in Clyro in the 1870s was still part of an order of immemorial antiquity: the poor gleaners set me thinking of the Book of Ruth, though I note that individualism has taken over from communal right and that the gleaners have been expelled from the field to the road. But the acorns must have rotted undisturbed under the oaks for a good long time now.

> I went to Allt-y-Fedwas to learn the real story of the death of the little boy who was killed by the horse last week. Price wishing to describe the child's size said that 'he stretched out a good deal of a long boy after he was dead.' A little chubby-cheeked girl sitting on the settle proclaimed aloud in a triumphant voice as if she were repeating a well learnt lesson, 'Charlie's dead and in the grave', and then fetched a deep long sigh. The low grey woman with the grotesque face sat by the window sewing. A comely girl in russet brown swept up the hearth with a goose's wing and set on the kettle, and a large black and white sheep dog pushed open the door and wandered into the room and was sent out again.

We have seen already how much commoner death was at Clyro then, as everywhere; and, as everywhere, it was especially the children who died, as the tombstones in the churchyard attest clearly enough. Has a child ever died in the 'The Archers', and what kind of a hullaballoo would there be if one did? This passage from the Diary is surely a marvellously vivid picture of the stoic attitude to death natural to a society where it was still a common hazard: the complete absence of emotion, the phlegmatic description of the dead boy, the child's ritual comment, the anonymity of the girl and the grey woman, the household tasks going on, and the unheeding dog – the images he selects couldn't be better chosen to convey the mood. Was this totally unselfconscious on Kilvert's part? I think it was; there *are* passages in the Diary that reveal a degree of self-consciousness in his writing, but none that suggest his literary technique was ever as deliberate as would be implied by such a conscious selection here. I think the selection was instinctive: he would have said he was just describing what he saw.

The Diary records another encounter that day with the traditional economy of the rural poor – up at the farmhouse of Wern

Vawr on Clyro Hill, where Mrs. Morgan of Cold Blow was waiting to have a gallon tin filled with milk, and Kilvert explains that it was an old custom for the poor to go round the farmhouses begging milk 'between and about the two Michaelmasses' – another indication of how strong the memory of the old Julian calendar still was in Clyro – to make puddings and pancakes for Bryngwyn and Clyro Feasts, on the Sunday after old Michaelmas Day (for these feasts traditionally fell on the day of the patron saint of the parish church, and the churches of both Clyro and Bryngwyn are dedicated to St. Michael). The custom, he notes, was still kept up in Bryngwyn and at some of the hill farms in Clyro, but 'at comparatively few houses now, and scarcely any-where in Clyro Vale'. Of course there is the obvious point, of the desperately thin margin of adequacy on which the poor lived at all (milk here is a rare luxury), but for me that is not the main interest of the passage, which lies in what it has to say about charity, and the decay of charity. Charity, if only for the deserving and respectable, was a virtue held in high regard, much practised and still more talked about by the Victorian upper classes. But this – Kilvert giving Mrs. Corfield a blanket out of the Communion Fund, Daisy Thomas sending the footman for a bunch of grapes for Alice Davies – is something very different from the traditional charity that Mrs. Morgan was seeking at Wern Vawr. This older form was almost as much a right as a favour: it is a survival from a pre-individualist, communal order of things in which tradition ruled absolute, as compelling on giver as on receiver, an order whose memory lingered far into the individualist nineteenth century: for instance, it lay behind the inarticulate protests against the individualism of the reformed Poor Law, protests which included the idea that the poor man had a right to an ungrudging charity. The acorn gleaners, expelled from the fields to the roadside, are another instance of the new attitude to poverty, according to which charity was a favour, and apt to be resented accordingly. There is a good deal to be said for the older, traditional form of charity, which not only excluded condescension, but guarded against the sort of abuse to which its modern equivalent, social security, is liable. Not, of course, that it would be thinkable anyway in a modern society; and already even in 1870 Victorian individualism was advancing fast into the hills, it seems. In the valley it was already victorious: it is interesting to note even in this instance how it has always been up the valleys that conquest and change have come. The Romans and the Normans came that way: it is there that the town stands, there that the railway runs, there that the bigger and wealthier farms and the country houses lie, there that the modern trunk road swaggers triumphally and insensitively through the landscape. Even as you turn off the valley road and climb into the hills, you are conscious of turning from the twentieth century into an older country, where the past dies harder.

On his return to the village, Kilvert called in at Hannah Whitney's cottage, just across the lane from his lodgings, gone now, and sat with her for an hour 'talking over old times, and listening to her reminiscences and tales of the dear old times, the simple kindly primitive times "in the Bryngwyn" nearly ninety years ago'. This is not a very common note in Kilvert, and a useful reminder not to exaggerate his immunity from nostalgia for the communal past. The past whose loss he is lamenting is a past in which people gave freely to their neighbours in need, and in winter evenings told stories of fairies by the fireside. Hannah Whitney in her childhood had heard them all, from her grandfather and his friends, men who had been born before the turn of the eighteenth century and still believed in the fairies – stories of the Wild Duck Pool where on Easter morning you could see the angels of the Resurrection playing before the sun, of Hob with his lantern who haunted the 'sheep cot pool' below Wernwg, of the old man who slept in the mill trough at the Rhosgoch mill and used to hear the fairies come in at night and dance to sweet fiddles on the mill floor. Hannah herself, I think, had never seen the fairies.

The longing for the old simple kindly times is something that we probably all feel occasionally: likely enough it is at bottom no more than a longing for our own lost childhoods. But here, clearly, it is not just subjective. Something was changing at Clyro. The kind of charity between neighbours that was sought at farm doors was fading as the bonds of community slackened, even on Clyro Hill; and village folklore was vanishing, the stories themselves being forgotten as belief in them died. What killed it, I wonder? Surely nothing of the Enlightenment can have soaked this far down in this remote Welsh soil? Nor is it likely that popular education had been going long enough to provide an explanation. Had Protestantism some long-term erosive effect on these beliefs, an effect that after three hundred years was beginning to wear them through? Whatever the explanation, the fairies are gone from Clyro Hill, not to return.

1870 *15 October*. Kilvert was visiting John Morgan again, listening as he loved to do to the old man's memories of his far-off days in Spain under Wellington, and of the size of the Spanish wolves,

> larger than any dog he had seen. 'We frightened them,' he said, 'by making a flash of powder in the pan of our muskets. When the wolves saw it they went away. They did not like to see that.' It is nothing to write, but the old man said it so quaintly as if the wolves disapproved of the proceedings and did not wish to countenance it, so they walked away.

Kilvert battling with the difficulties of his medium, and this time aware of it: there *is* a degree of self-consciousness in the Diary, though it arises not from the actor's consciousness of an audience, but from the craftsman's instinct for perfection. The world of actual sound and sight translates poorly into words on paper, and Kilvert knows as soon as he has put it down that he has missed the essence of what he wanted to record. It is the vexation of the diarist's job as against the novelist's: just because the novelist's is an entirely verbal world, it can have at times a completeness and a clarity that the diarist, whose verbal world is an attempt to translate a real one, cannot hope to equal. Compare Kilvert's characterizations with Jane Austen's or Dickens's: his are infinitely less sharp, less because he isn't so good at his job than because their characters are wholly expressed in the dialogue (and incident, and description), whereas real people express their characters as much in nuance of tone, expression, gesture, as in what they say, and these are modes that have no real verbal equivalents. Perhaps Kilvert could have got round it by cheating, and modifying the dialogue, putting words into the old man's mouth that would have the quaintness in them; but the diarist is a recorder, and recorders mustn't cheat.

The passion to record, to preserve, is one of the deepest roots of the diary-keeping impulse, and it is very strong in Kilvert; but the means of expression available to it have widened hugely since his time. Imagine what he could have done with a camera and a tape-recorder; Kilvert's is an exceptionally vivid verbal account of a landscape and a community, but a moment's reflection will bring home the enormous gap between it and the world that he heard and saw about him. Of that world almost no visual record at all seems to survive: the camera, of course, already existed (had done, indeed, for nearly fifty years), but it was still a clumsy instrument and an unusual one. Photographs of the 1870s are rarities, and those that do exist are mainly portraits: so it is very unlikely that any as old as this survive, or perhaps ever existed, of remote Clyro (the bottom picture on page 176 may be an exception, but I doubt it). We have photographs of Kilvert himself, and of a number of other Clyro figures mentioned in the Diary, but these are all either portrait photographs or formal groups, and, except for some taken many years after the period of the Diary, they are all of the gentry – the poor in the 1870s did not have their photographs taken. Nor have I ever seen a drawing or a painting of Clyro at this date, except for the sketch of the church by one of Kilvert's sisters, although we know Kilvert was given a painting of the village as a leaving present when he left in 1872. It is frustrating, this inability ever to *see* even a fraction of the Clyro world as it was, in the shapes that were so familiar to Kilvert's own eyes. Perhaps one day we will be lucky and something will turn up; but till then we are confined to what we can discern down the long narrow spyglass of the Diary itself. Here again, Kilvert lived on the watershed between two worlds: another generation, and from then on for the first time the past would be visible, and audible, for those who came after.

1970 *15 October*. In London.

> To the British Museum – struck again by the number of black faces you see in the streets, a good many of their wearers notably stylish and prosperous. Heaps of unsightly rubbish accumulating on the pavements as the dustmen's strike goes on. A beautiful morning though, bright and fresh. At the Museum I found my way to the Map Room, high up at the rear of the building, and spent a most

interesting day studying old Ordnance Survey maps of Clyro, the revision drawings of 1829 which clearly show that Ashbrook wasn't then built, and the first edition of the 6 inch and 25 inch maps, which date from the 1880s. Emerged finally about 4.30 and caught a bus along to Chancery Lane, where I went to the Record Office in pursuit of the 1871 census returns, only to find that they're not available till January 1st, 1972. So caught a bus back to Oxford Circus. As I waited at the bus stop, there was a strange sight – a procession of three youths, student age, with hair cut short to the head wearing an approximation to the costume of Buddhist monks, swaying in unison and wailing what was apparently a Buddhist chant. They attracted a few derisive smiles but not otherwise much notice – there's modern London for you.

Cosmopolis grows upon us as community and confidence disintegrate. Victorian England imposed its faith on half the world: what a piece of fantasy it would have seemed to Kilvert if someone had suggested that a century after his time English Buddhists would parade their faith in the streets of London! Psychologically at least, I suppose the last basis for the Victorian faith in the unique truth of Christianity was the assurance that it was going to overwhelm the other religions of the world when the two came into fair and open competition. Like the other great expectation of the last hundred years, the Marxist, it has not happened that way.

1870 *18 October*. Up the hill at Pentwyn, Kilvert found the old barn and cider-press being pulled down, and thought it a great improvement. This would be one of the old stone cider-presses, no doubt, and Miss Beynon, the middle-aged spinster who lived at Pentwyn alone with a single servant, probably had little use for it. Cider-presses were commonplace in those days, when nearly every farm in the parish probably made its own cider, and an old one was just junk. Since then their value has risen as their use has declined, according to a curious but common modern paradox. I have already suggested that cider-making died out at Clyro about the time of the Second World War, and I suppose it must have been about 1960 that cider-presses began to be seen as agreeable antiques, much coveted for the garden of one's restored country cottage. Perhaps there is a rule that it takes about a generation after an article has lapsed from common use before it begins to be valued as an antique: time enough for most of the old stone presses to be broken up and used for building stone or hard core, so that those remaining acquired rarity value. Made usually out of the soft red Herefordshire sandstone, they are fine monuments of pre-industrial technology and unselfconscious craftsmanship: modish enough for one to have been erected at the junction of the A49 with the new Hereford ring road just outside the walls of the old city, when the new road was built in the 1960s. This too would have astonished Kilvert: not just the notion that cider-presses might come to be valued as articles of beauty rather than of use, but the whole cult of antiques that is characteristic of our age, when Hay itself boasts something like half a dozen antique shops. I doubt if Kilvert ever saw an antique shop anywhere; that way of looking at the past was only just stumbling into life in his time. It is again the contrast between a society still so firmly attached to its past as not to be acutely aware of any gulf between then and now (though we have just seen that there are some occasional traces of such an awareness in Kilvert), and one so overwhelmingly conscious of living in flux that it clings on to any fragments of the past that it can lay hands on in the effort to retain its identity, to know where it came from; which is to know who you are.

> A wild rainy night. They are holding the Clyro Feast Ball at the Swan opposite. As I write I hear the scraping and squealing of the fiddle and the ceaseless heavy tramp of the dancers as they stamp the floor in a country dance. An occasional blast of wind or rush of rain shakes my window. Toby sits before the fire on the hearthrug and now and then jumps up on my knee to be stroked.

Clyro Feast Ball is interesting. These village festivals seem to have been widespread in the last century, and I should like to know when they died out – about the time of the First World War, perhaps? Certainly they have gone out of memory now, and there may be something in the obvious argument that this represents a decay of community life in the village; though I don't know: what with whist drives and the W.I. there may well be more communal social activities in the village now than there were in Kilvert's time, and certainly they are socially more catholic than they were then. Kilvert listening to the sounds of the Ball from his fireside is completely the outsider: it was unthinkable that he might cross the road and join it, and surely he would have been a better pastor without that inhibition? If the Ball was held nowadays, he could well be there.

1870 *19 October*. Went in to see Richard Meredith the Land Surveyor and sat talking to him for some time. He said the old folks used to rise very early, never later than five even in winter, and then the women would get to their spinning or knitting. His grandmother was always at her spinning, knitting, or woolcarding by 6 o'clock in the morning.

Richard Meredith the land surveyor was one of Kilvert's most prolific mines of local tradition and information, and must himself have been a man of curious and enquiring mind, to judge from the range of topics that the Diary records them discussing. He was a Hay man, living I think by the bridge into the town, which Kilvert had to cross whenever he went to or from Hay, so there was frequent occasion for a chat. His memories here remind us again that even in 1870 a gap was already opening between Clyro and its past. In my own time I have heard villagers draw the contrast between past and present in terms of later rising, as Richard Meredith does here, and I have already remarked that it may indeed be a good indicator of deep-lying social change. More precisely, perhaps, of a rising standard of living: sometimes the significance probably is that everyone can afford to light their house nowadays, and hence is no longer bound to observe the routine of the sun. But this cannot be the case here, for even in the old days the sun never rose at five in the winter; here the pressure must have been the necessity to start work at the earliest possible moment. The cottage industry referred to here is all the more interesting because it seems to have been all but entirely extinct by Kilvert's time – in all his perambulations of the parish, apart from one single isolated reference to a spinning-wheel, he never mentions spinning, knitting, or wool-carding. It could be, of course, that rising wages for labourers had made it unnecessary for women to bring in wages as well; but

remembering the acorn gleaners, it seems hardly likely. The true explanation must surely be that here as in so many other places the growth of the textile factories in northern England had driven the old rural industry into extinction. There is no indication that it had ever been a very great thing around Clyro, and it seems only to have been the smaller, simpler, and less skilled processes of the industry that had ever been pursued there; but the loss of them must have meant poverty rather than gain nevertheless, and if folk rose later by 1870 it was perhaps because there was no longer work for them to do.

1870 *20 October*. Visiting round the village, Kilvert called in on his neighbour, Hannah Whitney, as he loved to do. He not only liked to hear her memories of the Radnorshire of her youth, but revered her for her untaught wisdom, and was intrigued by her lineage, for there was a Durberville in Hannah. The Whitneys had been great folk in their day, taking their name from the next village down the valley, just over the border in England: they say that some fragments of what was once their mansion can still be made out at Great Gwernfythen, up the hill from Clyro, and Kilvert thought he could trace her blood in the fine lines of her features. The passage is a striking piece of precisely recorded observation and dialogue: the old woman standing in her doorway

> cloaked and with her rusty black bonnet fiercely cocked and pointed, crown uppermost, on the top of her head ... taking an observation of the weather, the world and the stream of water flowing fast down the gutter before the door.

Opposite: Hay, before it became Hay-on-Wye. This magnificent old photograph – dating, probably, from about 1890 – is taken from Broad Street looking over Hay bridge and up the road to Clyro. Clearly it is Thursday, market day; eggs are still sold on the raised pavement in the foreground. This is railway-age Hay, exactly as Kilvert knew it. Richard Meredith, the land surveyor, lived, I think, in one of the houses on the left, just above the bridge. The bridge, which has been replaced since the last war, spanned both the railway, on the near bank of the river, and the Wye itself, and it was a toll bridge: the gate can be clearly seen. Market folk, whom Kilvert so often mentions passing through Clyro, are on their way into town; to judge from the time of year as indicated by the trees, and the length of the shadows, it is still early morning. The Three Tuns on the right, incidentally, is still there.

She was indignant that no one now observed old Christmas Day; but

> she calmed down and went on to say philosophically, 'I do believe the Old Day is the right day, but them as have studied the matter say that we had gained too much time and that the new day is the right day. It may be, I don't know, not I, God only knows which day it is. If we keep one day and keep it in sincerity and truth that is the main.'

Finely recorded, and finely said: reading it today one can still sense the nobly free mind in that unschooled old woman of ninety, and her firm hold on the bedrock of right and wrong.

1870 *24 October*. Last night, when I went to the Vicarage to dinner ...

The Venables' were very generous in their hospitality to Kilvert: he dined at the vicarage more than once a week on average. These occasions are also recorded in Mr. Venables' diary, for he too was a diary-keeper, but his entries have a laconic quality entirely missing in Kilvert's – 'Kilvert dined,' says his diary for 23 October, and nothing more about the evening at all, and the same entry occurs for innumerable other evenings. Mr. Venables' entries, unlike Kilvert's, are made in a printed diary: each day he writes his dozen lines, and that is that, and one feels that the difference between the diaries is a good indication of the difference between the men. Mr. Venables was a man of affairs: he was vicar of Clyro, but he was also one of the leading country gentlemen of Radnorshire, one of the ruling and managing few, with the temperament to go with it. Much of his time was spent on the county bench, and on the boards of management of various local institutions. He clearly had a good head for business, and his diary is an appropriately businesslike document, a brief narrative record of things done, wasting no space on statements of opinion or observation of the world about him; very much the diary of a citizen of the world of telegrams and anger. There is no evidence that he took any part in the pastoral work of the parish, which seems all to have been left to Kilvert: Mr. Venables did what a gentleman parson was expected to do, took his share of the services and made the decisions – presided over the parish, one might say.

At eight o'clock, Mrs. Chaloner, his landlady, called Kilvert out into the passage to show him a strange rosy light in the sky, an aurora, through 'the great window' – the great Gothic window with wooden tracery that lights the staircase and the landings. It is still there today, spelling doom to any attempt to keep the house warm, as it faces north-east down the valley; but it is a noble thing, far the most striking feature of the house – it is said to have been thrown out of the church at the time of its restoration, as we have seen – and we would not be without it.

1870 *26 October.* Kilvert went visiting the Gores of Whitty's Mill, in the deep sudden dingle below Crossway. There were, I think, two mills in the parish in Kilvert's time, Clyro Mill at the end of the lane that runs past Ashbrook, and Whitty's, up on the hill. The mill was still an essential cog in the rural economy, at any rate here in rural Radnorshire: nearer London, steam-milling may already have been the rule. I imagine the village still grew enough wheat to feed itself, though very little grain is grown there today – here again, centralization and mass production have taken over from self-sufficiency. It was the coming of the railway that made the change possible, but in 1870 the railway was still a novelty in the Wye Valley and had barely begun to work its long-term consequences. So the millers were still prominent figures in the community, and it would seem prosperous ones: I cannot answer for Miller Minton, down at Clyro Mill, but according to the schoolmistress (a prime source of village gossip then, one senses) the Gores of Whitty's Mill made at least £200 a year and had £300 in the bank – 'very well-off' according to Kilvert, and so they may well have looked to him on his £100 a year and apparently no bank account at all. £200 was in fact about the salary of a senior clerk in a London commercial office, and doubtless went a lot further in Radnorshire: below the gentry, there can have been only a few of the wealthiest farmers in the parish making as much. So the Gores were prosperous people. While Kilvert was there that day, the eldest daughter, Mary – they were a family of girls – came in from a round on horseback among the hills, collecting debts for her father (no doubt this must have been one of the irritations of a miller's life), and one notes the tokens of prosperity at once. There is the horse, and Mary's costume – a 'dark riding habit' with 'a black jaunty pretty hat' – and Kilvert describes her as having 'the manners, bearing, and address of a lady'. Mrs. Gore, too, offered Kilvert gin. Gin was a liquid of lower social status (and relative price) then than now, and I suspect Kilvert thought it below him – certainly he accepted tea instead – but it is still the only record of his ever being offered it in Clyro (in fact, I cannot recall any other mention of it anywhere in the Diary). The Gores, one feels, were on their way up in the world.

Certainly the cosy mill kitchen, with the warmth of the welcome he received there, is a perfect image of that part of the Clyro world in which Kilvert above all delighted –

> the dear old Mill kitchen, the low, large room so snug, so irregular and full of odd holes and corners, so cosy and comfy with its low ceiling, horse-hair couch, easy chair by the fire, flowers in the window recess, the door opening into the best room or parlour. . . .

– an archetype of so many similar snug farmhouse kitchens where Kilvert was sure of a similar welcome from folk who were not painfully richer than he, who were grateful for what he had to give to them, the warmth of whose greeting was not inhibited by the decorum of Victorian genteel convention.

> I believe I might wander about these hills all my life and never want a kindly welcome, a meal, or a seat by the fireside.

It was a recurring dream with him: faintly one hears again the echo of Mouse Castle and Irish Mary, and of the Scholar Gipsy too – surely a poem that would have meant something to Kilvert if he had ever known it! – the lure of the picaresque, the idea of dropping out. In a small way, too, he proved the dream true on some of his later return visits to Clyro, after his curacy there ended in 1872: the doors of the farmhouses *were* open to him, and the welcome and the seat by the fireside were still there. He ends up:

> Blessings on the dear old Mill, and the brook that turns the wheel, and on the hospitable kitchen and the rooftree of the Gores, and blessings on that fair brave honest girl, the Miller's daughter of Whitty's Mill.

(Mary, one presumes.) Well, yes; but one notes without enthusiasm the tendency to revert to the stereotypes of sentimental novelettes.

It is a pleasant picture nevertheless, of Kilvert in the midst of this prosperous and happy family in the snug domesticity of their kitchen, and it would be pleasant to leave it there; but later time was harsh on the Gores and on Whitty's Mill. It was to be a theme for Hardy or Wordsworth, not for sentimental novelettes. When Kilvert came back to Clyro for a visit in March 1873, he noted that one of the sisters, Margaret, was already dead, at twenty: when he came again, in April 1876, he found another of them, Hannah, dying –

> dying of consumption in the same chair set in the same chimney corner where her sweet sisters Margaret and Mary had sat waiting so long and patiently for death.

Consumption was a mighty killer in the close damp hovels of the poor in the nineteenth century, in Clyro as elsewhere; and, cheerful though the mill kitchen sounds, nobody who knows the dark narrow dingle where Whitty's Mill stands will be surprised to hear that it was at work there too. Or was it some occupational lung disease of the miller's calling, due to the particles of flour in the air? However that may be, the three pretty girls, all dead in their twenties, lie side by side in the churchyard now, on the left of the yew avenue as you go in through the lych-gate. And their home?

1970 *8 March*. For our afternoon outing, we drove up the hill to Whitty's Mill. A raw grey afternoon, just coming on to rain thinly. We parked the car and scrambled all over the ruins of the mill that K knew as a happy family home. A messy business, for the little wooded dingle is a mass of slippery wet clay. It looks to me as though the culvert is new since K's time, and the road then crossed the brook at a lower level, by a ford perhaps, and passed below the house, whereas it's now above it. To make matters worse, there's a fallen fir tree across the front of the building, and at the back a great mass of raw soil and clay has been bulldozed out from the field above, obliterating everything almost up to the back wall. However, a little further up the dingle the remains of the old leat are very plain. The interior of the ruin is just a mass of fallen mossy stones – all the rooms looking tiny, as they do when a new house is rising from the ground. Both millstones are there, lying in the ruins of the old grinding room – one beautifully made of six or seven pieces of a very white quartzy-looking stone, tightly locked together by an iron tyre, the other a single slab covered in moss. A fragment of the floor above, ground level on the road side, remains, with a fireplace arched by an enormous rough-hewn wooden beam with old square-sectioned nails in it – very probably indeed, I think, the kitchen where K sat on October 26th, 1870, ninety-nine and a half years ago.

The land belongs to Crossway now: the Harrises tell me the mill was still standing till the 1950s, when they unroofed it to save the rates, in the days before old Clyro cottages started fetching fancy prices; and the roof once gone, ruin soon comes.

1970 *28 October....* I went to a village meeting in the hall at 7 – the adjourned meeting to discuss the proposal to make the village a 'conservation area'. M had told me that the previous meeting had stirred up much heat, and this one was no anti-climax. I arrived with Gwen Tong and Hannah Clarke, and found nobody in the hall but Mrs. Lewis, the vicar's wife and secretary of the parish council, while the men gathered round the gate outside. There were about 30 of us finally, one from most of the village households – the women and I all together on the chairs in the middle of the hall, the men, when they finally came in, sitting at the back all round the walls, till Mr. Cook, who had come to put the county planning committee's case, urged them to come forward, and they reluctantly moved up to the back row of chairs at the opposite end of the semi-circle from the women – but nevertheless did all the talking.

Mr. Cook didn't speak, but invited questions, and it was obvious at once that feeling was hot and strong against the idea. Mr. Cook's general line was that the main effect of being made a conservation area was to give the village a right to be consulted on all proposals for development in the area – but as a selling line it was a complete nonstarter, for everyone clearly regarded it as a mere excuse for 'they' meddling in their private affairs, and nobody showed any sign of wanting a right to be consulted – what they wanted was the right to do as they pleased with their own property, which is no doubt healthy enough in a way. The vicar was particularly vehement from the back: he thought it was 'the thin end of the wedge', and was highly resentful of the interference of 'outsiders' – which in this context reflected an obviously widely held suspicion of Kilvertians and other week-enders who wanted to put the village in a glass case. Peter Jones, the policeman, also had a lot to say, and was excellent – he had a copy of the Act, and questioned Mr. Cook very closely about its provisions. Mrs. Dworski made an acute point too – that consulting local opinion would inflame feuds in the village. Something in that, though to judge from the affair of Bob Price's garage, there would be practically unanimous support for almost any kind of development. Stan, from the hotel, was more judicial, but still hostile, obviously scenting checks on his right to extend his premises, and Mr. Watkins, from the cottages, could also see some merit in the idea; but Bob Price and Tom Lewis and all the others could obviously see none at all. Nobody spoke definitely in favour: the officers of the parish council, Mr. Walker, Mrs. Lewis, Mr. Griffiths (Gwernfythen) didn't speak. I suppose I ought to have said something – but the question and answer form of the thing made it difficult; and then again, I hadn't been at the first session of the meeting, and I was a newcomer to the village and very conscious of being isolated, and I've never been able to put a case well when speaking without preparation. M could probably have done it better. The gist of the case, I think, is that the intention is obviously mainly to conserve the *look* of the place – and I couldn't see any indication that any of the real village folk cared tuppence about the look of it, or even knew that it looked like anything at all. From this point of view, it's fatal to entrust conservation to local communities, it's not what they want – several of them made it clear that what they wanted, and no blame to them, was amenities, jobs, shops, business, a factory. Personally I think that anyway Clyro's beauty, such as it ever was, has already been ruined by the buildings of the last hundred years, and that it's an odd choice for a conservation area. But I also think that far worse can, and probably will, happen in the future, and for that reason I summoned up the courage to put up my hand and record the only vote in favour of the proposal.

Still, however wrong I thought they were, it was an impressive bit of village democracy – something I've never witnessed before, something you can't have in towns. Something too that would have been unthinkable to K. Except from the women to the men, there was no sign of deference to a ruling caste – everyone said their say and meant to have their rights. Though it was noticeable that, of the gentry present, only the vicar voted with the majority. We've had some kind of a visual education: we can *afford* to bother a bit about the look of things; and also we're birds of passage compared with most of the villagers, and to an extent share the outsider's notion of the village – as scenery.

1970 *3 November*... about 10 the electricity failed and plunged all the village into darkness. We sat up in the sitting-room over the fire, reading and working by candlelight – as K must surely have done in this room ...

Indeed: every night, probably. Electricity was still for the distant future, and there has never been gas in Clyro. The gentry used oil lamps, but most of the village must still have used candles, and I rather doubt if Mrs. Chaloner had lamps in Ashbrook – though she may have done. Like all Victorians, Kilvert was used to living at night in oases of light scattered through a house full of dark: the lighted corner in the dark room, the candle that you carried along the dark corridors up to bed. Except for the very rich, the idea of a house full of light came only with gas and electricity – in Clyro, that is, only after the Second World War. Now, we have not only expelled the dark from our houses, but are rapidly driving it from our main roads too, carrying the counter-offensive deep into the dark's country: then, it reigned unbroken in the village out of doors, clung tight round the cottages, and penetrated deep within them.

1870 *11 November.* The day that a successful Penny Reading was held at the school, according to William Plomer's note – the entry itself has not been preserved. Penny Readings were held regularly in Clyro school that winter, and seem to have been popular elsewhere in the neighbourhood too – certainly their popularity in Clyro is not in doubt: at the February one, according to the Diary, people were 'almost standing on each other's heads', and even trying to get in at the windows, and Kilvert, after reciting Jean Ingelow's 'Reflections' and his own 'Fairy Ride' (the holder of a twentieth-century Eng. Lit. degree purses his lips in a soundless whistle), emerged with a bad headache from the heat and foul air. I suspect that the November Reading was the first ever held in Clyro (the idea may very well have been Kilvert's own), so the attendance may have been smaller then; but large enough, clearly, to encourage repetition.

I do not know whether anyone has ever written the history of Penny Readings, nor where or when they originated (not long before 1870, surely?), nor for that matter when they died out, which might be almost as interesting; but as a feature of mid-Victorian rural society they're worth a moment's reflection. They must represent almost the very first attempt at popular entertainment in the countryside, and clearly there was a demand for it – 1*d.* cannot have been a negligible sum in 1870 for many of the audience – though likely enough an unconscious and an unrecognized demand, until somebody thought of trying the experiment. And immediately the questions throng clamorously into the mind – had the demand always existed? had it never had any satisfaction before? what prompted the start of Penny Readings? what purpose were they supposed to fulfil? and so on.

To all of them I've nothing to offer but vaguely informed guesses, and they deserve better than that. Way back, I suppose, the traditional providers of popular entertainment in the country-side were the Church and the alehouse; but the Church for all practical purposes had abdicated the function at the Reformation (whether it had ever performed it with any real degree of success even before then I don't pretend to know), and as for the alehouse, its presumable contribution of conviviality and a bit of beery singing was both limited and expensive – I've already suggested that it's unlikely that many Clyro labourers spent very much time at the Baskerville Arms in Kilvert's day. It does look as if the Penny Readings were attempting something nobody had ever tried before, presenting the poor with a literature more self-conscious and much more dependent on the written word than they had ever encountered in their traditional folk culture. And they came to hear it – though perhaps one shouldn't put too much emphasis on that, when one remembers the glamour with which the sheer novelty of the occasion must have invested it, and the emptiness that must often have been the main quality otherwise of winter evenings in the fireless and ill-lit cottages on Clyro Hill.

As for the motives, they may have been more complex. Note, for one thing, the place of the school in all this: with its building, the village had for the first time acquired a meeting-place where occasions of this sort *could* readily be held. It's likely too that the growth of popular education during the century had created both a thirst for its fruits and a concern among the rural upper classes to provide edification for adults as well as children. There is other evidence too for a growing sense of social responsibility, however one interprets it, among clergy and gentry in the second and third quarters of the century – one thinks of Evangelicalism, of the Oxford Movement, of the influence of Carlyle; and motives like a desire to provide alternative and more edifying entertainment than the pub may well have come into it too.

Edification, anyway, was certainly what was provided: the diet at Clyro Penny Readings, and one suspects elsewhere, seems to have been genteel to a degree – anodyne might not be much too harsh a word. There were songs as well as poetry recitals, but when on one occasion Charlie Powell, the blacksmith's son, proposed to sing a song that Kilvert regarded as 'low and coarse', Kilvert threatened to leave the platform and when Charlie Powell replied with 'insulting remarks', he was put out of the school by the village policeman. Traditional social discipline was clearly firmly in the saddle: this was improving entertainment, provided *for* the poor *by* their betters. It is true though that nobody else would have provided it at all, and that it was eagerly received. There is pathos in that picture of the many faces for whom there was no room clustering round the lighted windows of the school, so eager to get access to the culture that was on offer within – a widely applicable image of Victorian society.

Today, of course, there is television in all the cottages, and maybe there is some argument as to how far that is preferable to

Penny Readings; but there is a good deal else too – whist drives, the W.I., children's parties, amateur theatricals. The repertoire is far wider than in Kilvert's time, and there is far less disproportion between the few performers and the many audience, which is very much to the good: Kilvert himself, I fancy, would have thought so too.

1870 *15 November.* Kilvert had letters from home, enclosing a letter to his father from one of his former pupils, Augustus Hare. Robert Kilvert had taken in private pupils in his younger days as vicar of Hardenhuish – a common enough practice among the Anglican clergy in the middle decades of the nineteenth century, when the callings of priest and schoolmaster were hardly thought of as distinct and when the public schools had not yet established their monopoly as the only thinkable education for the sons of the upper middle classes. Francis Kilvert himself was to take a private pupil for a time in his later days as vicar of Bredwardine. It could be a very useful supplement to a clerical income, particularly for a young man with a growing family and no great private means such as Robert Kilvert was in the 1840s; and by degrees this group of pupils grew into a small school, enough to justify taking on an assistant tutor. Kilvert's father must have had good contacts, probably dating from his Oxford days, for his school attracted several sons of the aristocracy; but the only one of his pupils to have made any kind of a niche for himself in later memory was this Augustus Hare, a soft middle-aged bachelor who lived comfortably in Italy with his adoptive mother, writing guide-books and gentle over-leisurely biographies, some of which still survive faintly on the fringes of Victorian literary history. The interest of his letter on this occasion was that it contained reminiscences of his Hardenhuish schooldays, and that gives it an interest to us too, for they are one of the very few shafts of light on the world of Kilvert's childhood: Kilvert himself may have taken early lessons with his father's pupils, and there is no doubt that he was a child in the household at the time. Kilvert always remembered his childhood at 'dear old Harnish' as a happy time, so he was pleased that Hare's memories in the letter were fond ones – memories of the cook handing little hot cakes of bread out of the window, of collecting bits of tobacco-pipe on the roads, of dressings-up on the Fifth of November.

It throws a wry light on these nostalgic fragments that, when Hare came to publish his memoirs in 1900 – a work in six volumes, about a life in which effectively nothing happened – the passage about his Hardenhuish schooldays had a far different tone. In it, Robert Kilvert appears as a good man indeed, but a very unsympathetic figure: a man with 'no knowledge whatever of the world, still less of the boyish part of it'; 'a good scholar, but in the hardest, dryest sense, so this his knowledge was of the most untempting description'; a very hot-tempered man who 'slashed our hands with a ruler and our bodies with a cane most unmercifully for exceedingly slight offences', of whom his pupils walked in intense and abject terror. Hare's schooldays now appear to him as 'monotonous', his lessons as 'trash', his school-fellows as 'a set of little monsters' among whom 'all infantile immoralities were highly popular'.

Hare's readiness to say one thing to Robert Kilvert's face and another to the world after Robert Kilvert was dead is unattractive, though human. But it seems fair to say that what he wrote in his memoirs is more likely to represent his real feelings than what he wrote in his letter, and that people's memories are not usually embittered by the passage of time; and if so, the implications for Francis Kilvert's childhood are interesting. They suggest that, happy though his later memories of his childhood may have been, his father is unlikely to have been a very sympathetic figure; and one remembers again those capital Fs with which he always refers to his Father, the obedient deference which runs through all his references to him. Kissing the rod is a recurring pattern of Victorian father–son relationships – not, I think myself, an appealing one – and one looks further afield too, to other characteristics of Kilvert that were also widespread among his contemporaries: acceptance of traditional order and beliefs and of hierarchy, both upward and downward (for submission to those above goes with dominion over those below).

1870 *17 November.* The trees blazed with the diamonds of the melting hoar frost. The wet village roads shone like silver below, and the market folk thronged past the Vicarage and the School. A railway engine shot up a bright white jet of steam over the bank from Hay Station, the oaks were still tawny green and glittering with diamond dews, Hay Church in a tender haze beyond the gleaming of the broad river reach and rapids above the Steeple pool. How indescribable, that lovely brilliant variegated scene. A rook shot up out of the valley and towered above the silver mist into the bright blue sky over the golden oaks, rising against the dark blue mountains still patched and ribbed with snow.

1970 *15 November*. M and I set off for 9 o'clock communion at Llowes, but discovered half-way there that we were too late, and decided to go up to Brynyrhydd Common and do a bit of worshipping there instead. There were patches of ice on the road as we went up, and the view was marvellous. The dead dry bracken and grass were crusted with frost, the air tinglingly cold and dry. The sun was just up over the ridge of the Black Mountain, the near face of it all in shadow, the hedgerow trees throwing a comb of long spiky shadows over the fields, which were grey with frost: over Llowes the smoke of one or two chimneys hung lazily, hardly moving. There seemed not a soul stirring, all the crisp cold world to ourselves. But most marvellous of all, the view that made me exclaim as it first broke on us, rounding a corner below Clyro Court – away on the horizon the Brecon Beacons, the children's 'ice-cream mountains', in all the immaculate dazzling purity of new-fallen snow, the shadows lying deep and blue in the cwms, and the curving lines of the ridges sweeping up with an artist's grace to the pointed, volcano-like peaks. A more graceful group of mountains you can't conceive: they had this morning, absurd though it sounds, much the same serene unearthly beauty as Kanchenjunga seen from Darjeeling.

... We set out in the car about 4, the sun still brilliant, though declining. Up to Cusop Hill, and we all walked over to the old quarry. There was ice on the pools, and in the hedges the abundant holly berries seem to shine a brighter and brighter scarlet as the leaves fall. The face of Hay Bluff was all in deep cold shadow, but on Cusop Hill the sun was bright, and on all the illimitable plain north-eastward: you could see not only Clee Hill, but also, very clearly, Caradoc, forty miles off. We followed the hilltop to another quarry on its point, then scrambled down the steep sunward face of the hill to the white house that catches the evening sun from Clyro – half of it seemed shuttered up and rather sleazy, but from the other half two noisy Labradors came bounding out after us. The face of the scarp is rough ground with trees and bracken, but below the house it levels out into fields, shining in the path of the sun with spiders' gossamer. In the late sun, the dead bracken, the brown twisted leaves of the oaks, and the bare trunks of trees, the whole hill face, glowed a common ruddy orange: there wasn't a breath of wind, and a spray of dead oak leaves hanging in front of the deeply ribbed bark of the trunk had an artificially precise unmoving clarity of outline and of three-dimensional definition that suggested a bronze ...

Stillness is timelessness and hence changelessness, and here in the Clyro landscape little has changed in a hundred years, either in the abiding line of the hills or in something as ephemeral as a dead oak leaf. By the human time-scale, one is immutable, the other is repeated so often, so exactly, and so multitudinously that it's the persistence of the type, not the brevity of the one, that is noticed. Pascal remarks on it in the *Pensées*. What changes is the arbitrary human consciousness in the midst that does the seeing: the oak leaf, as it were. There are the quarries too, where the ephemeral took a chip out of the enduring, and now the grass has grown over.

1870 *18 November*. Went into the Tump to see young Meredith who has had his jaw locked for six months, a legacy of mumps. He has been to Hereford Infirmary where they kept him two months, gave him chloroform and wrenched his jaws open gradually by a screw lever. But they could not do him any good ...

1970 *28 November*. Got back to find E had kicked herself out of M's arms and had a very nasty fall. M put her down to sleep, and went off with C to the sale of work in the village hall. I had a late lunch, and E woke at 3.30 – still very shaken, wanting to be carried everywhere, and unable to use her right arm. I took her along to the sale of work, where she cheered up a bit. It was an animated scene, stalls all round the hall, and a steady stream of village folk drifting in and out. M, helping Mrs. Walker on the sweets and books stall, had even sold books to three hippies (who, when she was in doubt which to give the change to, said 'We are one'). Sat there with E till the end. We decided we had better take her to a doctor, and since she would probably need an X-ray, might as well go straight to the hospital in Hereford, so we drove off there at 5, rather weary, and had trouble finding the General Hospital. But it was a good time to go, for there was practically nobody there, and we got attention at once. They were all very pleasant and helpful, though E didn't like having her arm handled: on seeing an X-ray, they finally decided that there might possibly be a chip fracture, and put the arm in a sling, which E took to quite kindly ...

What a contrast of worlds! Even in 1870 medicine was already well on the hither side of the transition from barbarism and superstition to science; but the gap between a world in which a man's jaws have to be wrenched apart by a screw lever and the world of X-rays is all but unplumbable – in this field, our world is very young indeed. Our G.P. tells me that he has never heard of lockjaw as a complication of mumps, and that almost certainly young Meredith's trouble was an infection of the hinge of the jaw: in other words, the diagnosis was wrong and the treatment aimed at the symptoms, not the cause. Yet in the most fundamental sense young Meredith's case *is* on our side of the great divide: even in 1870 there was a hospital in Hereford that gave free treatment, and that treatment, however crude, was at least positive and rational. Social responsibility and science had taken over, and the assumption of both is one of the basic facts of the world we know as ours today. And among all the unfulfilled hopes and the disillusionments of the last hundred years, and God knows there are enough of them, I suppose modern medicine is about the last knight of the order of Progress who still wears his shining armour, and deserves it at that. There is less pain and less death in Clyro now than there was in Kilvert's day, and it is science and the idea of social responsibility, the doctors and the long arm of the welfare state, that have made it so; and good luck to them.

1870 *20 November*. I went back with Mrs. Venables to the Vicarage to tea and we had a long confidential talk between the lights and far into the dark, sitting by the drawing room fire, talking about the prevailing scepticism of the day. I said if I had children I should teach them to believe all the dear old Bible stories. She said she hoped to see me some day with a number of children about me, my own children. Never, I said, adding I did not believe that I should ever marry. Then came out by degrees my attachment to C. She was very much surprised when she guessed the right name after trying Mary Bevan, Fanny Higginson, Flora Ross, Lily Thomas. 'She'll never marry', she said gravely. 'I know it', I said.

He was wrong about his marrying, right about his children. The chronicle of Kilvert's romances weaves tantalizingly in and out of the pages of the Diary, broken all too frequently by lost volumes and by what he did not record. Who the strongly celibate C was, we do not know and probably never shall: Kilvert's attachments shifted with some regularity, as one love after another receded into hopelessness or tepidity, and within less than a year of this evening of fireside confidences with Mrs. Venables he was launched on the longest, best-documented, and most pathos-laden of all the romances to which his Diary bears witness, with Daisy Thomas of Llanthomas, younger sister of the Lily Thomas who figured on Mrs. Venables' list of candidates. Poverty, one imagines, was the bar to most of these affairs – apart from the vagrancy of Kilvert's fancy. Socially, he could not look for a wife outside the ranks of the upper middle classes – all Mrs. Venables' candidates are of this class – although, as we have seen, his sentimental fancies might wander farther afield. But no daughter of the Radnorshire gentry was going to be allowed to marry a penniless curate, with only his stipend of £100 a year to his name and no firm expectations for the future. There was a real need, I think, for Mrs. Venables' motherly sympathy, and I doubt if this was the first, as it was certainly not the last, time that Kilvert sought it.

There is also his encounter with scepticism, which is very much of the man and the time. Religious doubt was just becoming socially possible, not to say fashionable – not of course for the first time: there had been plenty of it in the previous century, but Evangelicalism and the grand rally of the aristocracy and the middle classes to the creed of respectability in the second quarter of the nineteenth century had put paid to all that for the time. Now scepticism was creeping back in again, helped along by such onshore winds as German biblical criticism, the development of geology, and of course Darwin's theory of evolution: the erosion of the grounds of faith was marked by such public scandals as the publication of Froude's *Nemesis of Faith*, and the recoil of the liberal wing of the Church of England itself by *Essays and Reviews*. So far as one can tell, the purely intellectual issues involved passed entirely over Kilvert's head: his reaction here can hardly be rated as anything higher than a nostalgic grumble, which reduces the issue not to the literal truth of the Bible stories – which was indeed one of the foremost points at issue between believers and sceptics of his generation – but to their age and their associations. The fact is simply that Kilvert was not an intellectual, and his instincts were deeply conservative. Teaching one's children to believe the dear old Bible stories is no way out, and is not a kindness to them: the issues have to be faced.

1970 *21 November*. Took the children into Hay to do some shopping, and got C's hair cut on the way home – the barber, a likeable talkative chap, on hearing I was writing about K, said he was the sort of person who might make him consider voting Socialist ...

– a comment not without ambiguity, but in context clearly not expressing approval. I note again that Kilvert these days is not very popular in his own neighbourhood, except among committed Kilvertians. But I confess that I find it hard to see the barber's reaction as a fair one – Kilvert's instincts were deeply conservative, as I've just said, and the Diary dismisses Radicals with the same implied snort as it uses for Dissenters, but he was a humane and sympathetic man, and not by the standards of his time a bigoted one – yet it would be interesting to know if any of the Clyro villagers, or for that matter the reigning Hay barber, thought that way about him in his own time. We know so little of how Kilvert appeared in the eyes of others, especially of his social inferiors.

1870 *25 November*. On to the Lower House where they had been killing a pig and the blood was streaming down the steep fold to the road. The farmer had rheumatic gout and was reclining in his easy chair with swollen hands and feet. I had a literary talk with Lewis Williams, about Byron, Scott, Wordsworth, Pope, Robert Montgomery, Clare, etc., till Greenway knocked at the door to ask him to come and help carry the pig indoors.

Lewis Williams must have been a remarkable man, and he can stand as a type of the frustrations imposed by the Victorian social and educational system, though also of the surprising oases of self-taught intellectual and literary culture which could be found in humble society then and which it might be harder to parallel today. He was the farmer's son, a bachelor of thirty living at home with his parents and no doubt helping with the work of the farm as farmers' sons normally did. He cannot have had much education – probably no more than the village school had to offer – and his love of poetry must have been a native irresistible instinct in him. Every mention of him in the Diary refers to it. Kilvert, ever ready to lend him books and to discuss them, must have been a godsend to him; and then you had to go and carry the carcase of the pig indoors. He would have gone up the educational ladder a century later, got to the university probably – and then what? A teacher's job, perhaps. Even in the 1870s, that might not have been beyond his reach, admittedly; but in the 1970s he would have come to it with a far richer academic training and equipment, and the result surely would have been a better use of his abilities for society, and a better fulfilment for himself, even if it left Clyro society a little the duller for his absence.

1870 *29 November*. Perch gives a good account of his own position in the Inland Revenue which he considers now to be safe and he thinks he will shortly have an increase of salary.

Perch, Kilvert's younger brother, was a portent of things to come. A hundred years after his time Civil Service careers would be commonplace, the Service itself a major vested interest, much envied for its inflation-proofed pensions by those in private employment. But in 1870 such a career was still a rarity for a son of the upper middle class. In that age of triumphant and ubiquitous private enterprise, the number of government employees was minute: indeed, the birth of the Civil Service in its modern form might be placed in that very year, when the entry to most branches was thrown open to competitive examination – did this perhaps have some bearing on the fears which Perch had apparently felt as to the security of his position? There cannot have been many jobs going in the Inland Revenue, in an age when income tax stood at fourpence and neither super tax nor death duties had been heard of. I know nothing of Perch's later career, but he should have had a good future before him, for from almost exactly that point onward the expansion of government activity, and especially of government revenue, has been steady, and cumulatively awe-inspiring; and its servants, as we all amply know, have risen with it.

> A letter from my mother ... She tells me that Maria Kilvert of Worcester died last week after a few days' illness. Mr. Hooper, her Worcester lawyer, wrote to ask my Father to come immediately. He and my Mother went to Worcester yesterday ...

Kilvert too went to Worcester for the funeral – staying at the Star Hotel, which is still there, under the Foregate Street railway bridge. His account of the occasion is one of the great set-pieces of the Diary, above all perhaps his description of the funeral procession and the mourners' struggle to carry the coffin into the cathedral, which is a masterpiece of slightly black comedy, related with an almost completely straight face. It was an occasion invested with a good deal of significance and feeling for Kilvert and his parents. Maria Kilvert was the only child of Kilvert's great-uncle Richard Kilvert, a prebendary of Worcester

Cathedral, and therefore herself Kilvert's first cousin once removed. She died unmarried, in the house in the cathedral close where she had presumably lived all her life. There was money in this branch of the Kilverts, and there is more than a suggestion that Maria Kilvert represented the only hope of real wealth for the diarist's branch of the family – wealth that would be regarded as such by their social equals, wealth perhaps comparable to Mr. Venables', wealth that might enable Kilvert's father to establish himself as a country gentleman of estate and independent means and not merely a country vicar without property of his own; for the money it seems came from her father, and Robert Kilvert was her nearest male relative on that side of the family. It would be surprising if the prospect of the old lady's death had not made its mark on the diarist's imagination, as well as on his father's, and on his dreams of the future; and great was his wrath accordingly when another letter from his mother the following day brought news of the contents of Maria's will –

> £15,000 left to charities, Clergy widows and orphans, Home Missions and S.P.G., by a right but by no moral right and a most unprincipled unnatural act and piece of ostentation and a most erroneous injustice. Still more monstrous, £600 had been left by the will to Lord Lyttelton and his son. Happily this had been revoked by codicil . . . To my Father she left her *rose trees* and to my Mother her furs and lace, which my Mother thinks may be worth a few shillings. . . . A most iniquitous will, not a shilling was left to any of the Francis Kilverts, the old grudge and malice against Uncle Francis for Writing Bishop Hurd's life ruling strong in death.

There are things here which are hard to understand – how exactly Lord Lyttelton came into it, for instance, and why Maria Kilvert should hold it against the diarist's branch of the family that his uncle had written the life of Bishop Hurd of Worcester, a perfectly decorous piece of Victorian clerical biography. But these are details: it is the attitude revealed that is fascinating. It is fair though to remark first that the passage is a fine example of another of Kilvert's great merits as a diarist: that on occasions his emotions keep their heat on to the paper. Diaries are reflective, self-conscious, retrospective documents, and one's own emotions, so often embarrassing and tawdry when recollected, tend to get filtered out of them; but Kilvert is not plagued by self-consciousness, and not ashamed to write his anger on to the page, and it comes out in passages as vividly human as this.

But what a text for a sermon on wealth! A priest of the Christian Church, a publicly committed follower of Jesus Christ, losing his temper with his aunt because she has left the bulk of her wealth to the work of that Church, and not to his family! Morally, I suppose, that must be the reaction. Not that one implies in this any suggestion that Kilvert's reaction is unusual – far on the contrary, it is wholly and endearingly human, the reaction most of us would probably feel in the same situation, and if he had the guts and the honesty to admit it to himself in his Diary, so much the better for him – though perhaps he ought to have noticed that the sentiment did sit a little oddly with his profession? Still, Christianity does have something to do with morality, and as a standing instance of the contradiction between its moral demands and apparently only partly redeemed human nature, the passage takes some beating.

But perhaps the passage makes an even better text for historical comment, for it says something far-reaching about the Victorian conventions of wealth, property, and family, and something that makes one see the formidable weight of the Marxist view of these things. Notably, as we've already seen, it shows how a man's moral consciousness can be shaped and in part dominated by these conventions. A Marxist might say with some justice that the whole implication of this passage is that the family is an instrument for the transmission of capital: translate it out of Marxian, and it is at least quite clear that Kilvert thinks that there is a moral bond between wealth and the family, that whatever the law may say, a man has no right to leave the bulk of his capital to anyone or anything outside the close circle of his blood relatives; and I think this does mean that to a very large extent the family is seen not as a unit of blood or of sentiment, but of money. Again, I am sure there was nothing peculiar to Kilvert in this view; it is because it is a quintessentially Victorian view that it is interesting.

I say that, and as soon as I write it I know it's wrong. It is not quintessentially Victorian at all, but much older, and its relevance to Marxism is limited. What we at least are pleased to think of as the typical *Victorian* attitude to wealth is the crude laissez-faire belief that the pursuit of profit is the sole end of man, the Gradgrind-and-Bounderby belief that wealth is the measure of human worth, the philosophy of go out and get it and never mind how; and this is Marx's notion of bourgeois society, that he sees as epitomized by Victorian England. But this is not at all what Kilvert is saying. He never says or implies, here or elsewhere, that life is making money, and he is fastidious and disapproving when a friend takes him to visit the Liverpool Exchange and he sees those who do live by that creed. The implication of his outburst on Maria Kilvert's will is that wealth is something that you inherit rather than something that you make: a hierarchical, aristocratic view of wealth in fact, not a bourgeois view. It assumes a stable social order, and wealth is that which enables a family to maintain the position to which it is entitled. There is little to wonder at in this, when one remembers that Kilvert's family had no connection with commercial or industrial occupations in his own or his father's generations; they had all followed professional or clerical callings, callings whose practitioners took their conventions and their assumptions much more from the aristocratic classes above than from the bourgeois classes below them – we have seen already how Kilvert, as an Anglican parson, was socially the equivalent of the landed gentry. Aunt Maria's offence was that by leaving her money outside the family she was endangering the fragile ability of the Kilverts to maintain themselves in that niche.

It remains true, though, that wealth is central to Kilvert's notion of family and of society, as it was for almost all his contemporaries. I have no passage of my own diary to set beside this one, but one must ask the obvious question – how far have things changed today? For myself, coming from exactly the same social stratum as Kilvert did, I find it difficult to say that it has changed very much, except in two closely related respects, both of which go back to the fact that since Kilvert's day there has been a major shift of power, especially political power, toward the propertyless in our society. One result has been that attitudes to wealth are increasingly conditioned by *their* opinions rather than by those of the propertied, and that wealth is consequently less reputable (though not necessarily less desired) now than then. The other has been the imposition of increasingly heavy taxes on inheritance, so that the hereditary element of wealth is no longer as strong as it was in Kilvert's day, and its ephemeral element stronger. But all that said, the gulf between those with capital and those without, though less precipitous than it once was, remains enormously significant; and I see no reason to think that the attitude of today's Kilverts to today's Aunt Marias has changed all that much.

It is true finally, of course, that Kilvert's reaction to the news of his aunt's will is not just family snobbery: he himself was going to suffer as a result of it. He would continue to be a penniless curate, with all the embarrassments that that brought, including the apparent hopelessness of marriage with anyone of his own station: next year, Daisy Thomas's father was apparently to reject his suit for her on precisely these grounds. This in spite of the fact that to a modest degree there was a happy ending to the story of Aunt Maria's will: it turned out that she had after all made Kilvert's father her residuary legatee, and in the end this seemed likely to bring him some £7,000 out of a total estate of £36,000. Perhaps this had some bearing on the fact that Kilvert did later get married – though not to Daisy Thomas.

1870 *3 December*. Kilvert caught the train from Worcester back to Hay.

> It was very cold travelling and I was very glad to walk through Hereford from Barrs Court to Moorfields.

– changing stations: Moorfields lay out on the Brecon road, so the walk would have taken him right across the city. As for the apparent *non sequitur*, trains were still unheated in the 1870s – a reminder again of the luxuries we take for granted.

> Near Barton station [another of them, in a city with less than 20,000 population!] I met a tall black-whiskered man coming along the street followed by some children. The man looked like a gardener [note the minutiae of Victorian class distinctions that could make such a judgement possible]. The children had been loitering or misbehaving in some way, for the man was very angry. He turned round and went back to them and I heard him say to one pretty girl of 10 or 12 years old, who seemed to be his daughter, 'If

I have to speak to you again I'll smack your bottom in the street.' There was something exceedingly refreshing in the simplicity and plainness and entire absence of reserve with which the man spoke and asserted his parental authority. He was evidently no convert to the doctrine of the dignity of the person and the immunity of the feminine flesh from corporal chastisement. The young lady whose bottom was in danger of being publicly bared and smacked seemed a good deal confounded and crestfallen at the prospect of the proposed castigation and not at all desirous of affording so curious and interesting a spectacle to the passer by.

A typical example of the born diarist's constant curiosity and acute observation of the world about him – as he quite often does, Kilvert even preserves an actual fragment of speech, which is always interesting, for few things are more ephemeral than colloquial speech. However, I think Kilvert's reasons for noting this particular incident may go a little deeper than a mere gift for observation. It's no surprise to find him coming out strongly on the side of parental authority; but I don't think it's entirely the fruit of my own prurient imagination to say that the ideas of bare feminine flesh and of chastisement, especially in conjunction, had an appeal for Kilvert – a minute textual critic might note that it's he, and not the gardener, who appears to introduce the idea of bareness in this incident. It would be unjustified to read very much into this instance taken by itself, no doubt, but if one takes it together with a number of others in the Diary, some of them much more explicit, the point seems to me fairly clear. Again it's not easy in the 1970s to assess fairly these indications of unconscious eroticism in Kilvert. Contemporary sophistication will classify it cheerfully as a bit of flaj, and visualize Kilvert as a raincoated figure in the back streets of Soho. But this is absurd,

---

Opposite: Barton Station, Hereford: one of the three stations that Hereford boasted in Kilvert's time, and seen here at almost exactly that date. Of the three stations, it was in fact the one that Kilvert used least; the trains from Hay in those days ran into Moorfields Station, a short distance west of Barton, and on his journeys home to Chippenham he walked through the city (passing across the bridge here just visible in the background) to catch a train from Barr's Court, today the only station in Hereford. But this picture conveys an idea of rail travel in the 1870s, which played so large a part in Kilvert's life, so vivid that it seemed impossible to omit it.

for an essential part of the nature of Kilvert's reaction to such incidents as these is his total and obvious unconsciousness of the instincts they represent: his total *naïveté*, in fact. It is, to my mind, completely clear from the way he describes them that no shadow of guilt attaches itself to these incidents in his mind, as it unquestionably would do if he had the faintest notion of any sexual significance in them. It is we, whom Freud tried to emancipate, who feel the guilt – though guilt is the corollary of knowledge. I think my previous definition of Kilvert's attitude is right – erotic in origin, innocent in fact.

1970 *3 December*. Took C to the village hall to see the W. I. dress rehearsal of their entry for the county drama competition – the last scene of 'A Christmas Carol'. About 25 there to see it, a mixture of W. I., children, and youths, and it was a gorgeous bit of village amateur dramatics. It only lasted 15 minutes, but the curtains stuck, and the actors, looking entirely incongruous, acted with marvellous woodenness. Someone from the council houses was Scrooge, practically the only speaking part – with a wig composed of a rubber bathing cap covered with hair from a white horse's tail – Kate Powell was Bob Cratchit, Mrs. Griffiths (Gwern-fythen) his wife, the eldest Ingram girl in short trousers a very attractive, though surprisingly adolescent, Tiny Tim. But it was all a brave show for a village W. I., and C was delighted by it . . .

Here one sees the change in village life over the last hundred years at its best. Nothing of this kind could have happened in Kilvert's Clyro; if it had, it is certain that the actors would have been the gentry, the village only a passive, though perhaps an eager, audience. But now this sort of village republicanism, which I've mentioned before, has taken over; here are people doing their own thing, or, better than that, working together to produce their own communal thing. And the village *women* at that, the least likely of all the groups of the village to do such a thing a hundred years ago. There seems no appropriate reaction but to be thankful for the last hundred years and for the W. I.

1970 *7 December*. In Hereford.

There was a power cut in mid-morning – today was the first day of a 'work to rule' in the power stations – and when I went with E to the fine old-fashioned ironmongers in Union Street, I found the whole place in darkness: it has no windows, and the deep cave was lit only by one or two torches and candles, little oases of light in the blackness. This sort of effect indoors is something totally unfamiliar and rather exciting, though it must have been normal, I suppose, a hundred years ago: the sort of enormous difference that colours all your image of the external world, yet which goes unmentioned and forgotten in almost all accounts of the past. A useful reminder of K's world. People were more amused than irritated, though folk kept coming in and asking for candles, which had been sold out long since: I bought lampwicks, something else they're hardly ever asked for nowadays. The lights came on again while I was there.

Two days later, tempers were shortening.

The cold made the threat of power cuts more alarming – they were widespread, and the go-slow was the universal topic of conversation (and execration) – it does seem wrong that a small body of men wanting more wages should be able to inflict so much inconvenience on the whole country.

It is interesting to compare Kilvert's reactions to a similar situation – he is writing at Langley Burrell in the winter of 1872–3.

1873 I found old Giles without coal, thanks to that strike of the South Wales colliers and the baneful tyrannical influence of that cursed Union. The poor old man had borrowed bits of coal from his neighbours till he was ashamed to borrow more, and had now just been picking up a few sticks rotten with the wet. He was shivering with cold and the damp sticks were burning feebly at the bottom of the grate.

And then a week later

Coal still rising. £2.11 a ton in London now. We are burning coke with wood and find it answers very well. The poor people are very badly off for Wales seems to have entered upon a desperately bitter and obstinate struggle with the masters, a struggle to be fought out now to the death and till one party or the other is utterly exhausted. Meanwhile innocent men, non-unionists, and women and children are dying of cold and hunger.

The frame of mind is not very different, but the differences are nevertheless instructive. Kilvert himself and his family are apparently suffering no hardship on account of the strike, and one notes again with envy the immunity of his private life from perturbation by public events. On the face of it anyway, his concern is on account of others, the poor of his parish (it is interesting to note the extent to which rural labourers in Wiltshire were dependent upon coal as a fuel by the 1870s: presumably wood was harder to come by in that heavily cultivated countryside than in Clyro) and elsewhere and the families and dependants of the colliers themselves, and to that extent at least his attitude is more generous, though it is natural to add that it could afford to be. The strike, too, is far less effective than a coal strike nowadays, let alone a power strike: partly because there was no central source of power (except gas, which was only available in towns and still exceptional in private houses even there) to be paralysed by it, mainly because union organization was then infinitely less effective. The strike was confined to South Wales, and there was no question of support from workers in other industries. So coal does not cease to be available as it would today; instead the market mechanisms work, and it merely becomes more expensive – not that it makes much difference as far as old Giles is concerned.

One difference, therefore, is that it was only the poor who suffered then, whereas now we all suffer together – some movement in the direction of social equality. However, this doesn't seem to do anything to mollify Kilvert's judgement on the strikers and the union, which is a great deal more outspoken and less mealy-mouthed than mine in 1970 – mostly I suppose because unions were not yet a hallowed feature of the social landscape, partly perhaps because unlike me he had actual physical suffering before his eyes. There is no sign that Kilvert made any attempt to see the colliers' side of the case – an indication of the limited reach of his sympathies. So far as the evidence goes, he had never seen mining or industrial working conditions at first hand: he was certainly capable, as indeed we see here, of sympathizing with the condition of the agricultural labourers that he worked among, though whether he would have sympathized with the formation of a union among them – as was in fact starting to happen at this very time – is a different matter altogether.

Anyway, both Kilvert's indignation and mine, I suppose, are an indication of the success of the strikes in question. Or are they? Mine is, certainly: coal strikes and power strikes nowadays work by making life so unpleasant for the population at large that they bring pressure to bear on the government to grant the concessions demanded. But in 1873 things were rather different. The colliers were up against the coal owners, not the government; and it may be doubted whether the coal owners lost much sleep over old Giles's sufferings, while the thought of channelling his indignation into a demand for government intervention clearly never occurred to Kilvert in that age of dominant laissez-faire. And in fact the South Wales colliers in 1873 lost, while the power workers in 1970 won: since Kilvert's time that particular balance of power has shifted a great deal, not to the advantage of his class and mine.

1870 *17 December.* That liar and thief of the world Sarah Thomas, Mrs. Chaloner's servant, is gone. The evening she went no one knew what had become of her all the early part of the night. Probably she passed it under some hedge and not alone. At a quarter before midnight she asked for a bed which Mrs. Price very properly refused. I hope she has cleared out of this village. Beast.

Oh dear. There are other instances of these slightly inexplicable outbursts of fury in the Diary – inexplicable, no doubt, only because we do not know the story behind them, but suggesting clearly enough that Kilvert had a volcanic temper buried somewhere within him. There must have been some reason for his vehemence here, but we shall never know what it was any more than we are ever likely to know what did become of the unfortunate Sarah, for whom there was no room at the inn – Mrs. Price being the landlady at the Swan. Kilvert apparently had his wish.

There is no Sarah Thomas in the Clyro entries of the census that was taken four months after she had fled from Ashbrook. The waters had already closed over her.

1870 *18 December*. I could not get out of my head a horrible story Wall was telling me this evening of a suicide committed by an old man named William Jones in the old barn, now pulled down, which stood close by Chapel Dingle cottage. The old man used to work for Dyke at Llwyn Gwillim, but becoming helpless and infirm he was put upon the parish. It is supposed that this preyed upon his mind. He was a very good faithful servant and a man of a sturdy independent character who could not bear the idea of not being able any longer to maintain himself and hated to be supported by the parish ... And he went into the barn and cut his throat from ear to ear – 'Heaven send that I never see such a sight again' said Wall.

We have seen already more than once that life at Clyro in the 1870s could wear a very hard face for the poor, and Kilvert does not burke the fact. But there is also visible in this entry the very deeply ingrained Victorian notion that a man should stand on his own feet, the notion that underlies the characteristic Victorian distinction between the 'deserving' poor, those who at least did their honest best to support themselves and their families and deserved help accordingly if they failed, and the 'undeserving' who didn't. Not surprisingly, it was especially an attitude of the upper classes, but William Jones's story is proof enough of how strong a hold it could have on the minds of the poor themselves. Kilvert's Clyro was a tightly knit and humane community by contrast with the great anonymous cities – no doubt it still is – but the shadow of 'the parish' always hung over the old age of the poor who made up the great bulk of its population, even of those as conscientious as William Jones had been, for saving on an agricultural labourer's wages was hardly a possibility. 'The parish' meant applying to the Board of the local Poor Law Union for help, and depending on their cold and not unduly generous charity – Wall, out of the goodness of his heart, used to bake for William Jones 'the little bit of meat that was allowed him by the Board' once a week; it meant being regarded in the eyes of the law as a pauper (and recorded as such for posterity in the census records too), and it meant all the village knowing it. It could dig deeply at the roots of a man's pride, and the presumed justice of the Victorian order of things was here at its most inscrutable.

All this is not quite a vanished world, for there are many still whose pride forbids them to seek help outside their own resources, but it is nevertheless one which looks pretty strange to us. The belief in the inevitablity of poverty has gone utterly; the state increasingly becomes the universal provider of help for the needy, and pays for it out of taxes to which we all contribute, and most of the sting of accepting charity has gone in consequence; an old age pension is a very different matter from Poor Law relief, because everybody gets it and there is no invidiousness about it. Hence the long-standing resentment of means-tested benefits; and before we condemn it, it might be as well to remember the story of William Jones. In that respect we do things better than Kilvert's society – at a price: a heavy financial price, of course, but also at the price of eroding that belief that a man ought to stand on his own feet, a belief which I, anyway, admire.

1870 *21 December*. Some ragged men were cutting the golden green mistletoe boughs [the description of the colouring is typically exact] out of the Cabalva orchards where they grow in thick bushes and bunches on the apple trees, and carrying them away to Hay for sale [the commercialization of Christmas, which we're wont to lament, had already started in a modest way even in rural Radnorshire, you note]. From Court Even Gwynne I cut across the field to the lane above Penllan and down the Further Bron to Brookside – through a little scrap of old Penllan orchard, with mistletoe growing on all the trees. I made several highly unsuccessful and undignified efforts to scale a very easy one, but finally found an accessible branch on another tree . . .

The cider orchards have all been abandoned, and the apple and pear blossom no longer makes the Wye valley a glory in the springtime, as it did then; but many wrecks of gnarled old trees still survive, and the mistletoe still grows on them – indeed, this area of the Welsh border is the only place where I've ever seen mistletoe grow in any quantity.

1870 *25 December*. As I lay awake praying in the early morning I thought I heard a sound of distant bells. It was an intense frost. I sat down in my bath upon a sheet of thick ice which broke in the middle into large pieces whilst sharp points and jagged edges stuck all round the side of the tub like chevaux de frise, not particularly comforting to the naked thighs and loins, for the keen ice cut like broken glass. The ice water stung and scorched like fire. I had to collect the floating pieces of ice and pile them on a chair before I could use the sponge and then I had to thaw the sponge in my hands for it was a mass of ice.

A spartan age! I've already mentioned that Ashbrook had no bathroom (there may well not have been a bathroom in the parish): Kilvert bathed in a hip-bath in his bedroom, and obviously made no concessions to the rigour of the seasons. There must have been a lot more cold, as well as a lot more darkness, a lot more pain, and a lot more death in Victorian houses then there is in ours. And more assurance, more optimism, less anxiety? – so I was going to write, and so it is conventional to think. But what about Edward Evans, and William Jones, and Sarah Thomas?

It's a fair question; fair, but not unanswerable. Edward Evans and William Jones and Sarah Thomas led wretchedly hard, narrow, and impoverished lives; betterment may well have seemed inconceivable to them, and anxiety never-ending. Their descendants today live infinitely more secure and more comfortable existences, and can face illness and old age with a degree of assurance unthinkable to the villagers of 1870. And moreover, we not only have luxuries undreamed of by the Victorians, but we assume that the passing of time will bring more of them: it is we, not they, who in that sense are the optimists, the believers in progress. Yet we pay a price in our neurotic awareness of history, of the precariousness of things: an awareness that brilliantly infects a book like John Fowles's *The French Lieutenant's Woman*, as I know it infects my own, and that Kilvert never felt at all. What Kilvert had, and what he shared with his villagers, was not a vulgar belief in progress, but a confidence in the future, a belief that the world they knew would go on. It was a hard world for many of them, but it would at least endure: 'Pain that lasts can be borne,' remarks Marcus Aurelius, with stoic grimness, and that faith buoyed up the villagers of Kilvert's Clyro as it buoyed up the folk of Flora Thompson's Juniper Hill and had similarly supported every generation before them. But that has changed now; to us the future by definition is golden, but untrustworthy; we are walking into fog. I think these may well be the only terms on which a belief in progress can be had – a future growing continually more comfortable is a future which by definition may not exist. And perhaps it is worth it at that price. All I say is that there is a price; that even Edward Evans and William Jones and Sarah Thomas had at least one good thing, and that we, who have gained so much else, have lost it.

1970 *25 December*. A dark, still, cold Christmas day, iron-hard with frost, a light powdering of snow on the ground. The children up soon after 7, delighted with their stockings, and M and PGP went to 8 o'clock communion ...

And so it went on; but here the courses begin to draw apart again. There are few records of Christmas celebrations anywhere in Kilvert's Diary. He was after all a bachelor living away from home, and Christmas was a working day for him as a parson; and above all, of course, there were no children. He and his own brother and sisters were all of age, and even when they were at home for Christmas, one knows the increasing slight flatness of family Christmases when you are no longer young: the only grandchildren were generally in India; and Kilvert himself, who would surely have delighted so much in a child of his own, was never to have one. So all we know of his Christmas of 1870 is that he went to church and to Sunday School (it was a Sunday; but I still wonder a little how many children were there that day), and that in the evening he dined at the vicarage with the ever-hospital Venables – whose first child was not yet one. On Boxing Day he went home for a fortnight's holiday, as he usually did at Christmas. The frost held, and from then on till the New Year there were great skating parties, high-spirited affairs with the local gentry, a notably bluer-blooded company than the gentry of remote Clyro. But the courses have crossed, and the ships are dropping out of sight of each other below their own private horizons.

1970 *30 December*. After lunch I went into Hay with C for a little quick shopping. The valley is all green and clear of snow, but the snow isn't conquered: it has fallen back to about the 1,000 foot mark, lying secure like a wild tribe in the hills. The top of the hills behind Clyro is crested with it, and Cusop Hill and the Mountain are still solid white. When I got back M took the children and drove into Presteigne to arrange with a butcher there to supply meat in bulk for our deep-freeze. Remarkably, he turned out to know Ashbrook well: his grandfather was the Moses who was steward of the Clyro Court estate for years between the wars, and he remembers all the Baskerville valuables being stored in the house when the estate was let – a chest of jewellery in the boxroom, C's attic room crammed with pictures ...

It's an addiction, this passion for the past: not, I've already noted, one that Kilvert shared, for all his study of History and Jurisprudence at Oxford, and maybe he was better off without it. But I can't shake myself free of this fascination with a dimension in which it's impossible to avoid moving and equally impossible to travel at will. We live in this house because Kilvert lived in it before us, and because of that all those who have lived here between him and us are of interest too; but what kind of a link is this? It isn't tradition: I don't claim to be *like* Kilvert, or *like* Moses (what a name for a predecessor!) because we've all lived at Ashbrook. We have shared some experiences because of it – the strangeness of the great window, the lovely sound of the brook always in your ears – but all in all, there's nothing more passive, more submissive to totally different regimes, more impersonal than a house; and Ashbrook, perhaps, more than most. Looking back on it, it strikes me what a withdrawn, aloof house it is: for most of its life it seems to have been a house of lodgers, and it has no strong family link because, being the official house for the steward of the estate, it has never passed down from generation to generation. Even Kilvert's Diary looks outward from the house, and gives hardly any impression of it. All of us who have lived here, Mrs. Chaloner and her daughter, Kilvert, the solicitor's clerk, Mr. Moses, and I do not know how many others unknown to me, have left it as anonymous, as impartially receptive to the next dwellers, as to ourselves. I am reminded by contrast of the little church at Newchurch, over the hill, that was tended for fifty years by Kilvert's friend David Vaughan – whose daughters he was once shocked to find castrating lambs – where there is a memorial tablet that sadly records the death of the last of many Beavans of Ty'n-y-cwm: 'at his death Ty'n-y-cwm passed to strangers.' As though nobody but the Beavans could ever be anything but strangers there. There is nothing of that quality about Ashbrook; we have all equally been strangers here. Yet whether in spite of that or because of it, I feel a kinship with Mr. Moses and the rest of them. He lies buried in the churchyard, incidentally, in a spot isolated from all other burials; his stone stands by itself, just inside the lych-gate opposite the post office. The only reason I can think of for this position is that it's the closest possible spot to Ashbrook, and that from it you can see the house, just across the road; and I like him for that.

1870 *31 December.* On the last night of the old year, Kilvert sat up with his mother and his brother, Perch,

> to watch the old year out and the New Year in. The wind was in the North and the sound of the bells came faintly and muffled over the snow from Chippenham and Kington. We opened the dining room window to 'loose in' the sound of the chimes and 'the New Year' as they say in Wales. It was bitter cold, but we went to the door, Perch and I, to hear better. I was carrying my travelling clock in my hand and as we stood on the terrace just outside the front door, the little clock struck midnight with its tinkling silvery bell in the keen frost. We thought we could hear three peals of Church bells, Chippenham, St. Paul's, and very faintly Kington. 'Ring happy bells across the snow.'

He was deep and content in a well-accustomed routine, memories of sitting up with his family for other New Year nights punctuating the memories of the five happy years he had already spent at Clyro; no doubt tacitly assuming, as one does, that it would go on for ever.

There were nine years to go, as it turned out. He left Clyro in

1872, on Mr. Venables' retirement, and went back home to Langley Burrell to act once more as his father's curate, as he had done before he came to Clyro. It does not sound like a step forward, though his observation of life and landscape in the Diary continues as full and as lovingly rendered as ever: there was an obscure, unhappy, apparently passionate love affair, the record of it mostly lost; but one suspects that his heart was still set on the Clyro country, which he often revisited, and in 1876 he was offered and accepted the living of St. Harmon's, in extreme north-west Radnorshire – a poor enough living, worth not so much more than his curacy at Clyro, but the first chance of independence he had had. The presentation belonged to the bishop (of St. David's, who still ruled over the whole of Radnorshire from his remote fastness), and one might hazard a guess that Mr. Venables, in retirement at Llysdinam, had jogged the bishop's memory about the deserts of his former curate. But in the following year he moved to another parish much nearer to his dearly remembered Clyro – Bredwardine, ten miles lower down the Wye, and only a couple of miles from his sister's home at Monnington, where his brother-in-law was now the vicar. As well as these advantages, the move to Bredwardine brought him much greater financial security – held in plurality with the vestigial parish of Brobury across the river, it was worth about £350 a year, a modest but comfortable clerical living at the prices of the 1870s. It was not an episcopal living: the presentation was in the hands of a local family who had known Kilvert while he was at Clyro. Bredwardine lies, very beautifully situated, in orchard country rising steeply from the south bank of the Wye to the top of Dorstone Hill, a thousand feet above it. Close though it is to Clyro, it lies in a different county, a different country, and a different diocese – in lush grazing Herefordshire rather than tough hill-farming Radnorshire. Kilvert seems to have been happy and to have made himself much loved in the two short years that he was there; but the Diary by now is thinning out and has less to tell us, as diaries do when an end is coming.

One consequence of Kilvert's presentation to Bredwardine, though, was that he was at last in a position to marry. All we know about his wife is that she came from a family of Oxfordshire gentry, for the volumes of the Diary which presumably described their meeting, courtship, and marriage, had all been destroyed before the manuscript reached William Plomer's hands. They were married in August 1879; shortly after their return from their honeymoon in Scotland, Kilvert went down with peritonitis and, as the Victorians did, died of it. The village buried him with great lamentation. His widow outlived him over thirty years, never marrying again, presumably treasuring the diaries, but to later generations still dumb. She returned to her family home; but when she died, she too according to her will was buried at Bredwardine. She lies under a similar monument to her husband's but in a separate burial plot, across the rutted track that runs, under the shadow of the big horse-chestnuts in the churchyard, to the broad nettle-grown platform of the old castle. Immense sweet-chestnut trees grow in the ditch around it, and spill their abundant harvest among the nettles: beyond it, where we went that day in August, you come to the place where the blackberry bushes grow.

1970 *31 December*. We got up later than ever as a cloudless morning was breaking, the sun rising in a splendour of intense saffron light over Cusop Hill, the fields everywhere white and crusty with frost. I did handyman jobs round the house in the morning, but the day insistently called you out, and after an early lunch we all set off up the Black Mountain in the car with the toboggan. The road was clear of snow till we got up on to the plateau near Twyn y Beddau, and what a sight it was from there! The whole Mountain was wrapped in shining snow under brilliant sun. And whereas from Clyro the world looked clear of snow, with only a crust of white on the higher hills, up here you saw the error of the lowland view. Whichever way you looked, the world was white and pure: the valley with its soft human browns and greens was a solitary gash, and beyond it the Radnorshire uplands stretched away for miles snowy and austere and inhuman. We were up in the cold world of the gods, and the human world looked a small exception. Up there, there hadn't been a hint of thaw since the snow fell: it lay dry and feathery, with just a glaze on the surface where the sun had melted it. On the open hilltop, the wind had swept it thin: the spiky dry bracken fronds stood up above it, the little gorse bushes were encased in miniature humped snow drifts, like an army of crouching dwarfs in snow-cloaks. The Tumpa, usually so black and ominous, looked particularly incongruous in spotless white. The air was still and dry and exhilarating. The road was open, and we drove on some way toward the Gospel Pass, then did some tobogganing: the view was glorious, the going splendid and very fast down the slope above the road, but also very bumpy, and M, C, and E successively had tumbles and bruises and retired discomfited to the car. They drove off home about 3.30, and I struck off across the plateau to walk home by the Esgyrn dingle. In drifts the snow lay deep, but the going was quite easy. The dingle is steep and narrow, and full of scrub and woodland: normally it would be very wet, but today the frost was hard, and the patches of bog and mud were safe to walk on. The streams full of bundles of icicles. I scrambled down to an old quarry, then found a track which led across the brook, past a ruined cottage, and through a forestry plantation, down to the Craswall road just above the Capel y Ffin junction. The valley was in cold shadow, but the last sunlight still glowed purplish on the formidable scarp of Cusop Hill opposite. At the New Forest farm I turned off on to what may once have been a lane, but is now mostly a watercourse and sometimes a ravine, that leads down past Llangwathan into Cusop Dingle, coming out where the road up the dingle ends. I followed it down in the sharpening chill of the dusk. It's a charming little valley, the Dulas splashing over rock ledges in sudden waterfalls and woods clinging to the hillsides above: there are houses scattered along it, latterly the big ugly villas of 19th century Cusop. Through Hay, over the bridge, up the hill, and across the hard frost-bound Tir Mynach fields home: the sun was down, but the west, streaked with clouds, glowed rose and salmon-pink behind the stately peak of Pen y Fan and the bare trees of Wye Cliff, while, behind, the Mountain glimmered colder and more blanched than ever through the twilight and the lights came pricking out in Hay below. There went 1970, and above, a sliver of new moon gleamed brighter and brighter as the afterglow faded.

DECEMBER

The Mountain dominates the landscape at Clyro as it has always done, and for beginnings and endings it seems natural to turn to the thing that more than anything else remains the same. In a way you are closest to Kilvert up there for that reason, because so much less has changed than in the human valley below, but as I said, it is the world of the gods – you buy the immunity from change at the price of remoteness from men. There are other ways too to interpret the immense parable that the Mountain continually presents. The green world I saw from the valley and the white world I saw from the hill, both equally objective ways of seeing the same landscape and yet totally different – they remind me, a little uncomfortably, of how much both Kilvert's record and mine are the green view, and of how different a version might be given, especially of Kilvert's Clyro and the contrast between the two, in a record written from Edward Evans's cottage then and from one of the council houses now. I have sometimes thought that nobody ought to read *Kilvert's Diary* without reading Flora Thompson's *Lark Rise to Candleford* immediately afterwards – a similarly rural society, seen only a few years later, but from the underside, not from the top. And yet *is* her valuation in the end so very different from Kilvert's? If Kilvert could be bigoted, perhaps the hardest temptation to resist in the 1970s is to have too little faith in your own values.

Like Kilvert at the end of 1870, we in 1970 had something like eighteen months left to live at Clyro, though we did not know it then. But this is not our story, which in any case is not finished yet, and I have nothing more to say about that. Kilvert came to Clyro to do a job, but we were secondary and derivative. We were there only because Kilvert had been there before us. We had three happy years at Clyro and were grateful for them, but that was really incidental. We were after Kilvert.

Epilogue

1976 *31 December*. So it seems that the book is going to be published after all; and after so long a gap, I thought I'd better pay a final visit to Clyro, to see how much it's changed since we were there, and to take my leave of K. So I set off in the car at 10.30: a very fine midwinter morning, brilliant sun, no wind, and quite mild, though there was still snow speckling the upper slopes of Caradoc and the Long Mynd. I drove south down the A49, out of Shropshire, passing Condover, where Kilvert's family came from three generations before his time: the same route through Ludlow and Leominster as we took on that day in April 1969 when we first went to Clyro to look for a house. The same road, but what was new and fresh then overlaid with seven years of familiarity and memories. Beyond Leominster, where you turn west, I hadn't been since we left Clyro four years ago; and all along that road, I had the uneasy experience of the revenant, of coming back to a once-familiar place and recognizing it at the same time as realizing that it's years since you turned up the memories; like going through a pack of old index-cards. The shapes of the hills to the south were familiar, but I'd forgotten the names; and I realized with a shock as I came to the villages along the road, Dilwyn, Sarnesfield, Kinnersley, that their names too had gone from me, though the instant I saw them on the roadside signs they were back with all their everyday flavour. And at once too there was that other uneasy experience, of finding that though you can go back in place, you can't go back in time: that things have changed. The road bypasses Dilwyn now, though for auld lang syne's sake I went through the village, round the three right-angle bends. At Whitney I came to the Wye, brim-high, and gleaming like a river of mercury in the sun. The Black Mountain beyond the river was dim and hazy under a bank of cloud and behind a dazzle of sunlight. The road now sweeps past the Rhydspence into Wales on an embankment, in such lordly fashion that I was past it before I realized where I was, and had to turn back to take the steep lane up the hill, past the trim little modern bungalows ('Two Hoots' and 'Janannie') that step up beside it, up into the narrow-laned high-banked country that has still changed little since K's time, the sun gleaming here and there on the river in the broad valley opening below. Round Chapel Dingle, past Bettws Chapel itself, the last fragment of Emma Griffiths' cottage, and the site of the barn where William Jones hanged himself, past the Tump and the ruins of Whitty's Mill in its dark wooded dingle, and up to Crossway, that K used to call Cross Ffordd to show off his knowledge of Welsh. Called on Joan Harris to tell her the news about the book and ask her if she was prepared to do the rest of the typing, and picked up a good deal of village news in the process. Then down the long hill to the village.

I already knew of a good many of the changes that had taken place since we left of course; but short though my look at the village was, it brought home to me how much of our Clyro is already as much history as Kilvert's. Cae Mawr is in new hands; Clyro Court is no longer a school, but a health farm(!); Mr. Evans, the headmaster of the village school in our time, is dead, and the school itself has left its old building and moved to a new one built on a corner of the Clyro Court grounds. The lane down to the ruined mill, where Kilvert walked that Easter morning, has been tarmacked, and now leads to a sewage treatment plant for the mains drainage that has come to the village. The council house estate has spread across the road into the field below Castle Clump, and a new private estate of unsurpassable hideousness is springing up on the hillside opposite Miss Beynon's Pentwyn (one up to the county council, whose own contribution to the suburban-ization of the village is a great deal more reticent). Clyro isn't even in Radnorshire these days, but Powys, and one can no longer make the boast that we used to be so proud of, that we lived in the only county of England and Wales that had no traffic lights. Looked over the wall at Ashbrook, which has changed hands twice since we left, with the special brand of nostalgia that you keep for houses where you once lived and were happy, and was pleased to see it apparently kindly cared for; and went up the avenue of yews for a look into the church, which was cold as ice, and at the visitors' book, which continues true to form ('Kilvert was a lovely soul' – 'Agreed!'). The sun had fallen behind the cloud-bank over the Black Mountain, which I could see was speckled with snow, and the day was darkening as I drove on into Hay, where there is little change in architecture since 1970 but much in atmosphere – then it was just a small Breconshire market town, with much the air of Kington or Knighton, now it's being more and more taken over by the second-hand book empire, with a parasitic fringe of antique shops and whatnot.

I had a hasty lunch in the very same café where I had tea that day in 1962 when I paid my first visit to K's country, coming up by train from Three Cocks, left the car, and set out on foot to climb Hay Bluff. Up the Capel y Ffin road, familiar landmarks falling into place all the way: crusts of ice in the gutters, though water running beneath them – it was obviously going to be cold on top. At the top of the dogleg bends above Llangwathan, I doubled back along the track to Upper Dan-y-fforest, through the little farmyard, and up the very steep pitch across Henallt Common, very slippery with hard ice across the full width of the track. Past Cadwgan, and out at last on to the great grassy plateau around Twyn y Beddau, with Hay Bluff itself confronting me grimly across it. There were patches of snow and ice here and there on the plateau, and the Bluff itself was white, hatched and stippled with darker lines where rocks and bracken showed through – just like the old First Edition Ordnance Survey maps. The grazing sheep and I seemed to have the entire place to ourselves.

I crossed the plateau and struck up the lower slopes of the Bluff, and found two parties of tobogganers having good sport in the folds of the hill, where the snow lay deepest. A small icy south-east wind blowing across the hill: thin skeins of mist trailing over the saddle from Craswall and along the eastern face of the Bluff. I made my way up the sunken path that slants up the western face, which was filled with snow and very slippery, and looking back, the view was desolate enough: the valley roofed from side to side with heavy dark grey cloud, the Mountain sterile in black and white and dead-bracken-brown, the dingles and lower slopes fertile but sullen in heavy sodden green. Across the river on K's side there was nothing to be seen: it was all lost in gloom and darkness below the ridge of Clyro Hill, itself barely discernible in the mirk. I went on. The upper slopes were hard going under very slippery frozen snow: I climbed up on to the prow of the Bluff just about half past three, and was no sooner there than I was surrounded by swirling grey mist. I could just make out the concrete trig point that marks the summit, and made my way over to it. Well, that was it. A desolate place to end at, and to be brought to finally by picking up a second-hand book in a shop in Adelaide. The world up there consisted of a fifty-yard radius of snow and black and withered heather, walled in by an impenetrable grey gloom. I stared out into the mist, and thought what a good ending it would make if a phantom black-bearded figure took shape out of it for a moment; but didn't expect it. So that's the last K walk, I thought, and turned back.

I was soon out below the mist, and charged down the slope in fine style, digging my heels into the snow. Found too late how treacherous the lower slopes were, frozen hard as rock just beneath the surface and wet and muddy on top, when I came down a terrific crack on the back of my head; but I did myself no harm, and made my way more circumspectly down to the cattle-grid at the entrance to the long narrow lane past Cilonw. The dusk was falling fast now, gleams of light from the sky reflected in the wet road between the bare spiky hedgerows. The lane tumbles abruptly over the edge of the lower escarpment by Pen yr Henallt, and far below the orange street lights of Hay shone out industrial and incongruous in the country gloom, while behind the Mountain was gone in night. It grew darker and darker between the deep hedges, and the lane stretched on and on, haunted strangely as the whole wintry walk had been by stray scents of June, where farmers had been scattering hay for their sheep. It was just on five when I got back into Hay, and found the car – touched for a moment by that old dream, that if I walked on to Clyro and back to Ashbrook, M would be there and tea would be ready. But having come this far, I decided I had better see where for K it had all ended.

So I took the road under Mouse Castle, past Hawkswood, where K on the way home from dinner after midnight once frightened the ladies by telling ghost stories, past Hardwick, and down the valley to Bredwardine. It was fully dark now, very dark in the avenue leading up to Bredwardine Church; so I left the car headlights on, and in their stark light found the pallid cross under the yew that marks K's grave, the old Norman tower looming overhead.

I left it at that: turned back to the car, crossed Bredwardine Bridge, and went north: for Letton, and Almeley, and Lyonshall; for Mortimer's Cross; for Aymestry, and Wigmore, and Leintwardine, and home.